barossa
wine traveller

we're here to
share the barossa

WINE PRESS

Brisbane, Australia
www.winepress.com.au
stelzer@winepress.com.au

First published in Australia by Wine Press 2009

Edited by Tyson Stelzer

Design, typesetting and layout by Tyson Stelzer

Proudly printed in Australia by Openbook Howden Design & Print

National Library of Australia Cataloguing-in-Publication entry:

Author:	Stelzer, Tyson, 1975-
Title:	Barossa Wine Traveller / Tyson Stelzer ; Grant Dodd
ISBN:	9780980640007 (pbk.)
Notes:	Includes index
Subjects:	Wine and wine making - South Australia - Barossa Valley - History
	Wine and wine making - South Australia - Barossa Valley - Guidebooks
	Wineries - South Australia - Barossa Valley - Guidebooks
	Restaurants - South Australia - Barossa Valley
	Barossa Valley (S. Aust.) - Description and travel - Guidebooks

Other Authors/Contributors: Dodd, Grant, 1967-
Dewey No: 641.22099423

Cover Photograph Gnadenfrei Lutheran Church and
Gnadenfrei vineyard, Marananga.
Photography by Dragan Radocaj and Tyson Stelzer

Previous page Gnadenberg Lutheran Church and Hill of
Grace vineyard, Moculta.
Dragan Radocaj Photography

This page Mengler's Hill Panorama.
Dragan Radocaj Photography
dradocaj@optusnet.com.au, 0412 707 019

We could not imagine being anywhere else.

*Even during the difficult days of years past
we were just walking, eating, living,
breathing, being Barossa.*

In the words of Martin Luther,

'Here stand I, I can do no other.'

Peter and Margaret Lehmann

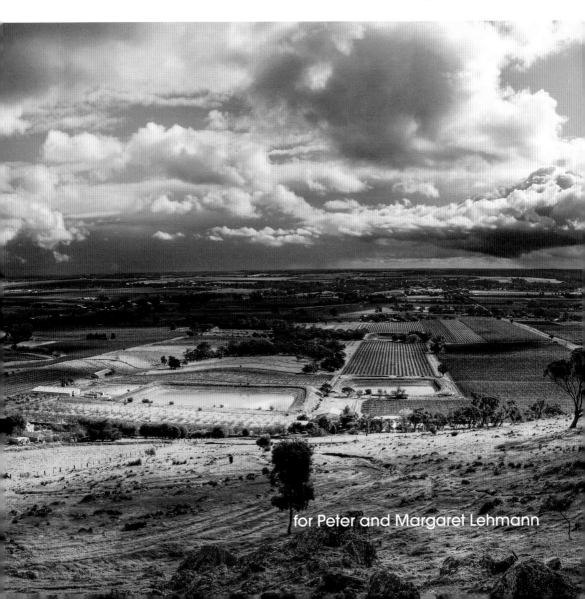

for Peter and Margaret Lehmann

barossa wine traveller

contents

Directory of Recommended Places to Visit

There's no better place to taste wines than at a cellar door, standing in the Barossa, vineyards all around you, winery out the back.
Dave Powell, Torbreck

Sunrise over Barossa Valley Way. Dragan Radocaj Photography

5

the barossa you never knew

There's a lot more to the world of the Barossa than it first seems. Turning off the highway, lines of ancient date palms stand as sentinels to guard the road to Seppeltsfield. The spires of fairytale churches stretch heavenward, competing with grand old gum trees on every side. Ancient bluestone cottages watch over lines of primordial vines, their twisted trunks bearing the laughter lines of a century and a half of life in the Barossa.

Century-old barrel halls dot the countryside, ripe with the heady perfume of vintage. The main street of Nuriootpa is filled with the exotic aromas of redgum burning in the smokehouse at Linke's butcher. Around every corner, the delicate scent of rose gardens lingers; the Barossa truly lives up to its name, 'Hill of Roses.' As night falls, the fragrance of the day dissolves into the crystalline purity of breezes that bring in the twilight from the cool of the ranges.

A local passes by in a 1950s Bedford truck, returning home from a day in the vineyards.

On another day he'll polish it up, don his traditional German 'lederhosen' outfit and wave at the children from the vintage festival parade.

It's a different world in the Barossa. At a glance, it would be easy to presuppose that these fairytale appearances are little more than a façade to lure the tourists to Australia's most famous wine destination; an Aussie attempt to replicate kitsch German traditions in a half-hearted fashion. But there's a lot more to the Barossa than it might seem.

This book is about folding back the layers and experiencing what really lies below the surface. It's the Barossa you never knew.

As a child growing up in Adelaide, I (Tyson) first visited the Barossa when I was younger than I can remember, and I've returned in most years since. For me (Grant) it's been my wine pilgrimage destination for more than a decade. We've always felt at home in the Barossa, but between the pages of this book, in digging below the surface, we have been astounded by the Barossa that has been unearthed.

There is an authenticity to the culture of this place that runs as deep as the roots of its archaic vines. It is a surprising truth that the Barossa's grand festivals, its traditional produce and its quirky idiosyncrasies are upheld not for the tourists at all, but for the locals themselves. That visitors are welcome to join in is a bonus for the Barossa and a windfall for the rest of us.

Since its settlement in 1842, the Barossa has treasured its German and English heritage, while at the same time infusing its own unique Australian flavour. "It's very unusual anywhere in Australia to find a community with such strong links to its European origins," says Philip Laffer, Chief Winemaker at Jacob's Creek. "This is because the Barossa was one of the poorest rural communities in Australia, most people just had a few vines and a cow, and this explains why so many people stayed here — they simply couldn't afford to go anywhere else."

And then there is the wine. That potent, deep purple glue that binds this community together. "There are very few communities that are driven around one thing," says Wolf Blass Chief Winemaker, Chris Hatcher. "In the Barossa, wine is at the core of everything."

More than any other Australian wine region, the Barossa is its own. There is no other precedent to which it aspires, and there is no Old World wine to which it pins its allegiances. In its own inimitable way, the Barossa marches to the beat of the drum of its own Oom-pah band.

It is a beat that sets the pace for the wine industry across the country. The winemaking landscape of the Barossa is rich with iconic names who have carved out the directions of some of Australia's most influential companies. Many of its most celebrated boutique wineries have their home here, as do most of the big names. In the words of Penfolds' Chief Winemaker, Peter Gago, "The Barossa is our engine room."

If anything is new in the Barossa today it is a renewed recognition of the old. Winemakers have recently launched their 'Barossa Old Vine Charter' to recognise and protect the oldest Shiraz and Cabernet vines in Australia, and most likely the oldest Grenache and Mourvèdre, too. These rank among the oldest vines in the world. At the same time, there has been a

Marananga and Seppeltsfield Panorama
Dragan Radocaj Photography

resurgence in the food heritage of the Barossa. 'Food Barossa' was established in the mid-1990s "to first identify the food culture of the Barossa, and then to conserve it," says founding chair, Margaret Lehmann.

Wrapped in these many layers of heritage is a unique Barossa that is today one of the most remarkable communities to visit anywhere in this country.

In its places, faces and never-before-told stories, this book will take you to the Barossa wherever in the world you happen to be enjoying its fruits. For the first time, the inside stories of each of its 150 wineries are told, leading you through a behind-the-scenes tour of the Barossa like you've never known it. Along the way you'll discover all the favourite haunts of the Barossa and Eden Valleys, according to those who know them best, the wine folk who call the Barossa home.

If you had all the time in the world to plan the ultimate trip anywhere, you might look up a few locals and find out about the most authentic places to visit, to stay, to eat and to drink. You'd get the local tips on the best shops, the best golf courses, the best walks, the best coffee, the best places to take your kids and, of course, the best wines. In these pages, we've done all the hard work for you and put together the inside secrets, not just from a few people 'in the know,' but from every winery worth visiting and every wine personality worth talking to across the length and breadth of the Barossa.

You'll find a lot of fun around every corner and plenty of good old yarns to make you smile.

We wish you an exciting journey. We guarantee you will discover a Barossa you never knew.

Rowland Flat vineyard. Dragan Radocaj Photography

The Barossa Vintage Festival Parade
Dragan Radocaj Photography

the barossa valley way

There is a small and unusual thing in the Barossa that epitomises the hospitality of the region toward visitors. And if you don't get into trouble you'll never discover it.

I (Tyson) only know about it because I got into trouble. I was researching this book and I was running late for an appointment with Peter and Margaret Lehmann. On one of those Barossa back roads that becomes a little too boggy when it's wet, before I knew it my little hire car was stuck in the mud. There was nothing I could do to get it out and the RAA (South Australia's motoring rescue crew) doesn't come out this far.

Then I noticed it. So improbable that I thought it could only happen in the movies. On the fence along the road, exactly opposite my car was a little sign. "Bogged? Call this number...

Minimum charge: One carton of West End Draught."

Before long a ute was towing my car out. His name was Phillip Neldner, he grew grapes for Yalumba just down the road and he'd lined the fence all the way along that road with little signs. He told me that he pulls tourists out at all times of the day and night.

It's the small things that make the biggest impression. I know of nowhere else where someone would advertise that they'll crawl out of bed at midnight to help a stranded stranger.

And he refused to accept that case of West End Draught.

9

four seasons in one valley

The weather in the Barossa makes it a comfortable place to visit at any time of the year. Cool to mild winters call for a warm coat, and don't forget to pack your hat and sunscreen in the height of summer. Spring and autumn are delightfully mild. It's always a little cooler in the higher reaches of the Eden Valley.

Harvest at Langmeil Wines
Dragan Radocaj Photography

a year in the life of a wine

Winter (June - August)

Having lost their leaves, vines are dormant for the cooler months, making this the ideal season for pruning. In the wineries, wines are being bottled or rest in barrels to age.

Spring (September -November)

Budburst signals the start of a new season as the Valley explodes in a sea of verdant green.

Summer (December - February)

Summer brings flowering in the vineyards and the onset of fruit, which ripens through the warmer months until harvest begins in late January.

Autumn (March - May)

Harvest continues throughout autumn. Their work complete for the season, vine leaves begin to turn glowing shades of gold and red before starting to fall. Meanwhile, wineries are a buzz of activity with grapes arriving and wines bubbling their way through fermentation.

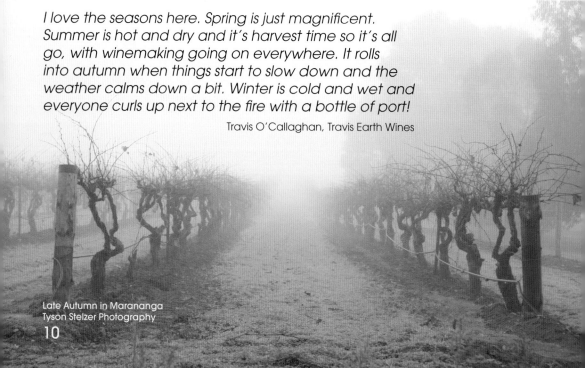

I love the seasons here. Spring is just magnificent. Summer is hot and dry and it's harvest time so it's all go, with winemaking going on everywhere. It rolls into autumn when things start to slow down and the weather calms down a bit. Winter is cold and wet and everyone curls up next to the fire with a bottle of port!

Travis O'Callaghan, Travis Earth Wines

Late Autumn in Marananga
Tyson Stelzer Photography

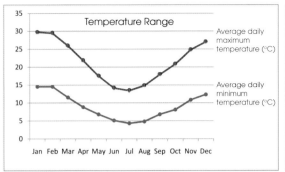

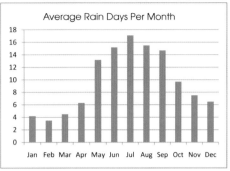

a note from the authors

This book is written for you. It's not written for the winemakers of the Barossa — not one of them has paid to be included. It's not written for the advertisers — unlike most travel guides, you'll see that there are none to be found. It's not written for South Australian tourism and it's not even written by South Australians. It's written by two blokes from Queensland who love the Barossa, who have a ball every time they visit and who want to share a few secrets so that you can, too.

This is an independent guide that aims to be as inclusive as possible. You'll find almost all of your favourite Barossa wineries in these pages — 150 in all! You may notice that a few names are missing. Everyone was invited to be a part of this book through the Barossa Grape & Wine Association. Regrettably, a small number have elected not to participate. We hope that they will change their minds when they see the finished product and come on board for the next edition!

You will notice that there is no pattern to the space that we have given to each winery in these pages. We make no apology for this. We have simply provided the space to allow the people, the places, the history and, most importantly, the wines of the Barossa to tell their own stories.

Spring in Rowland Flat
Dragan Radocaj Photography

Mengler's Hill Panorama
Dragan Radocaj Photography

the best of the barossa

The best wines of the Barossa stand shoulder to shoulder with the great wines of the world. We've scoured the length and breadth of the Barossa and assembled our own hall of fame, a roll-call of heroes that represent the absolute epitome of quality and value, vintage-in, vintage-out. If money is no object, you must tick every one of these wines off your drinking list before you die. We've listed them in descending order of price

Shiraz reigns supreme as king of the Barossa, and it comes as no surprise that it leads our list, with seven epic examples. In second place, Riesling is queen, and Cabernet Sauvignon is the prince. The diversity of what follows is quite remarkable: Mataro, Grenache, Viognier, Semillon and Tawny are all worthy of a place in the king's court. For one region to produce such variety at world-class standard is a testimony to the unique terroirs of the Barossa and the hard-working hands that have for generations so meticulously tended them.

The Best Red Wines

Penfolds Cellar Reserve Cabernet Sauvignon
Penfolds RWT Shiraz
Teusner The Astral Series Moppa Mataro
St Hallett Old Block Shiraz
Peter Lehmann Stonewell Shiraz
Yalumba Tri-Centenary Vine Vale Grenache
Anaperenna by Ben Glaetzer Shiraz Cabernet
Spinifex Shiraz Viognier
Rockford Basket Press Shiraz
Fox Gordon King Louis Cabernet Sauvignon
Dutschke St Jakobi Single Vineyard Shiraz

The Best White Wines

Yalumba The Virgilius Viognier
Peter Lehmann Wigan Eden Valley Riesling
Peter Lehmann Margaret Barossa Semillon
Leo Buring Leonay High Eden Riesling
Pewsey Vale The Contours Eden Valley Riesling
Jacob's Creek Steingarten Riesling

The Best Fortified Wines

Penfolds Great Grandfather Old Liqueur Tawny
Seppeltsfield Paramount XO Tawny

barossa on a budget

When you're doing the Barossa on a shoestring, you'll be amazed at the quality you can afford if you know where to look. If $20 is your spend for a great bottle of wine, the Barossa will spoil you with some of the best value options anywhere in the world. Buy carefully and you needn't always spend a fortune to drink in style.

This is why we've lined up our top wines under twenty bucks. The best-of-the-best budget bottles of the Barossa! This is a roll-call of sensational wines made exclusively from Barossa fruit. Irrespective of vintage, you can rely on these labels for your everyday drinking, every day of the year.

It's the big companies who lead the way in the value-for-money stakes, and between them Peter Lehmann, Yalumba and St Hallett have snared close to half the places in our list. But don't underestimate the value that the Barossa's small makers can offer, with nine little producers more than deserving of a place or two in our list. They're ordered approximately in descending order of price.

The Top Reds Under $20

Fox Gordon By George Cabernet Tempranillo
Fox Gordon Eight Uncles Shiraz
Yalumba Bush Vine Grenache
Yalumba Barossa Patchwork Shiraz
Yalumba Barossa Shiraz Viognier
Kalleske Clarry's GSM
Teusner The Riebke Northern Barossa Shiraz
Yalumba The Scribbler Cabernet Shiraz
Glen Eldon Kicking Back Shiraz Mataro Grenache
Irvine Springhill Merlot
St Hallett Gamekeeper's Shiraz Cabernet

The Top Whites Under $20

Leo Buring Eden Valley Riesling
St Hallett Eden Valley Riesling
Peter Lehmann Eden Valley Riesling
Spinifex Lola
Pewsey Vale Eden Valley Riesling
The Willows Vineyard Single Vineyard Semillon
Peter Lehmann Barossa Riesling
Peter Lehmann Barossa Semillon
St Hallett Poacher's Blend Semillon Sauvignon Blanc

The Top Rosés Under $20

Charles Melton Rose of Virginia
Turkey Flat Rosé
Teusner Salsa Barossa Valley Rosé
Peter Lehmann Barossa Rosé
Spinifex Rosé
Irvine Breughel Cabernet Franc Rosé

the barossa old vine charter

With a history of grape growing and winemaking dating back to 1842, the Barossa is home to some of the oldest vines in the world. Vines of different ages throughout the world have been variously described as 'old' but it has never been defined as to precisely what qualifies a vine to be 'old.'

After many years of discussion, the grape growers and winemakers of the Barossa have established their own Barossa Old Vine Charter:

Barossa Old Vine
Equal or greater than 35 years of age

Barossa Survivor Vine
Equal or greater than 70 years of age

Barossa Centurion Vine
Equal or greater than 100 years of age

Barossa Ancestor Vine
Equal or greater than 125 years of age

Phylloxera is a tiny but deadly grapevine pest that wiped out millions of acres of grapevines across Europe in the mid-1800s. There is no remedy once it enters a vineyard, so the only way to protect the Barossa's famous old vines is to keep this menace out. You can help with this. Please do not enter a vineyard or winery without the owner's permission. Stick to designated paths and roads. Check your shoes for dirt when entering and leaving a vineyard and scrape them clean. If you have recently visited vineyards in the Nagambie, Mooroopna, Upton, Yarra Valley, King Valley, Albury-Wodonga, Rutherglen or Sydney regions, please clean any dirt from your shoes and vehicle before you arrive in the Barossa. With a little care, we can all help to preserve the heritage of the Barossa's treasured old vines.

We have a vineyard in the Angaston region that is a traditional horse-and-cart-delivered Saltram vineyard. The vines are about 119 years old. Can you imagine what was happening then, and who might have planted those vines? It's amazing to think that they're still productive. I don't think I'll be that productive when I'm 119!

Shavaughn Wells, Saltram

Moorooroo vineyard old vine
Dragan Radocaj Photography

the barossa old winemaker charter

Vines are important, but we reckon winemakers are equally important, so we decided to invent The Barossa Old Winemaker Charter. We stole the description of The Barossa Old Vine Charter and simply replaced every occurrence of "Vine" with "Winemaker."

Barossa Old Winemaker

Equal or greater than 35 years of age

These Old Winemakers have grown beyond adolescence and are now fully mature. Many have a trunk thickness that can be attributed to the Barossa's vast nutritional resources. Their worthiness has now been proven over many vintages, consistently producing the highest quality fruit for Barossa wines of distinction and longevity.

Key Barossa Old Winemakers: Stuart Blackwell, Rick Burge, Chris Hatcher, Geoff Schrapel, Louisa Rose, Richard Sheedy, Robert Hill Smith, Brian Walsh

Barossa Survivor Winemaker

Equal or greater than 70 years of age

These Very Old Winemakers are a living symbol of traditional values in a modern environment and signal a renewed respect for the Barossa's Old Winemaker material. They have weathered the worst of many storms, both man-made and naturally occurring, including the infamous 1980s Vine Pull scheme. A Barossa Survivor Winemaker has reached a significant milestone in Barossa and Australian viticulture history and pays homage to the resolute commitment of those growers and winemakers who value the quality and diverse flavour structures of old winemakers.

Key Barossa Survivor Winemakers: Wolf Blass, Don Ditter, Colin Gramp, Peter Lehmann, Max Schubert, John Vickery

Barossa Centurion Winemaker

Equal or greater than 100 years of age

These Exceptionally Old Winemakers serve as a witness to the Barossa's resilience in the face of adversity. The Barossa, unlike many of the world's great wine regions, is phylloxera free, which allowed these winemakers to mature into their thick, gnarly trunks and naturally sculpted forms without interference. Noted for their low yields, they produce fruit with intensity of flavour. Trained generations ago, when dry farming techniques demanded careful site selection, Centurion Winemakers have truly withstood the test of time.

Key Barossa Centurion Winemakers: Percival Burge, Albert Henschke, Benno Liebich

Barossa Ancestor Winemaker

Equal or greater than 125 years of age

An Ancestor Winemaker has stood strong and proud for at least one hundred and twenty five years. They are a tribute to the early European settlers of the Barossa, pioneers of our modern wine industry. These Very Exceptionally Old Winemakers and their genetic material have helped to populate this region with irreplaceable, remarkable old stocks and are the underpinnings of our premium viticultural tradition. These low yielding winemakers, with fruit full of intensity and flavour, are most often dry grown.

Key Barossa Ancestor Winemakers: Johannes Basedow, Johann Gramp, William Salter, John Ernst Seppelt, Samuel Smith, Samuel Elderton Tolley

While Barossa Centurion and Ancestor Winemakers have not lived as long as their vines, their legacy will live on forever in the Barossa.

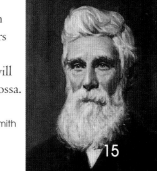

Samuel Smith

barossa wine routes

Keen to explore just one part of the Barossa?
We've devised the best wine routes for each of
the Barossa's subregions. Make your way to each
of these wineries in the order that they're listed
and experience what the diverse little pockets of
the Barossa have to offer.

Eden Valley
Peter Seppelt (Map 48)
Poverty Hill Wines (Map 49)
Irvine at Eden Valley Hotel (Map 28)
Fernfield (Map 16)
Mountadam (by appt) (Map 43)
Henschke (Map 23)

Angaston
McLean's Farmgate (weekends) (Map 41)
Yalumba (Map 73)
Thorn-Clarke (Map 63)
Small Fry (Map 58)
Taste Eden Valley (Map 14)
Saltram Estate (Map 54)

Williamstown
Fox Gordon (by appt)
Domain Day (Map 13)
Linfield Road (Map 37)

Lyndoch
Creed of Barossa (Map 11)
Tait (by appt) (Map 61)
McGuigan Barossa Valley (Map 72)
Charles Cimicky (Map 5)
Massena Vineyards (by appt) (Map 40)
Kies Family Wines (Map 34)
Burge Family Winemakers (Map 4)
God's Hill Wines (by appt) (Map 22)
Dutschke (by appt)
Schild Estate (Map 55)
Ross Estate (Map 53)
Kellermeister & Trevor Jones Fine Wines (Map 33)

Rowland Flat
Lou Miranda Estate (Map 39)
Jenke Wines
Liebichwein (Map 36)
Gomersal Wines (Map 19)
Jacob's Creek Visitor Centre (Map 29)
Grant Burge (Map 20)
Glen Eldon (Map 18)
Moorooroo Park Vineyards (Map 42)

Krondorf
St Hallett (Map 59)
Rockford (Map 51)
Villa Tinto (Map 67)
Charles Melton (Map 6)
Kabminye (Map 30)

Bethany/Tanunda
Spinifex (by appt)
Domain Barossa (Map 12)
Turkey Flat (Map 65)
Chateau Tanunda Estate (Map 8)
Bethany Wines (Map 3)
Murdock (Map 44)
Illapara Fortified Wine Store (Map 27)

North Tanunda
Langmeil (Map 35)
Peter Lehmann (Map 47)
Richmond Grove (Map 50)
Stanley Lambert (Map 60)
VineCrest Fine Barossa Wine (Map 68)
Cockatoo Ridge Wines (Map 9)

Seppeltsfield Road
Chateau Dorrien (Map 7)
Hewitson (by appt) (Map 26)
Rolf Binder @ Veritas Winery (Map 52)
Whistler (Map 69)
Heritage (Map 25)

Marananga/Seppeltsfield/Greenock
Beer Bros
Torbreck (Map 64)
Two Hands (Map 66)
Barossa Valley Estate (Map 2)
Seppeltsfield (Map 56)
Greenock Creek (late Sept – Nov) (Map 21)
Kalleske (Map 31)
Murray Street Vineyards (Map 45)
Hentley Farm (Map 24)
Sieber (Map 57)
Pindarie

Nuriootpa
Barossa Cottage Wines (Map 1)
Teusner (by appt)
Kaesler (Map 32)
Penfolds (Map 46)
Elderton (Map 15)
Rocland Estate
The Willows Vineyard (Map 62)
Gibson (Map 17)
Loose End (Map 38)
Wolf Blass (Map 71)
Craneford (Map 10)

BAROSSA
SOUTH AUSTRALIA

Business Name	Phone	# Map Ref.
WINERIES Cellar Doors		
1 Barossa Cottage Wines	(08) 8562 3212	E13
2 Barossa Valley Estate	(08) 8568 6950	D9
3 Bethany Wines	(08) 8563 2086	G11
4 Burge Family Winemakers	(08) 8524 4644	H7
5 Charles Cimicky Wines	(08) 8524 4025	H7
6 Charles Melton Wines	(08) 8563 3606	G11
7 Chateau Dorrien	(08) 8562 2850	E11
8 Chateau Tanunda Estate	(08) 8563 3888	F11
9 Cockatoo Ridge Wines	(08) 8563 6404	E11
10 Craneford Wines	(08) 8564 0003	B17
11 Creed of Barossa	(08) 8563 4046	H7
12 Domain Barossa	(08) 8563 2170	F10
13 Domain Day Wines	(08) 8524 6224	K7
14 Eden Hall	(08) 8564 2435	E14
14 Eden Springs	(08) 8564 2435	E14
14 Wroxton Barossa Boutique Wines	(08) 8564 2435	E14
15 Elderton Wines	(08) 8568 7878	D12
16 Fernfield Wines	(08) 8564 1041	J15
17 Gibson Wines	(08) 8562 4224	D13
18 Glen Eldon Wines	(08) 8563 3226	G10
19 Gomersal Wines	(08) 8563 3611	F8
20 Grant Burge Wines	(08) 8563 3700	G10
21 Greenock Creek Vineyard & Cellars	(08) 8562 8103	D9
22 God's Hill Wines (by app. only)	0412 836 004	H7
23 Henschke Cellars	(08) 8564 8223	F17
24 Hentley Farm Wines	(08) 8562 8427	E9
25 Heritage Wines	(08) 8562 2880	D10
26 Hewitson (by app. only)	(08) 8443 6466	E11
27 Illaparra Fortified Wine Store	(08) 8563 7575	F11
28 Irvine Wines	(08) 8564 1072	J15
29 Jacob's Creek Visitor Centre	(08) 8521 3000	G9
30 Kabminye Wines	(08) 8563 0889	G11
31 Kalleske Wines	(08) 8563 4000	C10
32 Kaesler Wines	(08) 8562 4488	D12
33 Kellermeister & Trevor Jones Fine Wines	(08) 8524 4303	H8
34 Kies Family Wines	(08) 8524 5333	H7
35 Langmeil Winery	(08) 8563 2595	E11
36 Liebichwein	(08) 8524 4543	H10
37 Linfield Road Wines	(08) 8524 6140	K7
38 Loose End Wines	(08) 8563 2507	D13
39 Lou Miranda Estate	(08) 8524 4537	H9
40 Massena Vineyards (by app. only)	(08) 8564 3037	H8
41 McLean's Farm Wines (weekends only)	(08) 8564 3340	F13
42 Moorooroo Park Vinyards	(08) 8563 0422	G10
43 Mountadam Vineyard (by app. only)	0427 089 836	J12
44 Murdock Wines	(08) 8563 1156	F12
45 Murray Street Vineyards	(08) 8562 8373	C10
46 Penfolds Wines	(08) 8568 9408	D12
47 Peter Lehmann Wines	(08) 8563 2100	E11
48 Peter Seppelt Wines	(08) 8568 2452	M14
49 Poverty Hill Wines	(08) 8568 2999	M14
50 Richmond Grove Winery	(08) 8563 7303	E11
51 Rockford Wines	(08) 8563 2720	G10
52 Rolf Binder & Veritas Winery	(08) 8562 3300	E11
53 Ross Estate Wines	(08) 8524 4033	H8
54 Saltram Estate	(08) 8561 0200	E13
55 Schild Estate Wines	(08) 8524 5560	H8
56 Seppeltsfield Estate	(08) 8568 6217	D9
57 Sieber Wines	(08) 8562 8038	E8
58 Small Fry Wines	(08) 8564 2182	E14
59 St Hallett Wines	(08) 8563 7000	G10
60 Stanley Lambert Wines	(08) 8563 3375	E11
61 Tait Wines (by app. only)	(08) 8524 5000	H7
62 The Willows Vineyard	(08) 8562 1080	D13
63 Thorn-Clarke Wines	(08) 8564 3036	E15
64 Torbreck Vintners	(08) 8562 4155	D10
65 Turkey Flat Vineyards	(08) 8563 2851	F10
66 Two Hands Wines	(08) 8562 4566	D10
67 Villa Tinto	0414 349 999	G10
68 Vinecrest Fine Barossa Wine	(08) 8563 0111	E11
69 Whistler Wines	(08) 8562 4942	E11
70 Wilderness Wines	(08) 8564 1254	J15
71 Wolf Blass Wines	(08) 8568 7311	C14
72 Yaldara Estate	(08) 8524 0225	G7
73 Yalumba	(08) 8561 3200	F14
74 Jenke Vineyards	(08) 8524 4154	H9
75 Pindarie Wines	(08) 8524 9019	F7
CELLAR MERCHANTS		
8 Barossa Small Winemakers Centre,		
Chateau Tanunda Estate	(08) 8563 3888	F11
14 Taste Eden Valley	(08) 8564 2435	E14
74 Tanunda Cellars	(08) 8563 3544	F10
RESTAURANTS/HOTELS/CAFES/ BAKERIES/FARMERS MARKET		
Bakeries		
1 Apex Bakery	(08) 8563 2483	F10
2 Lyndoch Bakery & Restaurant	(08) 8524 4422	H8
3 Tanunda Bakery	(08) 8563 0096	F11
Restaurants, Hotels & Cafés		
4 1918 Bistro & Grill	(08) 8563 0405	F10
5 Appellation at The Louise	(08) 8562 4144	D10
6 Barossa Valley Estate	(08) 8568 6950	D9
7 Café Y, Yaldara Estate	(08) 8524 0225	G7
8 Harry's, Novotel Barossa Valley Resort	(08) 8524 0000	G9
9 Jacob's Restaurant, Jacob's Creek		
Visitor Centre	(08) 8521 3000	G9
10 Kaesler Restaurant	(08) 8562 2711	D12
11 Keils Fine Food & Coffee	(08) 8563 1468	F10
12 Kies Monkey Nut Café	(08) 8524 5333	H7
13 Krondorf Road Café	(08) 8563 0889	G11
14 Lou Miranda Estate Restaurant	(08) 8524 4537	H9
15 Lyndoch Lavender Farm Café	(08) 8524 4538	I8
16 Maggie Beer's Farm Shop	(08) 8562 4477	D11
17 Nuriootpa Vine Inn	(08) 8562 2133	D12
18 Rumours Espresso, Wohlers	(08) 8563 3494	F10
19 Salter's Restaurant	(08) 8561 0216	E13
20 Tanunda Hotel	(08) 8563 2030	F10
21 Tanunda's Ice Creamery Café Diner	(08) 8563 3601	F10
22 The Branch	(08) 8562 4561	D12
23 The Clubhouse	(08) 8563 2058	D10
24 The Lord Lyndoch	(08) 8524 5440	H8
25 The Old Mill Gallery Café & Entice Boutique	(08) 8563 0222	F10
26 The South Australian Company Store	(08) 8564 3788	E14
27 Tonic Restaurant, Lyndoch Hill Retreat	(08) 8524 4268	H7
Farmers Market		
28 Barossa Farmers Market	0402 026 882	E13
Saturday 7.30am - 11.30am		
ACCOMMODATION with 10 rooms or more		
1 Barossa Motor Lodge	(08) 8563 2988	E11
2 Barossa Valley Tourist Park	(08) 8562 1404	D12
3 Gawler Caravan Park	(08) 8522 3805	H3
4 Kapunda Tourist & Leisure Park	(08) 8566 2094	A8
5 Lyndoch Hill Retreat	(08) 8524 4268	H7
6 Novotel Barossa Valley Resort	(08) 8524 0000	G9
7 Nuriootpa Vine Inn	(08) 8562 2133	D12
8 Nuriootpa Vine Court	(08) 8562 2133	D12
9 Tanunda Caravan and Tourist Park	(08) 8563 2784	F10
10 The Louise	(08) 8562 2722	D10
11 The Vineyards Motel	(08) 8564 2404	E13
12 Top Drop Motel	(08) 8562 1033	D12

one day in the barossa

If you have just one day in the Barossa, here are the cellar door destinations you mustn't miss:

St Hallett (Map 59)

Rockford (Map 51)

Charles Melton (Map 6)

Turkey Flat (Map 65)

Peter Lehmann (Map 47)

Penfolds (Map 46)

Seppeltsfield (Map 56)

Yalumba (Map 73)

© COPYRIGHT 2009
BAROSSA PRINTMASTERS, TANUNDA

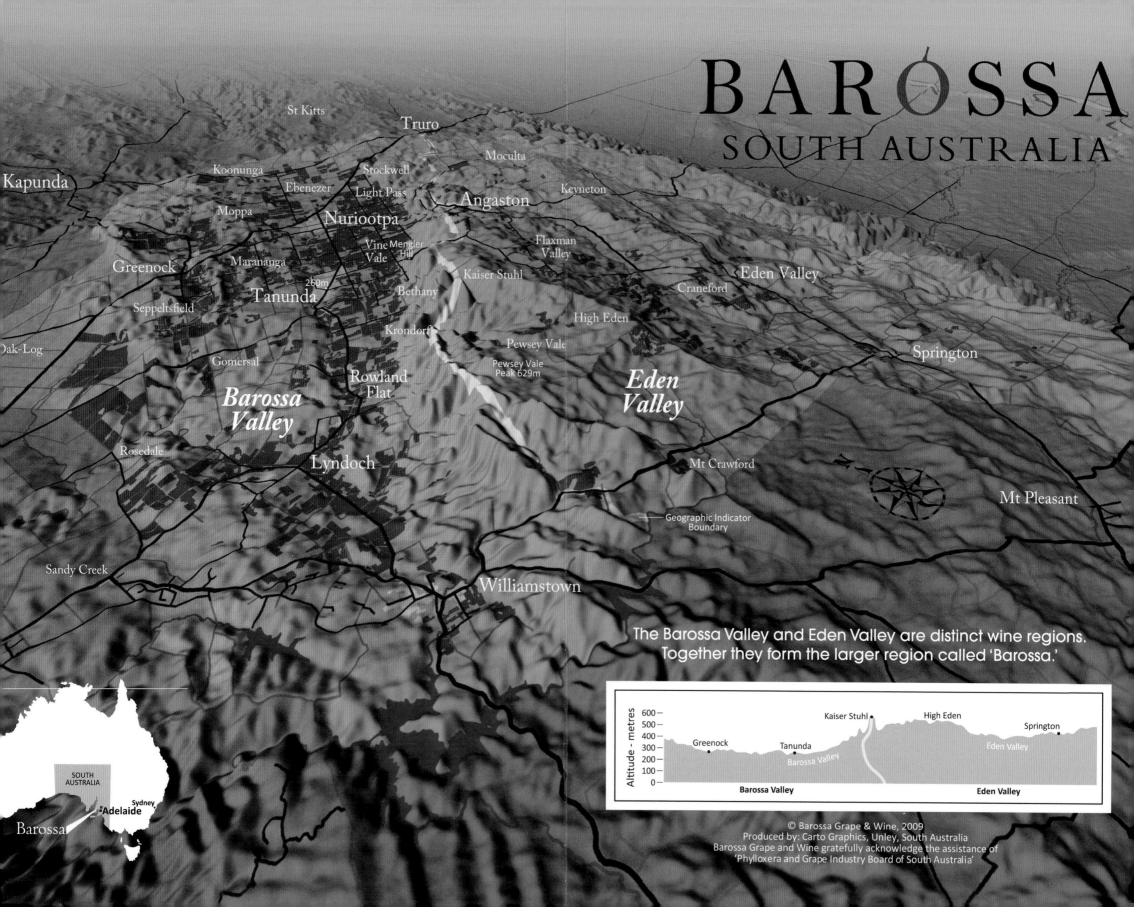

BAROSSA
SOUTH AUSTRALIA

St Kitts

Truro

Moculta

Koonunga

Stockwell

Keyneton

Kapunda

Ebenezer

Light Pass

Angaston

Moppa

Nuriootpa

Flaxman Valley

Eden Valley

Vine Mengler Vale Hill

Greenock

Marananga

Kaiser Stuhl

Craneford

260m

Bethany

Tanunda

Seppeltsfield

High Eden

Springton

Krondorf

Pewsey Vale

Oak-Log

Gomersal

Pewsey Vale Peak 629m

Eden Valley

Rowland Flat

Barossa Valley

Rosedale

Lyndoch

Mt Crawford

Mt Pleasant

Sandy Creek

Geographic Indicator Boundary

Williamstown

The Barossa Valley and Eden Valley are distinct wine regions. Together they form the larger region called 'Barossa.'

SOUTH AUSTRALIA

Sydney

Adelaide

Barossa

Altitude - metres

600 —
500 —
400 —
300 —
200 —
100 —
0 —

Kaiser Stuhl

High Eden

Springton

Greenock

Tanunda

Eden Valley

Barossa Valley

Barossa Valley

Eden Valley

© Barossa Grape & Wine, 2009
Produced by: Carto Graphics, Unley, South Australia
Barossa Grape and Wine gratefully acknowledge the assistance of
'Phylloxera and Grape Industry Board of South Australia'

Travel times in minutes

	Mount Pleasant	Springton	Eden Valley	Keyneton	Williamstown	Lyndoch	Rowland Flat	Bethany	Moculta	Angaston	Tanunda	Seppeltsfield	Marananga	Greenock	Nuriootpa	Stockwell	Truro	Gawler	Adelaide CBD*
Adelaide Airport*	75	80	85	105	70	75	80	95	110	105	90	80	85	80	90	95	100	60	10
Adelaide CBD*	70	75	80	100	65	70	75	90	105	100	85	75	80	75	85	90	95	55	
Gawler	45	45	50	50	25	15	20	35	45	35	30	25	30	25	30	35	40		
Truro	50	45	40	35	40	35	30	20	10	20	20	25	25	25	15	10			
Stockwell	45	40	35	30	35	30	25	15	15	15	15	20	20	20	10				
Nuriootpa	40	35	30	25	30	25	20	10	15	10	10	15	10	10					
Greenock	50	40	35	30	35	30	25	20	25	20	15	10	10						
Marananga	45	40	35	30	30	25	20	15	25	15	10	10							
Seppeltsfield	50	45	40	35	40	30	25	20	30	20	15								
Tanunda	45	40	30	25	25	15	10	5	25	15									
Angaston	35	25	20	10	35	25	20	10	10										
Moculta	45	35	30	15	45	35	30	25											
Bethany	40	35	25	20	30	20	15												
Rowland Flat	35	35	40	35	15	5													
Lyndoch	30	30	35	40	10														
Williamstown	20	20	25	35															
Keyneton	35	30	25																
Eden Valley	15	10																	
Springton	10																		

I would recommend driving to the southern end of the Barossa from Adelaide through the hills – through Lower North East Road, Tea Tree Gully, Chain of Ponds, Kersbrook and Williamstown. It takes almost the same amount of time and it's sometimes quicker than going through Elizabeth. And it's so much more scenic!

Wayne Dutschke, Dutschke Wines

* Allow additional time during heavy traffic periods.

Stockwell Road. Dragan Radocaj Photography

an eventful barossa

There's always something going on in the Barossa and the internet is a great way to stay in touch with the latest. Log on to www.barossa.com to find out about upcoming Barossa events, and keep an eye on the web sites of your favourite wineries listed in this book to see what they're planning.

Here are some of the events you can look forward to...

The Barossa Vintage Festival – A week-long festival with more events than we can list! Parades, horses, music, scarecrows, family days, exhibitions, balls, food, wine and more. It begins on Easter Sunday every second year (2011, 2013, etc). See www.barossavintagefestival.com.au

Barossa @ Home (last weekend in June)

Gourmet Weekend (August)

Eden Valley Spring Riesling Tasting (September)

Barossa Wine Show Public Tasting (September)

Barossa Slow (October)

Barossa Farmers Market (Every Saturday 7:30am-11:30am. See full details in the Directory of Recommended Places to Visit on page 220.)

Top left and middle top Ziegenmarkt ('Look at the size of my sausage!') **Top right** Dave Lehmann at the Shiraz Alliance **Above** Barossa Farmers Market **Below and right** Vintage Festival Parade. John Kruger Photography and Dragan Radocaj Photography.

The Barossa has a real sense of community. This is a fully integrated wine region where everybody is involved in the wine industry, whether they work in the supermarket or the baker's shop. If you go to fill up your car with petrol and there's been a frost that night, you can guarantee that when you pay your bill the person will ask, 'Was last night a problem?' or 'How's vintage?'"

Peter Schulz, Turkey Flat

Yalumba Producers Market
Dragan Radocaj Photography

23

You'd be surprised how many cars stop at Jacob's Creek for that photo with the sign. All of those English people who've had bottles of Jacob's Creek are suddenly standing at Jacob's Creek. And it's an epiphany for them, it's bloody brilliant!

The same people who've been buying Basket Press Shiraz for years stand in Rockford's courtyard on a cool, misty winter morning and go,

'Oh gees, here I am! Here I am! Here I am in the Barossa and I've got vines all around me. I can see the hills and I've got a good red in my hand. This is what I've dreamt of!'

Charles Melton, Charles Melton Wines

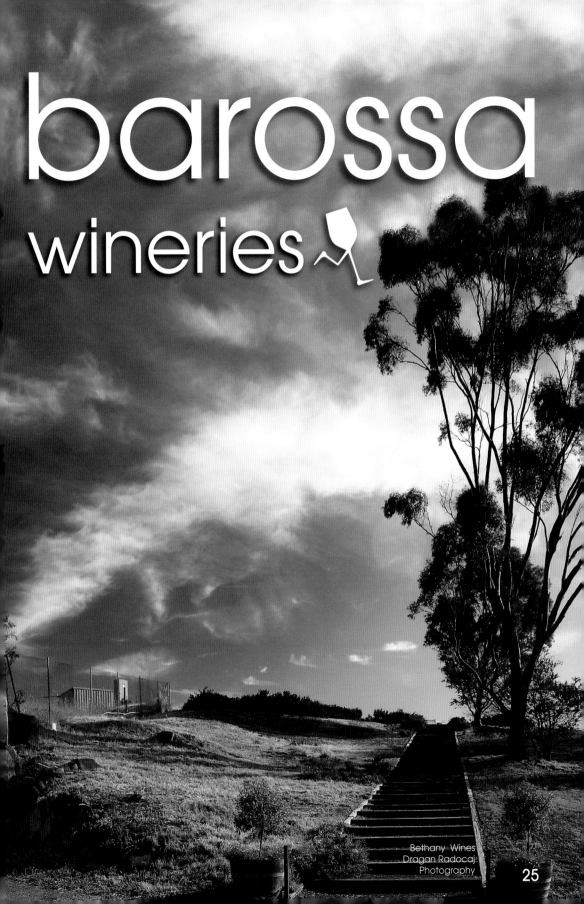

barossa
wineries

balthazar of barossa

Anita Bowen's route to the wine industry was a little less orthodox than most, but the former relationship counsellor and sex therapist has quickly made a name for herself beyond the confines of her previous vocation. Balthazar

of Barossa sources grapes exclusively from an estate vineyard that Anita helped to plant in 1999.

My Place

"At a dinner in Melbourne in the early days of the brand a restaurateur said to me, 'You know, you don't look like a winemaker!' It was a strange statement to make, but I guess I don't! I make wine that I'm intensely proud of because I love wine, I love this region and I love the wine industry and its lifestyle. I like to think that this passion somehow resonates in the Balthazar wines."

Stonewell Rd Marananga

Ph (08) 8562 2949

www.balthazarbarossa.com

anita@balthazarbarossa.com

Est 2001

Tastings by appointment

Price range $20-$50

Key Wines: Balthazar of Barossa Shiraz, Ishtar Barossa Goddess White Viognier

Local knowledge

"Murdock Wines does Tapas better than anyone in the Barossa. It's a favourite of mine for a funky, laid-back lunch."

barossa valley estate

Barossa Valley Estate enjoys a stunning vista from its state-of-the-art winery and ultra-modern cellar door in Marananga. "What's special about this place is its history," explains Winemaker Stuart Bourne. "It's the '80s and a whole bunch of third and fourth generation growers can't sell their fruit. What are we going to do? Take life into our own hands, form a co-op, bring our fruit in, get a winemaker and take it to market. Cracking idea! That's how we started life as a 100% cooperative owned winery. And then Hardys came along during the 90s. 'Great place! Can we go you halves?'

So it's not a takeover. Growers say, 'Great, this will give us a chance to build a new facility.' Hardy's say, 'Great, we've got the Barossa brand that we've always wanted!' Grower needs a distributor, distributor needs a winery. Perfect!"

My place

"I'm not a fifth generation local," says Stuart. "And, although there is a degree of localism in the Barossa, as there would be in any country area in Australia, it's a very accepting community toward change. The influx of new blood into the district over the last twenty or thirty years makes us all look

Seppeltsfield Road Marananga

Map D9 Winery 2

Ph (08) 8568 6950

www.bve.com.au

bve@bve.com.au

Est 1985

Cellar door tastings open 10-4:30

Picnic facilities, crafts, local produce, café, restaurant

Price range $15-$90

Key Wines: E&E Black Pepper Shiraz, E&E Sparkling Shiraz, Ebenezer Shiraz

Barossa Valley Estate cellar door

at things differently, bringing in fresh ideas and new concepts, but still keeping the traditional Barossa heart. I think what we've got today is a really good blend of very traditional Barossa Lutheran, Germanic roots, but with a modern flair. It's got a very good cohesive feel. 'Brand Barossa' is bigger than everyone, and we're just a piece of that."

Barossa Character

Stuart Bourne says he only makes wine to pay for golf. "When I was a younger man, golf was going to pay for my wine. My plan was to get on tour and be a pro. Look what happened – now wine pays for golf! The best place to play golf is the Barossa golf course, out north of Nuriootpa, near Kalimna vineyard. That's a cracking joint! Tanunda Pines is a beautiful golf course, too. They're the two majors in the district. If you want to drive a bit further, there's Mt Pleasant, out the back of the Eden Valley, set on the hill, with cherry orchards around it. It's a cracking golf course! The view off the first, and whoosh, down the hill! It just makes you think, 'I'm going to get that blinding white light and smack the cover off it.' And, on a hot day, on unirrigated fairways, you can drive 300 down a hill!"

You wouldn't read about it

"One thing I love about this district are the gorgeous old trucks that they pull out at harvest. We've got an old '56 Bedford restored in the shed. Well, restored on the outside! We use it as our stalk truck. The thing's more than fifty years old and it starts first time, every time. And all she has to do every year is carry the stalks around, and then we'll put her back in the shed

for the rest of the year. That '56 Bedford is a cracking old bus!

"The most interesting sport in the Barossa is playing Kegel in Tanunda. It's the Germanic ten pin bowling, but with nine pins and a really thin alley. It's open to the public when they play once a week. And you can hire it out any time you want. For a fun event, get ten people in and play Kegel. It's like going back 100 years!"

Barossa dirt

"For us, northern Barossa has been where the best fruit comes from. You get the occasional snippet of sheer brilliance pop up from somewhere else, but the theme for us is north of the highway."

Infamous growers

"You name it, if it can carry grapes, we've seen it! This chap from out north has a beautiful old truck. He's actually got four or five trucks that are the same, but only one works. The others he butchers to pieces. As a piece goes, he goes out to the other wrecks and pulls a bit off. One day he pulls up over the weighbridge and the fuel pump's gone! So, we pull it off the weighbridge with a tractor, get if off to one side, still full of fruit. 'Don't worry,' he says. 'I'll just nip off home and I'll butcher one of the other ones!' And he comes back with a fuel pump off one of the old wrecks, sticks it on and away it goes! Then he goes to tip it. The ram won't go all the way up to the top because the seals are pretty knackered, it's so old. So the crew here got ingenious and put a forklift either side and lifted the tray up to throw the fruit into the crusher. They pulled the forks out, and he was good to go!

Stuart Bourne on the coffee machine in cellar door
John Kruger Photography

"I love harvest time. Some weather-beaten old grower in his old terry towelling hat comes pottering in the door in the afternoon after he's been picking all day. And he stands around and wants to have a chat. And another chat. Nothing moves too quick. We're like, get it in, pump it over, get the yeast into it! And he's there, 'Nah, do it later!'"

Local knowledge

"I'm an Angaston boy and there is only one Schulz's butcher! But the ham from Linke's kills it! For a quick snack, I'd go to Sunrise Bakery in Angaston or the Wurst Haus in Tanunda!

"1918 is good for a quiet drink. You can sit outside and have a nibble. The Tanunda club is a good joint and the Brauhaus Hotel in Angaston is a good pub. For a really good feed, you can't go past a degustation at Vintners, Barossa smoked pizzas at Roaring 40's Café in Angaston, or whatever Mark McNamara has decided is fresh that day at Appellation just up the road here. The guy's a freak - he's done some incredible things! And he hosts stay-in tuition weekends, where he'll take you down the Barossa Farmers Market Saturday morning. You literally have no idea what's coming out for dinner Saturday night until you've been down the markets in the morning and had a poke around!

"One of the undiscovered gems of the district is the Barossa Farmers Market on Saturday morning from 7:30 to 11:30, down the back of Vintner's old shed. You'll find whatever's come out of the ground the day before. Great stuff! Steicke's dried fruit is always represented – dried pears, apricots, peaches and prunes. Grab a mixed bag! Low sulphur, dried on site, still vibrant in colour. They supply our restaurant here. You can also get it at Gully Gardens in Angaston, which is open during the week for limited hours. They're a lovely family, the Steickes.

"Kaiser Stuhl National Park is a good place to go for a walk. At Mengler's Hill you can sit and chill and look over the district – that is a priceless view!

"For accommodation, The Louise is stunning.

There are two races in the world that make incredible smallgoods – Germans and Italians. There aren't a huge number of Italians around here. But, man, that German blood!

Stuart Bourne, Barossa Valley Estate

Barossa Slow

Novotel is good if you like that larger format. It has beautiful views, especially at harvest, when you'll see Orlando lit up like a Christmas tree! We use Lindsay House in Angaston, which is a great place and it overlooks the whole valley. It's a massive house, two storey with multiple bedrooms and it looks down the hill of Angaston, across the plain. It's three B&Bs in the one joint, so you can either take an individual portion of the house that you don't have to share, or you can take the whole house for ten people. It's all interlocking rooms, which shield you if you don't want to see others, or you can open the whole place up. It's a very flexible design for a B&B!"

Wining kids

"Country sport is pretty big to us. If kids come into the district, the train park in Nuri is good for littler kids and next to the train park is a full skate park for the older kids. Angaston oval's got a skate park, full playground, oval, cricket nets, basketball court, tennis courts, netball courts, the whole bit!

"When kids come to Barossa Valley Estate there's plenty of open space to run around. For the little kids there's a toy box and they can get bikkies. A little bit of Seppeltsfield red cordial always arcs them up! We've got a bit out the back, just in case, and it's proven to be very popular. The kids feel like they're doing something with their parents. We put a little bit of red cordial in a glass and they stand there and feel like they're part of the tasting, even though they've only got cordial. When they've drunk it they can go outside and run!

"During vintage time, my boys go down to Angaston twice a week and sit on the train and watch all the grape trucks and tanker trucks go by. And they'll see the occasional tractor and machine harvester go past. It's hours of fun. Really cool big boys' toys, petrol, happy days!

"I take them up to the quarry to see all the big trucks and loaders. You can't get into the quarry,

Barossa Valley Estate cellar door

but you can see it all from outside. There's a public weighbridge where you can park off to the side and see all the big machines working. Linke's earthworks, big graders and tip trucks – they love it!"

Food matches

"When someone's coming into cellar door, they can try local produce with local wines," explains Venue Manager Tom Fotheringham. "Our Estate Platter is all local, except for some of our cheeses. We've got Linke's butcher, who smoke all their own meats – ham, chicken and mettwurst. Zimmy's provides us with dill cucumbers and onions. Lyndoch bakery bread. Pear chutney, which goes really well with the cheese. Barossa grown Kalamata olives made by the same guy. And, of course, Maggie Beer's paté. We have a good relationship with all the local suppliers. They drop off their produce for us, and stop and have a chat, so we hear what's new."

"My favourite food and wine matches are seared scallops and Semillon, King George Whiting and Eden Valley Riesling, and Garfish and lemon with Chardonnay," says Stuart. "A real classic is E&E Black Pepper Shiraz and slow braised lamb shanks from either Linke's butcher or Schulz's butcher. Just the other day I did Ebenezer Shiraz with kangaroo back strap, pan fried with dark chocolate and chilli as a glaze. Great combo! I also do slow-roasted Spanish neck pork. Linke's put it in a net and I roast it for about eight hours with spicy BBQ sauce. Serve it with coleslaw and Apex bakery buns!"

barossa valley roennfeldt wines

Barossa Valley Roennfeldt Wines is a single Shiraz wine producer from a single vineyard near Greenock.

"Although we produce wine grapes for some of the biggest wine names in the Barossa Valley, we elect to only make our wine when the vintage is of the highest quality," explains Brett Roenfeldt. Six generations ago, his forebears settled on the property in 1849. "This was 'The Genesis' for our family in Australia, hence the name of our wine."

Barossa dirt

"Turn over the earth at our 'Poplar Holme' Homestead and you're just as likely to pick up yet another Clydesdale horseshoe for the collection. The property boasts over 150 years of continuous farming so it's fairly common to unearth all sorts of farming relics from yesteryear."

Local knowledge

"We suggest a visit to Linke's Bakery for some traditional German Kuchen (German cake) or Bienenstich (to die for!) and then off to Linke's Butcher for some Mettwurst (garlic or Brandy)."

Greenock Road Greenock

Ph 0411 180 960

roennfeldtwines@gmail.com

Est 2005

Tastings by appointment or at the Small Winemakers Display at Chateau Tanunda

Price $38

Key Wine: Genesis Barossa Valley Roennfeldt Shiraz

Brett Roenfeldt

beer bros

Colin Beer has been a grape grower and wine producer for more than thirty-six years. Together with his wife Maggie he is a formidable force in the Barossa. They have built the Maggie Beer brand into a gourmet institution and established Maggie as one of the country's foremost culinary identities. In 1997,

Maggie Beer

Colin and his brother Bruce launched a small portfolio of hand-crafted wines under their Beer Bros brand. They are sold at Maggie Beer's Farm Shop in Nuriootpa and at selected local restaurants.

My Place

"The process of grape growing has always held a great fascination for me," says Colin. "You prune vines, watch them grow, keep an eye out for trouble, then pick when you think the time is right. Observing that evolution is exciting, and after all these years it's still the aspect of the business that I enjoy the most."

Pheasant Farm Road Nuriootpa

Ph (08) 8562 4477

www.maggiebeer.com.au

Farm Shop@maggiebeer.com.au

Est 1997

Cellar door tastings open 10:30am-5pm daily

Conferences, functions, crafts, local produce, food available all day

Price range $12-$48

Key Wines: Beer Bros Old Vine Shiraz, Pheasant Farm Home Block Shiraz

bethany wines

Johann Schrapel arrived in Bethany, the first settlement in the Barossa, in 1844 and planted vineyards in 1852. After more than a century and a half of continuous grape production, the estate remains very much under the care of his fifth and sixth generation descendants, with brothers Robert and Geoff Schrapel at the helm. Their wives and children lend an active hand in the daily running of the vineyards, winery and cellar door. Tucked into one of the most unique and spectacular winery locations anywhere in the country, Bethany Wines is a sight not to be missed – and don't forget your camera!

My place

"The Schrapel land has never been for sale and has only ever transferred," explains Geoff.

"They must have been pretty serious in the early years, and they were making wine here and selling it by the late 1800s." It wasn't until 1981 that the first wine appeared under the Bethany label. "That was our first Bethany vintage," says Rob. "And the cellar door was opened in 1982."

The first wines were made from grapes that the brothers couldn't sell. "One of those was our White Port, or Old Quarry Fronti, as we call it now," says Geoff. "Now we get people coming back for it over and over again! They can buy it in bulk as well, in large containers for a barrel at home. Maintaining our fortified wines is an important link to our history."

You wouldn't read about it

The winery and cellar door

Bethany Road Bethany via Tanunda

Map G11 Winery 3

Ph (08) 8563 2086

www.bethany.com.au

bethany@bethany.com.au

Est 1977

Cellar door tastings open Mon-Sat 10-5, Sun 1-5

Picnic facilities, tutored tastings, crafts, local produce

Price range $10-$85

Key Wines: GR Reserve Shiraz, Riesling, Shiraz Cabernet, Old Quarry Fronti, Cabernet Franc Rosé

at Bethany are nestled into a historic bluestone quarry in the Barossa Ranges, overlooking the family vineyards. "The quarry was operated by the Schrapel family from 1846 and its stone was used to build all

Bethany Wines
Dragan Radocaj Photography

31

of the cottages in Bethany, the Bethany church in 1862, the Langmeil church in 1888 and Chateau Tanunda in 1890," explains Geoff.

"The quarry was abandoned in 1930 and our father put a big wall across the front of it and it filled with water," recalls Rob. "In 1981 when we built the cellar door and winery, we had to do quite a lot of digging to get them into the quarry!"

Geoff points out that "not only is the winery nicely hidden in the hollow, but it allows us to process the fruit by gravity flow, and this is important to us. We drop the grapes off at the top of the hill and they go through the process by gravity without the need for pumps. The more gentle the process, the less we do to the wine and the better it is."

Visiting Bethany Wines

"We've got the best overall view of the Valley of any winery in the Barossa!" says Geoff. "The beauty about this hill is that you are high up but also close, so you can see the vineyards through to Tanunda. Eden Valley begins just at the top of the hill behind you, and the view extends from Rowland's Flat right through to Kalimna and all the way out to the ocean."

"It's a short walk up the steps from the car park to the top of the hill to take in the view," adds Rob. "And then you can walk across to look down into the quarry at the winery. A lot of visitors enjoy the chance to have a look at a working winery and see a bit of action.

"We have a number of wines at cellar door that aren't commercially available. There's a Quarry White and a Quarry Red as well as back vintages of various wines. Our GR Reserve Shiraz is available for tasting on most days and there is no tasting charge.

"Private tastings are available in the area behind the barrels for our GR Wine Club Members. We have quite a few back vintages of both whites and reds that we have held back for special tastings. Email or phone in advance to make a booking."

Local knowledge

"You can pick up a copy of the Bethany heritage walk brochure from our cellar door," says Rob. "It gives a really good run-down of all the old buildings through Bethany. You can visit the Pioneer Cemetery and Bethany church.

"The church still rings the bell at sunset on Saturday evening. This is unique to the Lutheran communities here in the Valley. It goes right back to the early traditions as a reminder of worship on Sunday morning. Visitors are very welcome to attend any of the churches in the region. Communion is very open now.

"For accommodation in Bethany, I'd recommend Sonntag House. It's an authentic, traditional, old German-style cottage with two or three bedrooms as well as a spa and well fitted-out bathroom."

Wining kids

"Bethany Reserve is one of the best places to go for a picnic in the Barossa," recommends Rob. "There's a lot of history in this spot, where herds of cattle and sheep from up in the hills

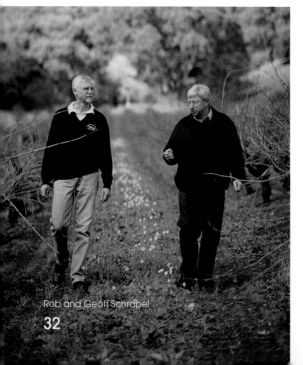
Rob and Geoff Schrapel

would be collected at night. The community got together and planted all the big gum trees during the depression in the early 1930s, when there wasn't much work around. The area is now open to the public for anyone to use. It has a well-sheltered area so it's great even on wet days and it has seats and tables, a fireplace and good toilet facilities. The community built a fully-equipped kitchen, which is available for hire for large groups through the Barossa Council (enquire at any Barossa library). There is also a great, open common area for families across the creek."

Bethany Wines

Food matches

"The dill cucumbers are unique in the Barossa," says Geoff. "Rob and I have judged them for years at the Tanunda Show. It's more of a party than a bloody judging! Zimmermann's, or 'Zimmy's' as we call them, are the best.

They have kept their dill cucumber style authentic. You can buy them in the Tanunda supermarket in Cryovac packs, to keep them fresh. Zimmy's pickled onions are very good, too, although I'm glad there weren't too many entries in that competition in the Show!"

biscay wines

Biscay Wines is owned and managed by the experienced John Hongell, former General Manager of Saltram Wines. A strong connection with his family is maintained through the brand, with all grapes sourced from the Hongell vineyard, which includes 1943 Grenache vines. Just 1000 cases of two wines are made each year, vinified by John's son, Trevor, and sold at the affordable price of $20.

My Place

"I started my working life as a brewer," recalls John Hongell, "but my focus changed when I discovered wine. I fell in love with the Barossa, moved

here in 1973 and I've never left. Biscay Wines is not a hobby, it's my passion and my connection to friends, family and food. Seeing my name on a wine made from grapes that I've grown myself gives me a great sense of pride. The only thing better is opening a bottle and sharing it with like-minded people."

You wouldn't read about it

"In the early days when we first bought the vineyard it was irrigated using town effluent. We used to wade in with bare feet and pass the soaker hose from row to row using a pitchfork. We didn't mind putting our feet it in but we drew the line at our hands! We like to think our Grenache had

646-647 Barossa Valley Way Tanunda

Ph (08) 8563 0297

hongell@ozemail.com.au

Est 1998

Tastings by appointment

Price: $20

Key Wines: John Hongell Old Vine Grenache Shiraz, John Hongell Barossa Valley Shiraz

a little more body back then!"

Local knowledge

"I love to drive the back roads through the hills. There's a real sense of intrigue and a great feeling of freedom there."

Trevor and John Hongell

33

burge family winemakers

Fifth generation grape grower Rick Burge was born in the family home on his Draycott vineyard and started working the property on a tractor when he was ten years old. "I'd like my tombstone to say, 'He made good Lyndoch wine,'" he says. "That's all I'm trying to do. I'm a hands-off winemaker because I'm not clever enough to trick wines up!"

My place

"Our Draycott and Olive Hill Vineyards surround the cellar door and we only use genuine, estate grown fruit," says Rick. "Planted, ploughed, pruned and picked by the producer! I still do it myself and I spend forty percent of my time in the vineyard. I get out there with the pickers and taste most vines.

Barossa Valley Highway Lyndoch

Map H7 Winery 4

Ph (08) 8524 4644

www.burgefamily.com.au

draycott@burgefamily.com.au

Est 1928

Cellar door tastings open Fridays, Saturdays and Mondays. Sundays on long weekends and festival weekends.

Price range $20-$50

Key Wines: Draycott Shiraz, Olive Hill Shiraz Mourvèdre Grenache, Shiraz Rosé, Olive Hill Semillon

Rick Burge

"Our Old Vine Grenache is about eighty-five years old and the vines visible immediately in front of the cellar door are about fifty years old. As a grape grower I'm fifth generation but as a winemaker I'm third. We have had continuous winemaking in the family on this property since my grandfather, Percival, started in 1928. My Dad took over when my grandfather retired in 1950 and I've now done twenty-three vintages myself.

Visiting Burge Family

"We have a small cellar door with historic items and memorabilia on display. The old barrels along the wall are not decorative — they contain 1993 fortified wine.

Everything in the range is available for tasting, and there is no tasting charge. If people want to meet me personally, they should phone in advance to make a booking. Just not during vintage, because I'll be in the vineyard or the winery!"

Barossa Character

"Music is my other passion, and I won a producer's award about ten years ago. It has helped my winemaking, because making a good blues album is a lot like making a good red. Both have to be of interest and have balance. With every taste of a good album, like a good wine, you pick up slightly different nuances,

so it's beautifully balanced. Great musicians, like great winemakers, stand out for the bits that they don't overplay. When a wine is overworked and there's too much on the palate, it's overkill. A great wine is so simple, yet it's so complex and everything is there. The mantra I go by now is 'simplicity is a form of genius.' For the great old blues guitarists, it was the notes they didn't play that made their music so interesting. You imagined and allowed your brain to fill it in. Chris Finnen would just lay back and play, and you were enthralled. And a great wine is the same."

Local knowledge

"Linke's and Schulz's butcheries have the best bacon by far. Often when I have interstate guests I'll whiz up to the butchers and we'll have a bacon tasting. They just can't get over the bacon!

"I recommend that our visitors get off the bitumen and go sight-seeing. Go up into the ranges to Trial Hill and High Eden. Take Trial Hill Road out of Lyndoch or go through Williamstown, around the forests and up to Springton and Eden Valley. It's a great place to chill out."

35

b3 wines

B3 is a new venture for the three Basedow brothers, Peter, Michael and Richard. Johannes Basedow built the original wine business in 1896, which continued under the family name until the untimely death of John Basedow in 1975. Since then the Basedow name has seen various owners, with the brothers now working toward the next chapter in the Basedow story.

My Place

"Our place is about family, history and heritage," says Richard. "For all three of us, our first wages were in this business, picking fruit as kids for the family brand. Our great grandfather built it and more than a century later we carry on his passion. Perhaps this pride is a German thing, it's in our blood! We're making wines to be proud of and one day we want to do that with the family name back on the bottle."

Barossa Character

"Johannes Basedow was a true legend of the Barossa. He founded the Tanunda Club and, despite some trials and tribulations, it remains an institution in the valley and a favourite haunt of many winemakers."

You wouldn't read about it

"There's a real sense of brotherhood in the Barossa. When you need a hand, you pick up the phone and someone on the other end will be only too happy to help. You just know that when the time comes, you'll do the same. It's what makes the Barossa so special."

Local knowledge

"The best local tip I can think of is to get over to Maggie Beer's place. It's authentic, tasty Barossa food at its best!"

Light Pass Road via Basedow Road Tanunda

Ph (08) 8363 2211

www.b3wines.com.au

info@b3wines.com.au

Est 2001

Tastings by appointment

Price range $16-$49

Key Wines: Eden Valley Riesling, Grenache Shiraz Mourvèdre

Peter, Richard and Michael Basedow

charles cimicky wines

Hermann Thumm Drive Lyndoch

Map H7 Winery 5

Ph (08) 8524 4025

charlescimickywines@bigpond.com

Est 1972

Cellar door tastings open Mon-Fri, 10:30am-3:30pm

Price range $20-$45

Key Wines: Trumps Shiraz, Autograph Shiraz, Durif

"You wouldn't be in the wine industry if you didn't enjoy endless challenges!" says Charles Cimicky, who has seen a few himself in four decades in his family-run winegrowing business. The Cimicky brand specialises in Shiraz production and its 'Trumps' Shiraz has generated a loyal following of consumers seeking a value-for-money proposition.

My Place

"You never stop learning as a winemaker," says Charles. "It's a constant game of fine tuning and attention to detail. Every year and every vintage, you find something new and there's always the feeling that you can improve on what you've done before. It's been that way for us since 1973, and we're still striving to get that extra little bit with each passing year."

Local knowledge

"If you are looking for a quiet, peaceful place to relax and get away from things for a while, spend some time in the gardens here at our winery. I often use the area when I need to collect my thoughts and solve a problem or two!"

charles melton wines

Krondorf Road Tanunda

Map G11 Winery 6

Ph (08) 8563 3606

www.charlesmelton wines.com.au

cmw@charlesmelton wines.com.au

Est 1984

Cellar door tastings open 11-5 daily

Veranda dining 12-4 daily

Price range $19-$50

Key Wines: Nine Popes Grenache Shiraz Mataro, Richelieu Grenache, Rose of Virginia Rosé

Charles 'Charlie' Melton is a living icon of the Barossa, but he's as down-to-earth and friendly as any bloke you've met. One of the first champions of old vine Grenache, after twenty-five vintages his Nine Popes Grenache blend is recognised as one of the best in the country. He has also cemented a reputation worldwide for one of Australia's most consistent rosés. A beautiful outlook, walk-in winery and a café menu to die for make this little cellar door one of the best in the Barossa.

My place

"There is a community spirit here that is as strong as any other wine area in the world," says Charlie. "You can see it in the events in the region. Everything that happens during the Vintage Festival happens on a voluntary basis – the air show, dinners, tastings, parade, everything. There is one paid director and that's it. Not only are the parade organisers volunteers, the participants are all totally voluntary, and some of them spend months working on those floats. A community puts on a parade that stretches for six or seven kilometres with 120 floats!"

"The strength of the cohesiveness and cooperation in a community like this is a tremendous thing. Visitors see it when they come here. We've got our own recommended list of twenty or thirty wineries for when visitors ask where else they should go. I don't expect everyone who comes to the Barossa to only visit this place, buy my wine and nick off home again, so I send them to other places I know who have the same aspirations as us: people who make great wine, sell it at a fair price, look after visitors and are grateful that they made the effort to come to their place and support the Barossa. We send them to wineries where they'll get the same treatment that they get here.

"People often come here and say, 'Gee whiz! The last couple of wineries we went to have all been happy to recommend their opposition around the valley. We didn't think you'd do that! We thought you'd all keep the focus on yourselves.' The tourists pick up on that and see that this is a really friendly place to visit because we're all mates and happy to recommend each other and help out. It's a place built on good values of friendship and cooperation. And that makes a visitor's experience more enjoyable."

Barossa dirt

When you visit Charles Melton, the vines immediately in front of the cellar door are 1948 bush vine Grenache.

"People visit us far more readily for Grenache than they do for Shiraz here," Charlie points out. "Grenache is one variety that the Barossa does better than many other districts. Apart from McLaren Vale, there are no other areas in Australia that have the Grenache resources that we have here. We have a resource that resonates with the district, the climate suits it perfectly and the old bush vines make great wine.

"I remember taking the very first wine down to Rocky's (Robert O'Callaghan's) cellar door and having a drink with him and telling him that I'm going to call this thing 'Nine Popes'. It was a take-off of Chateauneuf-du-Pape, which I thought meant 'Castle of the nine popes'. I'd done my Alliance Français course and read a bit of history about the seven Avignon popes and I couldn't work out why it was 'nine popes' when there were only seven. I later learnt that it was 'chateau of the new popes', but by then it was too late to rename the wine!"

Local knowledge

"I'm involved in the air show. A school that has 70 kids puts on an air show that attracts more than 6000 people! For a little school fundraiser, that's incredible!

"Appellation has been a massive bonus for the Barossa. The quality and style of food that Mark McNamara is doing is extraordinary. The food is just stunning and the atmosphere and the mindset of Appellation is of an international standard. It's been a real godsend for the Barossa."

Visiting Charles Melton

"We have a particularly beautiful aspect here, one of the most beautiful in the Barossa. Krondorf Road itself is a fantastic road, partly because of the calibre of the people on it and partly because it's lovely and quiet. It's virtually a dead end so generally the only people who come up the road are wine lovers. People come

Charles Melton cellar door at sunset

here and it's a lovely spot to sit under the veranda. We live here every day and every now and then I watch the sun set or I go and sit up there and just have a glass or look out over the back and go, 'Gees, what a sensational place!

"People sitting here on the veranda want to feel that they're in the middle of the action. Like they can just get up from their table, wander over and be where all the hard work goes on. So we've set it up that they can come over to the winery shed and step in. We have a velvet rope two or three feet in, so you can walk to the door and step inside. During vintage you'll be able to see the whole process all in one spot. The storage tanks are down one side, the fermenters down the other and you can see the pressing going on, racking fermenters or tipping whole bunches into tanks. You feel like you're right in the thick of it during vintage, and the rest of the time you can look at rows of 600 or 800 barrels lined up. It gives visitors a thrill and enriches the experience.

"We have a unique way here. We've had a table in cellar door for 20-odd years. People sit down and we have the time to have a yarn, expound our philosophies and taste some quality wine. We've only been doing food for a couple of years, but it's been a monster success! We do simple lunches of vegetarian tarts, smoked salmon from the Mount Pleasant butcher who smokes it in his smoke house; Hutton Vale lamb and Hutton Vale beef pies are made by the fantastic local guys at Carême; our cheese

is from the Barossa Valley Cheese Company; lettuce is grown freshly over at Marananga; and in winter we add some peppered roast beef."

CHARLES MELTON
FINE   BAROSSA   RED   WINES

You wouldn't read about it

"As you leave here and head back down toward the main road, just after the railway line you'll see a little fibro shack on the left. It was always known as 'the shack' and it was the breeding ground for a number of young winemakers. A heap of us used to live there in the mid-70s. And we used to have Saturday afternoon beer kegs. They had those red plugs and for every keg we would take the plug and nail it on the facia of the shack, until there was this never-ending line of plugs. There used to be a railway platform at Krondorf and the train that runs twice a day would come up in the afternoon to take the ore back to Port Adelaide. The boys in the ore train got sick of driving the train past and seeing us all sitting out there every Saturday having this beer keg. So they stopped the train one day, came over, had a quick schluk, jumped on the train and continued on!

"Another story from the shack was kept secret for quite a while. A guy called Janis was the chief chemist at Orlando and he owned Lawley Farm. We shared the shack with Bill Seabrook and we used to keep a shotgun in the cupboard. One Saturday afternoon we were all just sitting

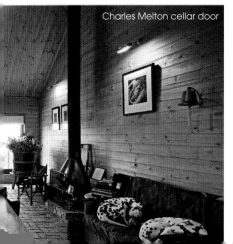

Charles Melton cellar door

Charlie & Virginia
hosting lunch
on the veranda

around having a drink when Bill came racing in saying, 'Where's the shotgun?! Where's the shotgun?!' We said, 'It's in the laundry where it normally is.' 'Ah, there's some ducks down on the creek.' And we said, 'Oh that's good,' because we used to have a Sunday stew. Whatever was left over from the weekend would go into a big stew pot on Saturday night for Sunday stew. So away he went, and we were thinking that he was going to come back with a couple of nice teals or wood ducks. The next thing we heard was, 'Boom! Boom!' And dead silence. And we thought, 'Gees, we didn't know Bill was such a hunting, shooting, fishing kind of guy! He said ducks, so there must have been two of 'em, and we've only heard two shots, so he's obviously not a bad shot!' A couple of minutes later, Bill walks in with two of the biggest,

fattest, tamest, whitest Muscovey's you've ever seen in your life! Monstrous, white, bloody, domestic ducks. We said, 'Bill, they're someone's ducks! They're domestic ducks, they're not wild ducks. We were thinking wild ducks!' He said, 'Oh! Doesn't matter! We'll still eat 'em!' So, we started dry plucking them in the kitchen. About two minutes later there's a knock on the door. And Janis was Swedish or Finnish or something, I can't remember. So someone opened the door. 'G'day Janis, how you doing?' 'I am well.' 'What can we do for you?' 'Ahem. Have you seen my ducks?' Meanwhile, the kitchen is awash with bloody duck feathers. 'Nope, sorry Janis, nope, haven't seen them, mate.' Bang! Shut the door and that was it. Bill had cleaned up Janis' bloody pet ducks! We did eat 'em, and we enjoyed the duck stew. We had some good times back then!"

Charlie Melton

Mist on the hills near Tanunda. Dragan Radocaj Photography

chateau dorrien

The Dorrien vineyard is one of the Barossa's most famous sites for Cabernet Sauvignon and this was the first variety that Fernando and Jeanette Martin launched under their Chateau Dorrien label when they purchased the estate from Seppelt in 1985. Having grown up in a wine and liqueur making family in Italy, fortified wine is a particular passion of Fernando's and today it forms a key component of the company's range.

My Place

"Like many producers in the Barossa, our place is about family," Fernando explains. "We're 100 percent family owned and operated, with a father and son winemaking team. For a point of difference, we also make honey liqueurs from local honey and we offer honey tastings to our visitors. Keeping things warm, friendly and personal has been the abiding theme of our place since we began."

You wouldn't read about it

Constructed in 1911, the Chateau Dorrien cellar is a landmark Barossa building.

Food matches

"We love to serve our Shiraz with game birds such as pigeon, quail and duck, plus plenty of roast garlic and pumpkin mash!"

Corner Barossa Valley Way & Seppeltsfield Road Dorrien via Tanunda

Map E11 Winery 7

Ph (08) 8562 2850

www.chateaudorrien.com.au

dorrienwines@ozemail.com.au

Est 1984

Cellar door tastings open 11-5 daily

Gallery, historical buildings, picnic facilities, crafts/local produce, tours, Pétanque

Price range $10-$22

Key Wines: Shiraz, Cabernet Sauvignon, Fortified White Frontignac

Below from left Ramon and Father Fernando Martin; Pétanque on the Chateau Dorrien grounds; Cellar door tasting

chateau tanunda estate

Chateau Tanunda is one of the Barossa's most spectacular historic icons, but it lay in a state of disrepair until South African-born businessman John Geber was inspired to buy and restore it in 1998. Five million dollars later (and counting), the Chateau has regained its former glory and is once again a landmark destination in the Barossa. Its grand event and function areas cater for more than 600 people and its sprawling grounds include 'The C.C.G.' - Chateau Cricket Ground. The cellar door is home to the Barossa Small Winemakers Centre where the wines of more than twenty small producers can be tasted.

9 Basedow Road Tanunda

Map F11 Winery 8

Ph (08) 8563 3888

www.chateautanunda.com

wine@chateautanunda.com

Est 1890

Cellar door tastings open 10-5 daily

Historical buildings, tutored tastings, tours, crafts, local produce, coffee, light meals, concerts, festivals, picnic facilities, functions

Price range $15-$160

Key Wines: Terroirs of the Barossa Greenock Shiraz, Grand Barossa Shiraz, The Chateau Eden Valley Riesling

My Place

"I was cycling through the Barossa in 1998 and was intrigued by the presence of a tower through the tree line," recalls John. "On closer inspection I found a magnificent but run-down building, boarded up behind a 'Do not enter' sign. Before I knew it, I had made an offer on the place. Not long later I jumped on the phone to my wife and told her, 'I think I've bought a Chateau!' Being European, she said, 'But there aren't any Chateaux in Australia!' It turns out that buying the building was the cheapest part of the next ten years. Restoring it to its former

Tim Smith and John Geber

Chateau Tanunda

glory has been a labour of love, and something to be proud of. I'm just passing through and am merely a custodian of this great building. It is Chateau Tanunda that must stay, because it is something of absolute iconic beauty in the history of Australia."

Barossa Character

"Some of the most famous names in the history of the Australian wine industry have worked here. Max Schubert, Bill Seppelt, Grant Burge, Robert O'Callaghan, the list goes on. If only the walls could talk!"

The Chateau Cricket Ground

"We have a cricket ground behind the winery that is recognised as one of the most spectacular in the world. A charity cricket match is played every year to raise money for the David Hookes Foundation, and we've had some of the biggest names in cricket joining us, including Bishan Bedi, Mike Gatting and Arjuna Ranatunga."

You wouldn't read about it

"At the time that it was built in 1890, Chateau Tanunda was both the largest building in South Australia and the largest winery in the Southern Hemisphere."

Local knowledge

"Being an avid cyclist, I love jumping on a bike and exploring some of the back roads of the Barossa. You might even discover a Chateau!"

Wining kids

"Our international standard croquet lawn is open to our cellar door visitors, including kids. That should keep them busy while you enjoy a platter of food and a glass of wine!"

Mike Gatting at Chateau Tanunda

43

cirillo wines

Marco Cirillo describes himself jokingly as a 'mad young Italian winemaker'. True or not, he's made a statement about his intent to be a serious player in the Barossa by holding back his only wine for ten years prior to release. It's made from an estate grown Grenache block planted in the 1850s.

My Place

"I'm first generation Australian but a ninth generation winemaker, with family roots buried in the Italian wine industry for as long as anyone can remember," says Marco. "Our Grenache vineyard is one of the oldest in the world. It produces very special fruit and my goal is simply to produce a wine that does this site justice."

Barossa Character

"The doors to my place are always open. It's the local drop in centre for a beer and a glass of wine with mates. Everyone is welcome!"

You wouldn't read about it

"I prune every one of my 5500 old Grenache vines personally, on my own. At ten to twelve minutes a vine it's a massive job. I don't let anyone else do it - one wrong cut and I'll pay for it for the next two vintages!"

Local knowledge

"There are a lot of local waterways here with plenty of perch and trout - you just have to know where to look. Once you've found your spot, the only decision you'll need to make is whether it's a one or two bottle Riesling day!"

Lot 298, Nuraip Road
Nuriootpa

Ph 0408 803 447

marcocirillo@adam.com.au

Est 2002

Tastings by appointment

Price $50

Key Wine: 1850s Old Vine Grenache

Marco Cirillo

Cirillo
18 50
OLD VINE
Grenache
BAROSSA VALLEY

1850 Grenache vines

44

clancy fuller wines

It was during the infamous 'vine pull' of the late 1980s that Peter Fuller and Paul Clancy arrived in the Barossa and acquired a couple of old vineyards with, in Peter's words, "a commitment to sustain these vines and make authentic Barossa wines which were a tribute to the hardworking pioneers who established them." Made in tiny quantities, their wines are available for tasting by appointment.

My place

"The tiny one acre Fuller vineyard alongside Bethany Creek is more than 120 years old," explains Peter. "In fact, it only survived the vine pull because the locals liked to harvest the leaves for their dill pickles! Today, it still produces very low yields of highly concentrated, distinctively chocolatey Shiraz."

"Clancy's vineyard is adjacent to Jacob's Creek, just a stone's throw from where Johann Gramp planted his first 'garden' in the 1840s," says Paul. "Here the red schist soils of this forty-year-old vineyard produce Grenache, Shiraz and Mataro which have a distinctively perfumed, elegant profile."

28 Murray Street Tanunda

Ph (08) 8563 3668

www.clancyfuller.com.au

peter.fuller@fuller.com.au

Est 1994

Tastings by appointment (24 hours' notice preferable)

Price range $15-$40

Key Wines: Two Little Dickie Birds Rosé, Silesian Shiraz, Three Hogsheads Shiraz

"We have also introduced a cheeky Grenache-Mataro Rosé called Two Little Dickie Birds to the portfolio - 'one named Peter and one named Paul' as the nursery rhyme goes," says Peter.

craneford wines CRANEFORD

Originally established in 1978 near Springton in the Eden Valley, the modern home of Craneford is in Truro. Revitalised by new owners in 2004, the busy and comfortable cellar door is open seven days a week.

My Place

"Craneford Wines is unique for its predominantly female staff," points out winemaker Carol Riebke. "Most were born and bred into the Barossa winemaking extended family. We crush, produce and bottle all of our products on site, and I like to think that it shows in the wines."

You wouldn't read about it

"We commissioned the well-known artist Allyson Parsons to design a label for a portfolio of wines under her name. Each year, a percentage of the sales of these wines goes to the Royal Adelaide Hospital Cancer Centre."

Local knowledge

"Brauhaus in Angaston serves hearty, great value meals."

Wining kids

"All of our staff members have kids and after 3:30pm on school days they enjoy our lovely cottage garden and feeding the fish in the pond."

27-31 Moorundie St Truro

Map B17 Winery 10

Ph (08) 8564 0003

www.cranefordwines.com

production@cranefordwines.com

Est 1978

Cellar door tastings open 10-5 daily

Café, coffee, tea, light snacks, olive oil, conferences

Price range $10-$130

Key Wines: Shiraz, Merlot, Private Selection Shiraz

The Craneford team

45

creed of barossa

Business partners Mark Creed and Daniel Eggleton established Creed in 2005 with a goal to build a wine business based around sustainability. Their philosophy is that minimalist winemaking produces individual wines that more accurately reflect their vineyard origins.

My Place

"Creed came about as a result of a desire to produce an organic, sustainable product," explains Daniel. "We work with our growers to achieve this, putting attention to detail first. When it comes to winemaking, we're untrained winemakers, but highly trained drinkers, so we've worked out from experience just how we want our wines to taste!"

Barossa Character

"My mum's family have been in the Barossa for 150 years and were originally stone fence builders in the Eden Valley. A lot of their amazingly resilient fences are still standing today!"

You wouldn't read about it

"My partners Mark and Mandy Creed operate about fifteen B&Bs in the Barossa as well as our wine business, so life is busy. The good news is that we can give you a great time on the wine and then give you a bed to sleep it off!

295 Barossa Valley Way Lyndoch

Map H7 Winery 11

Ph (08) 8524 4046

www.creedwines.com

admin@creedwines.com

Est 2005

Tastings by appointment

Accommodation, tours

Price range $15-$85

Key Wines: Pretty Miss Shiraz Cabernet Franc Viognier, Two Brothers Shiraz, The Bism Shiraz

Local knowledge

"There are great golf courses in the Barossa where you can always get a game. My favourite is Tanunda Pines, a top course and friendly place."

david franz

David Franz Wines is the creation of Dave Franz Lehmann, son of Barossa legend Peter Lehmann. That's where the connection ends, however, because this is an independent business driven by a fiercely independent individual, determined to craft his own legacy built around hand-crafted and exciting wines.

Nicki, Alex, Frank, Stella, David, Ben and Georgie Lehmann

My Place

"My place is an extension of me and it reflects the fact that I like to do things my way," says David. "I'm a self-taught winemaker (good genes notwithstanding!), and I've built David Franz from the ground up around the things I love – food, wine, friends and lifestyle. I like to think that my place is about flavours, not just of wine but of life."

Lot 43 Stelzer Road Tanunda

Ph 0419 807 468

www.david-franz.com

davelehmann@david-franz.com

Est 1999

Tastings by appointment

Price range $18-$85

Key Wines: Georgie's Walk Cabernet Sauvignon, Alexander's Reward Cabernet Shiraz

Barossa Character

"I may have grown up around wine, but I'm still as much in awe of the great winemakers as any punter."

David and Nicki showering in Sparkling Nicole NV
Inset from top David and Alex playing in the vineyard; Alex the copilot; The Barossa Vintage Festival Parade

You wouldn't read about it

"Seek out a small family winemaker, make the time to go and see them, embrace what they do and four times out of five you'll end up sharing the dinner table with them! That's just how the Barossa is."

Local knowledge

"I love to go to Appellation with friends, hand myself over to the chef and never make another decision for the rest of the night! It's one of the great dining experiences in Australia."

Food matches

"You can't beat real food that's cooked with integrity. Soulful, rich, slow cooked oxtail is magic with my Georgie's Walk Cabernet."

diggers bluff

Diggers Bluff is named after Tim O'Callaghan's dog, Digger, and the windy bluff on which they live overlooking Seppeltsfield. Here Tim prunes, picks, ferments, presses and labels his wines "with my own hands" to produce a style which he attributes to the influence of his father, Robert O'Callaghan at Rockford – "rich, soft and balanced."

DIGGERS BLUFF

My place

"In the winery I use a very slow crusher to carefully remove the berries from the stalks," explains Tim, "making sure that there is a minimum of stalks and leaves in the ferment. This also ensures we get no snails, lizards, nails, posts or even the odd push bike, believe it or not! I have an 1800s and a 1960s hand cranked press, and these play a critical role in achieving soft, smooth flavours and tannins."

Visiting Diggers Bluff

"We have a top view and awesome sunsets and if you're keen to come and have a look you're most welcome. Please call ahead. You'll enjoy a one-on-one tasting with someone who works in the winery and vineyard. If you're lucky it might even be me!"

875-876 Radford Road Seppeltsfield

Ph (08) 85631510

www.diggersbluff.com

diggersbluff@bigpond.com

Est 1998

Tastings by appointment

Price range $17-$45

Key Wines: Top Dog Shiraz, Watch Dog Cabernet Shiraz, Sly Dog Cabernet, Stray Dog Grenache Shiraz Mataro, Lap Dog Rosé

Local knowledge

"We enjoy a good beer and feed after a long day and we're lucky that the Greenock Tavern is just across the Seppelt Valley. It sports a fine brew from the local brewery, The Barossa Brewing Company, and some of the best pub food you'll find in Australia."

Darren Davis and Tim O'Callaghan making wine the old-fashioned way with a basket press and **inset** foot stomping grapes

Todd Riethmuller working the pizza oven in cellar door

domain barossa

"Trying to find something else to do with my life, I was reaching the end of the University of Adelaide course book when I turned the page and found a degree called Oenology. If only I'd known what it meant I wouldn't have wasted all that time on the first hundred pages!" says former accountant Todd Riethmuller, who traded in a career as a financial controller in Papua New Guinea to study winemaking. In 2002 he became the owner and winemaker of Domain Barossa and opened a cellar door on the main street of Tanunda.

My Place

"We started Domain Barossa with the idea of building something that was warm and casual. It also made sense to us to do it in the heart of town,

as you'll find in places like Champagne. We found a great spot and my Dad pitched in to help set it up while I was busy getting our wines ready. Actually, 'help' might be a little unkind - he reminds me that he did most of the work!"

You wouldn't read about it

"I used to attend at a lot of 'rock concerts' in Papua New Guinea. The only difference there was that there was no music, only rocks! On Friday afternoons the local lads would get a bit tired and emotional and start raining rocks down on the roof. I can handle anything that the elements and the wine industry can throw at me after four years of that!"

Wining kids

"My kids will play with anyone!"

25 Murray Street Tanunda

Map F10 Winery 12

Ph (08) 8563 2170

www.domainbarossa.com

rtodd@smartchat.net.au

Est 2002

Cellar door tastings open Weekends 12-5:30, other days by appointment

Coffee, light meals, tutored tastings

Price range $15-$34

Key Wines: Ruth Miller Eden Valley Riesling, Black Tongue Shiraz

Food matches

"We have a wood-fired oven in cellar door. My speciality is a lamb, basil and tzatziki pizza, with our Black Tongue Shiraz!"

49

domain day wines

Robin Day is a Barossa veteran, after a twenty-eight year career with Orlando, variously as a Winemaker, Chief Winemaker, Technical Director and International Development Director. In 2003 he set up his own operation on one of the highest and coolest sites in the Barossa Ranges. "Our vineyard is at an altitude of 450 metres at Mt Crawford," Robin says. "If you go any further in most directions you are no longer in the Barossa." This site has become home to an eclectic array of no less than ten different varieties, including virtually everything that you wouldn't expect – and not a vine of Shiraz, Cabernet, Grenache or Mataro.

My place

"In 1999 I was looking for a piece of cool climate land within driving range of home," recalls Robin. "I guess you could say that was slothful, because after roaming the world for 1.5 million frequent flyer points, I was over that! I found the site because the car that I had been building for twelve years was not always on my side. Toward the end of the gestation of the replica of a Type 59 Bugatti, the main mechanic had pointed me to an engineer at Mt Crawford who put his artisan skills and love into beautiful work with metal. Roger, who is now our de facto vineyard fix-it-man, was making some parts in polished aluminium for me. On my way up to pick them up I saw a For Sale sign. It looked as though the site would have excellent air flow and water drainage, so I rang the agent and asked if he had a soil auger. After we worked out that a posthole digger was a loose translation,

24 Queen Street Williamstown

Map K7 Winery 13

Ph (08) 8524 6224

www.domainday.com.au

robinday@domaindaywines.com

Est 1999

Cellar door tastings open 10-5 daily

Tutored tastings

Price range $7-$28

Key Wines: one serious Riesling, 'g' Garganega, Sangiovese, Saperavi

we checked out the soil and bought the property. Since that time there has never been a dull moment, but we keep working on new and inventive ways to complicate things! The most recent has been our oak and hazelnut/truffle venture and shamelessly manipulating the soil to plant Nebbiolo."

Relaxing in the Riesling vineyard at Domain Day

You wouldn't read about it

"Wyndham Hill Smith was showing some visitors around Yalumba. 'How many people work here, Mr Hill Smith?' one asked. 'About half of the bastards!' was the reply.

"Peter Lehmann was showing a group around Saltram. 'Do you make vinegar, young man?' a little lady asked. 'Not intentionally, madam,' was the reply.

"Jon Fechner of the Apex

Eden Valley
Dragan Radocaj Photography

Bakery would get my vote anytime for the best throwaway line which he repeated as frequently as required. Jonny was my right hand man in the red vintage cellar at Orlando. He was worth about five blokes as a result of a combination of work ethic, positive thinking, morale boosting and mastery of bulls**t. Time after time on a Sunday morning in vintage he would be there looking and feeling like death, pulling hoses and directing the cellar guys with the mother of all hangovers. 'Robin, I'm never going to drink again,' was the famous line."

Visiting Domain Day

"We always have some bin ends and an odd dozen or two of quaffers at the cellar door. There is a browsing rack for single bottle cheapies and back vintages of reds. If you call in advance to make an appointment we can arrange vineyard visits, master class tastings conducted by myself and group catering by Regency

trained chef, Jimmy Day."

Food matches

"My favourite combination is 'Domain Day one serious Sangiovese' with slow cooked Tuscan roast of beef. It is half a lifetime in one dish! We like the vibrancy of the Lagrein with duck, veal or gourmet sausages and we prefer to drink our 'one serious rosé' with Indian curries."

Local knowledge

"Roaring 40's Café in Angaston has the best pizza you will find anywhere. Keils in Tanunda is a great coffee spot. For a great meal, I really enjoy the inventiveness at 1918, the classic class that Peter Clarke produces at Vintners, and Appellation is a great dining spot for special occasions.

"Years ago I caught decent sized rainbow trout in Jacob's Creek and the Para and even managed to catch one during my lunch break once or twice when I was a young winemaker at Orlando."

Sunset over Rowland Flat
Dragan Radocaj Photography

dorrien estate

Dorrien Estate is home to the massive Cellarmasters Wine Group, a mail order and membership-based wine club that sells direct to consumers. There's no cellar door or sales outlet in the Barossa as their wines are only available through the club.

My Place

"No one knows much about us as our sales channel is unique but I'm always amazed at the affection the locals have towards Dorrien," says General Manager and Winemaker, Mark Robertson. "We've built up a fiercely loyal core of Barossa growers. The winemakers who've been here over the years read like a who's who of winemaking fame. This says something about the culture at Dorrien, and we'd like to think it shows in our wines."

You wouldn't read about it

"Without a cellar door we don't generally have visitors, but every now and then we have a bin end clearance where we get rid of all the mixed cases and loose ends. People line up with their trailers from 5am to get first access and we sometimes move over 2000 cases in a day!"

Local knowledge

"For a top meal, you really can't go past 1918. Anywhere that lets you take your own wine and is always pleased to see you gets my vote!"

"For a really good beer and good company, try the Snake Pit at the Angas Park (AP) Pub. Ignore the tats on

Corner Barossa Highway & Siegersdorf Road Tanunda

Ph (08) 8561 2200

www.cellarmasters.com.au

cellar@cellarmasters.com.au

Est 1988

Price range $10-$50

Key Wines: Mum's Block Shiraz, Bin 1 Barossa Valley Cabernet, Krondorf Growers' Barossa Shiraz Viognier

everyone — these are some of the most genuine people you will meet!"

Wining kids

"When the kids are getting a bit ragged, try Kathy's Sweet Shop in Tanunda. The bribe angle always works for me!"

dutschke wines

When Wayne Dutschke decided to crush grapes from his uncle Ken Semmler's old St Jakobi vineyard in 1990, it was red wines and fortifieds that would be his focus. Two decades later, the fruit purity and balance in his wines have established his reputation among the best winemakers in the Barossa. He also happens to be one of the most friendly blokes you will ever meet.

My place

"We love it down here in Lyndoch because it's so peaceful," says Wayne. "We don't have the busy tourism that they have up at Nuri and out Marananga way, which makes it much quieter here."

Barossa dirt

"Our vines still grow on the land that my mother's family, the Semmlers, settled on when they came out in the 1850s. A lot of the land surrounds the St Jakobi church and school, which were a big part of their life. Virtually everyone in four generations was baptised, schooled and married there.

"The St Jakobi vineyard was purchased by my grandfather, Oscar Semmler, in the mid-1930s. It was primarily dairy country then and there were no vines on it apart from some old Mataro near the house.

"We also take a bit of fruit from three of the six vineyards along God's Hill Road. To me, it's a unique little patch. There are many unique patches throughout the Barossa, but because of the soil variation along this strip, and because it's so small, I think it's quite exciting. I see more ripe plum up on the hill here and more dark cherry and spice and finesse in the more fertile soil down the bottom. There's a great deal of contrast in the styles grown along the road. It's our little project to see what God's Hill Road becomes over time. I feel that it is distinct from other fruit grown in the Lyndoch Valley.

"Our love of reds and fortifieds have led me to focus on these styles. With the Sun Dried

Lot 1 God's Hill Road Lyndoch

Ph (08) 8524 5485

www.dutschkewines.com

wayne@dutschkewines.com

Est 1990

Tastings by appointment

Price range $20-$75

Key Wines: Oscar Semmler Shiraz, St Jakobi Shiraz, WillowBend Shiraz Merlot Cabernet, GHR God's Hill Road Four Vineyards Shiraz

Shiraz, we pick the fruit as ripe as we can. We go through the vineyard with buckets a few weeks after the machine harvester and pick anything that's left on the vines. It's been shrivelled by the sun to two-thirds of its weight."

Visiting Dutschke

"If you'd like to visit, just give us a call or send an email, preferably with a few days' notice. We'll normally spend more than an hour in the shed, so allow plenty of time for the visit. We'll show you the inside of a working winery and taste samples out of tanks and

St Jakobi church, school and vineyard

53

barrels. Depending on what you'd like to see, we could jump in the vehicle and head down God's Hill Road to do a quick lap of the vineyard so you can picture where the fruit is from. Most of our fruit is taken from vineyards in three kilometres south of our front gate — any vineyard we drive past between here and uncle Ken's.

"We also have a guest barrel (instead of a guest book) for our visitors to sign. I'm up to about the ninth or tenth barrel now and I'm running out of space for them inside! I use the signature barrels for our Sun Dried Shiraz, but I only need eight or ten barrels for it."

You wouldn't read about it

"God's Hill Road is one of the earliest known stretches of dirt in the area," Wayne points out. "I don't know why it's named as it is, but there are a few jokes and rumours around. This is the highest point around here, perhaps they thought this is where God would sit? There's a huge, sharp crest on the track down a bit further where you get to a point and you can't see down the other side. Some people say that's what people used to sing out when they got to the top, 'Oh my God!'

"I think it might have something to do with early gold mining days. There's an old gold mining shaft in our front garden that we found just by chance when there was a heavy rain. It was a really wet few days in August and we had four-and-a-half inches in two-and-a-half days, which is a lot for us here. My wife Brenda was chasing a cardboard box that was blowing in the wind across the yard, and came across a depression that was 30 or 40 cm deep and almost a metre square. She came in and asked had I been out there digging? Not in this sort of weather! The next day it was three-and-a-half metres deep! We thought it might have been an old well. But I asked an old guy, Jack Filsell, who grew up as a kid in this area and lives just down the way. He said there's actually a vertical shaft, and there's another one on the other side of God's Hill Road, and a horizontal shaft that ran forty feet underneath the road. Years ago, before vehicles had pneumatic wheels, when there were steel rims on buggies, you could hear the change in note as the buggies went down the road. Maybe there was gold found in the area? Maybe there wasn't but they had a good look!"

You would read about it!

Wayne Dutschke and Paul Cassidy are the men with purple hands. Their children's book, 'My Dad has Purple Hands' was written by Wayne and illustrated by his mate Paul.

Wayne explains that "the book shows the steps of winemaking through the eyes of a little kid who grows up with a family in a vineyard and a small winery out the door, questioning why Dad comes home with purple hands. There are plenty of children out there who have parents who are winemakers. People can purchase the book from us, from the bookshops in the Valley and a good number of cellar doors. It retails for $24.95."

Wayne and Brenda Dutschke's children, Jackson and Sami, treading the grapes

Wining kids

"The Whispering Wall is just over the hill, 6km from here. It's a large concrete reservoir wall which, by pure chance, forms an amphitheatre. Just by whispering at one side, you can hear what's being said very, very clearly on the other side. It's more than 100m across, which is quite a distance for the sound to travel! It's marvellous! We take a lot of people there, and we still get a thrill out of it ourselves each time we go!"

Local knowledge

"In the area here there's something that I don't think is ever promoted. Just across the hill here is Sandy Creek Conservation Park. It's 10km around. And inside it is an old homestead called Sandy Creek Hostel that belongs to the Youth Hostel Association. It's an old homestead, done up beautifully inside and anyone can lease it out. It can sleep up to ten people, and it's $140-$170 per night – very inexpensive! For overseas visitors it's just ideal because you can go and visit the wineries and come back at night and have a glass of wine on the veranda and watch the kangaroos.

"Yaldara is a nice winery to visit. There's a lot of history there and it's a great building – a huge sandstone-fronted chateau with lovely gardens and a cheese and olive tasting room.

"If you want a really good steak, The Lord Lyndoch is great for Wagyu beef. They're decent-sized cuts and you can get a 600g steak. It's the pick of the restaurants in Lyndoch.

"Many people travel to Lyndoch just for the butcher. There are many good butchers throughout the Barossa, but when Brenda buys something from Lyndoch, most of the time I can pick that it's from there. It's got a particular character about it. Sometimes walking down the street, you can smell the smokehouse going, and it's that same character that's in the meat.

"The Lavender Farm is off the Lyndoch-Williamstown Road. There are big paddocks of Lavender and all sorts of oils and smelly things made from Lavender.

"Barossa Helicopters is a worthwhile thing to do while you're in the Barossa. Some days on the weekend they will advertise a quick flight for just $25."

eden springs

"Our belief is that good wine begins in the vineyard" is the philosophy of Ray Gatt, who bought Eden Springs and set about upgrading its facilities in 2006. This small, cool climate producer specialises in Cabernet Sauvignon, Riesling, and Shiraz and has recently added to its holdings with the purchase of the historic Siegersdorf vineyard.

My Place

"Quite simply, High Eden is a cool climate wine growing region like no other!" Ray exclaims. "With an area of just forty hectares it's also one of the smallest gazetted wine regions in Australia. What we lack in quantity, however, we make up for in quality. The thin, rocky soils and low-yielding vines of High Eden vineyards produce fruit of incredible intensity, making wines with varietal characters that set them apart."

Barossa Character

"Eden Springs' wines are made by the talented and terrific winemaker Jo Irvine. After many years as a nursing sister she studied winemaking and hasn't looked back since. Infamously known as the 'Queen of Zin' for her talents in the early days of Australian Zinfandel production, Jo was named 'International Red Winemaker of the Year' at the 2006 London International Wine Challenge. She's proof that the old glass ceiling has been well and truly shattered in the world of winemaking."

You wouldn't read about it

"'The Mushroom Tree' is a giant monkey nut pine tree high on a ridge of the southern Barossa Ranges. Its distinctive canopy is shaped like a mushroom and is visible for miles. Locals use it like a beacon to lead them up the pathways to High Eden. Look out for 'The Mushroom Tree' to find your bearings and you'll never be lost in the Barossa!"

Local knowledge

"The Mount Pleasant Hotel

Boehm Springs Road Springton

Ph (08) 8564 1166

www.edensprings.com.au

info@edensprings.com.au

Est 1972

Tastings at Taste Eden Valley in Angaston

Price range $16-$20

Key Wines: High Eden Shiraz, High Eden Riesling

and the Eden Valley Hotel are hands-on operations, both offering great quality, keen prices and no pretension."

Wining kids

"Throw your kids in the car with their bikes, boards or skates and let them explore the Barossa Valley Bike Path, an off-road route from Kroemer's Crossing near Tanunda north to Nuriootpa."

Food matches

"Our Eden Springs High Eden Riesling works well with food that has simple, clean flavours. A favourite match of mine is prosciutto and melon."

Morning mist over Eden Springs

eden valley wines

"Some time ago the brand 'Eden Valley Wines' was offered for sale by auction and twelve local grape growers and winemakers banded together and successfully bid to gain ownership of the regional name," explains one of the twelve, Brian Waples. "The principle is that wines are crafted for the label only from parcels of members' fruit, from vineyards spread throughout the Eden Valley." Fruit selection and winemaking duties are handled by Stephen Henschke and James and Joanne Irvine.

Local knowledge

"When we are not leaning on the neighbouring fence discussing the weather, politics or how to run the wine industry you may bump into us sharing a beer at either the Eden Valley or Springton Pub."

Ph (08) 8562 4590

www.edenvalleywines.com.au

contactus@edenvalleywines.com.au

Price range $25-$49

Key Wines: Eden Valley Wines Riesling, Eden Valley Wines Shiraz

eighteen forty seven wines

Located in the heart of Rowland Flat, 1847 Wines produces small volumes of wines made exclusively from estate grown grapes. John Curnow spent the majority of his career in the beverage industry before purchasing a block of land in 1995 that had first been settled in 1847.

My Place

"Our place is about making special wines," John says. "The goal that we set right from the start was to make wines that would be recognised internationally as fine quality."

You wouldn't read about it

"The great Johann Gramp was the first owner of our property, and it is the original site of the first winery to be built in the Barossa."

Vineyards of significance

"There's a funny thing about our 1902-planted old block. There is one row of this vineyard that the birds just love to attack each and every year. It seems like nature knows something that we don't!"

Local knowledge

"In the Barossa you don't need to go far to be immersed in history. You can feel it all around you everywhere you go. This place has a unique culture like no other."

Church Road Rowland Flat

Ph (08) 8524 5328

www.eighteenfortyseven.com

1847@eighteenfortyseven.com

Est 1996

Tastings by appointment

Price range $40-$100

Key Wines: Home Block Petit Verdot, Sparkling Petit Verdot, First Pick Shiraz

John Curnow

elderton wines

3-5 Tanunda Road Nuriootpa

Map D12 Winery 15

Ph (08) 8568 7878

www.eldertonwines.com.au

elderton@eldertonwines.com.au

Est 1982

Cellar door tastings open Mon-Fri 8:30-5, Sat-Sun 11-4

Picnic facilities, tutored tastings

Price range $13-$100

Key Wines: Command Shiraz, Ashmead Cabernet Sauvignon, Ode to Lorraine, Estate Cabernet Sauvignon, Estate Shiraz

Originally planted in 1904, the Elderton Estate vineyard has since been almost completely surrounded by the town of Nuriootpa. "The vineyard would be much more valuable as residential or commercial development, but the Ashmead family has a real passion for this wonderful resource of row after row of gnarled old vines," says Allister Ashmead, who heads up the family winery with his brother, Cameron. This vineyard is the site of their 104-year-old Command Shiraz block and 64-year-old Ashmead Cabernet block, providing the fruit for the two flagship wines of the estate.

My place

"Our cellar door is modern and comfortable, and staffed with friendly and informative ambassadors who can take you through the wines of Elderton," explains Allister.

"We have a comprehensive list of wines which cover multiple price points, multiple varieties and multiple sub-appellations of the Barossa. We generally will have quite a few of our elite wines on tasting. Our wines are served in Riedel glassware and we use specialised wine fridges in our tasting room to ensure that both reds and whites are served at the correct temperature. We don't mess around with merchandise – for us it's all about the wine."

Barossa Character

"There is a spot in our estate vineyard where about six vines are some forty years younger than the rest, as our late father Neil Ashmead, whilst naughtily combining his two great passions of wine and motorcars, rolled his HSV Commodore going very quickly up one of the vineyard rows!"

Elderton WINES BAROSSA

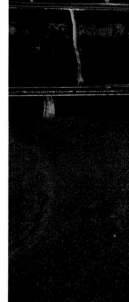

You wouldn't read about it

"Elderton began as a winery in 1982, but not many people know that Elderton was almost wiped out just before vintage in March 1983. A flash flood came in the middle of the night and basically 'knocked over' the entire estate vineyard. Each vine was painstakingly put up by hand and the winery was saved. As a result, we don't recommend drinking the 1983 vintage!"

Barossa dirt

"Elderton is proactive about sustainable operations. We were the first winery in South Australia and the second in Australia to be carbon neutral. We are turning our vineyards towards biodynamics to increase the biodiversity in the ecosystem, using solar power in our cellar door and we have an amazing water recycling capability in our winery. We believe in generational family wine companies and we want to ensure that this place is in good shape when our children hopefully take the helm in the future."

Wining kids

"There is an amazing playground with an old steam train across from the cellar door, so kids just love making our cellar door a 'must stop!' We have expansion plans for our cellar door, which will include activities for the kids."

Elderton cellar door

Food matches

"Barossa Shiraz goes with everything! Seriously, though, to keep things simple, a nice dry aged porterhouse steak cooked rare on the grill goes down well with Elderton Shiraz every time!"

Left Drinks on the veranda
Centre Allister Ashmead, Richard Langford & Cameron Ashmead at the Elderton winery
Right Elderton Winemaker, Richard Langford

59

fernfield wines

Bryce Lillecrapp, a fifth generation descendent of Eden Valley founder William Lillecrapp, gave his wife Bronwyn a present of a short winemaking course in 2001. This set off a chain of events that led her to further studies and to the formation of Fernfield Wines.

Rushlea Homestead, Fernfield Wines cellar door

My Place

"We are enjoying the opportunity to maintain a tradition here in the beautiful Eden Valley," says Bronwyn. "Our family-run business is about making hand-crafted wines that people can afford to drink."

Wining kids

"Kids are always welcome here. We're a family business and our kids are a part of it. There are always plenty of toys at cellar door to keep the young ones distracted."

Food matches

"Our Eden Valley Riesling works wonderfully with Thai.

Rushlea Road Eden Valley

Map J15 Winery 16

Ph (08) 8564 1041

www.fernfieldwines.com.au

rebecca@fernfieldwines.com.au

Est 2002

Cellar door tastings open 10-5 daily

Local produce platters

Price range $12.50-$30

Key Wines: Pridmore Shiraz, Juuso Merlot, CCC Cabernet Sauvignon

A touch of sweet fruit and fresh acidity is a perfect match for a little chilli and spice."

Homestead on Seppeltsfield Road
Dragan Radocaj Photography

Matt Gant and John Retsas

first drop wines

"My ambition is to make booze that turns me on, and enjoy the ride!" says winemaker Matt Gant. "First Drop is about passion for life, fun and flavour – a lifelong commitment to making kick-arse booze!"His partner in First Drop Wines is John Retsas. "While we have a lot of fun, it's really important to us to respect the history, the subregional characters and the traditions of the Barossa," he says. This philosophy has led the pair to create a range of contemporary Barossa wines that cleverly embrace the nuances of the Barossa and at the same time makes them accessible to a new generation of drinkers. "We make wines that we want to drink and that express the style of Australia," says Matt. Their labels and web site are as innovative and ground-breaking as the wines themselves.

My place

In keeping with its contemporary approach, First Drop focuses on an online emphasis rather than a regional presence. "We're too busy having fun to open a cellar door!" jokes John. "But, seriously, a lot of blogging happens online and punters are having a great time expressing themselves on our site."

In the Barossa, First Drop Wines are poured at 1918 in Tanunda and can be purchased at Tanunda Cellars and at the Brauhaus in Angaston.

Ph 0420 971 209
www.firstdropwines.com
matt@firstdropwines.com
Price range $18-$100

Key Wines: The Cream Barossa Shiraz, Lush Barossa Trincadeira Rosé, The Matador, Mother's Milk Barossa Shiraz

Local knowledge

"Our old favourite spot to eat is 1918 and we like to have a punt at The Valley Hotel or a really good beer at the Tanunda Club," says John. "The Valley Hotel is our local canteen, where we have great production meetings! It's the source of many a crazy First Drop idea."

flaxman wines

"Fiona and I used to visit a different wine region around Australia each year but we kept coming back to the Barossa," says Col Sheppard. "We built up some wonderful friendships with people in the wineries, and I worked a vintage with Andrew Seppelt five years ago. While I was here I was told about the Flaxman Valley property and I bought it without Fiona seeing it – a very brave move!" The old vine Shiraz, Riesling and Semillon from this site form the basis of the Flaxman range.

Tasting Flaxman Wines

"You can taste our wines at 'Taste Eden Valley' in Angaston but we welcome you to visit us at our property in Flaxman's Valley anytime. It is always nice for people to actually see where the wines are coming from and meet the people behind them.

Col Sheppard working hard in the vineyard

Appointments can be made either by phoning my mobile or emailing."

You wouldn't read about it

"My best kept secret was making our Shhh Cabernet. It was a wine I made with my mate Nathan Schultz without Fiona or Nathan's partner Lydia knowing. We wrote 'Shhh' on the barrels so nobody would let it slip to the girls. We showed them the finished product and luckily they loved it. There's a bit of a theme happening here with

Lot 535 Flaxmans Valley Road Angaston

Ph 0411 668 949

www.flaxmanwines.com.au

info@flaxmanwines.com.au

Est 2004

Tastings at Taste Eden Valley in Angaston

Price range $25-$45

Key Wines: Riesling, The Stranger Shiraz Cabernet, Eden Valley Shiraz, Shhh Cabernet, Dessert Semillon

flaxman wines

not telling Fiona things!"

Local knowledge

"A Barossa Burger at The Barossa Farmers Market is a great way to kick off the day if you've over indulged the night before! We also really enjoy lunch on a cold day in front of the fire at either 1918 or Kabminye."

Sunrise over Tanunda from Mengler's Hill. Dragan Radocaj Photography

fox gordon wines

There are few winemakers in the country with the talent to make a diverse variety of wines as consistently outstanding as Fox Gordon winemaker, Tash Mooney. A consultant winemaker for many brands, it is in the Fox Gordon range that Tash has the opportunity to craft wines that she can call her own. The business is a family enterprise run by three families with a history and passion for the Barossa Valley. Distinguished packaging and value-for-money pricing places Fox Gordon at the top of the list of Barossa boutiques that you must seek out.

Barossa Character

"As a winemaker with grandparents and great grandparents from the Barossa (and a maiden name of Shultz!), I grew up listening to stories about the region and its people and it gave me

a real sense of place. I have a deep connection to the Barossa Valley culture and this is why I choose winemaking as a career."

My place

"We're getting back to the community way of life in the world, with everyone planting gardens and getting back to the basics. And that's the way the community in the Barossa has always been here. It's a really simple and authentic way of life. And that's how we make our wine."

You wouldn't read about it

"In Springton, on the edge of the Eden Valley you can visit an historic red gum tree that housed a family of immigrants in the 1850s. The 'Herbig Family Tree' is about 300 years old now and it's still standing. It was hollowed out, probably by lightning, to offer a large area in the centre where

Lot 535 Flaxmans Valley Yettie Road Williamstown

Ph (08) 8524 7149

www.foxgordon.com.au

info@foxgordon.com.au

Est 2001

Tastings by appointment

Price range $20-$45

Key Wines: Hannah's Swing Shiraz, King Louis Cabernet Sauvignon, By George Cabernet Tempranillo, Eight Uncles Shiraz, Abby Viognier, Princess Fiano – yes, every wine is a standout!

Friedrich Herbig, his wife and the first two of their sixteen children lived. These are my ancestors on my Mum's side. It's a fascinating place to visit."

Vineyards of significance

"Fox Gordon and I have worked with some historical vineyards and one in particular I will never forget. It's in the Barossa backblocks and run by an elderly German couple who planted the vineyard eighty years ago. They can speak only a little English, wear the traditional German hats with the ear flaps that tie under your chin, use kerosene lamps and have two cows that they milk by hand each day. They're a lovely couple and their fruit is some of the best that I have ever made wine from."

Visiting Fox Gordon

"Fox Gordon doesn't have a cellar door, so we offer tastings

Tash Mooney and Rachel Atkins

to visitors in the Barossa at a local restaurant or wherever they are staying. We come to you! Give me a call if you'd like to do a tasting. We often end up going to dinner at somewhere like 1918. Then visitors are really relaxed, in their environment, and I really enjoy that. They get to really taste and appreciate the wines much more than in a standard cellar door experience."

Food matches

"Our Hannah's Swing Shiraz goes brilliantly with Lachsschinken, potato and goat's cheese pie. It's fantastic winter fare!"

Local knowledge

"Murdock is great for cocktails and sardines."

Wining kids

"I asked my kids for their favourite things and they said they love the Barossa Farmers Market because there is always lots of free stuff! The Whispering Wall at Williamstown has to be seen to be believed. And they love a wintertime fire and BBQ in the Mount Crawford forest that surrounds the southern end of the Barossa (but do check fire restrictions first)."

Rowland Flat vineyard.
Dragan Radocaj Photography

gibson wines

Rob Gibson is a mainstay of the Barossa and impossible to miss - not least for his signature moustache. After twenty-two years in winemaking and viticulture at Penfolds Wines, he utilised his intimate knowledge of the Barossa's best vineyard sites to establish his family label in 1997. He has since built a strong following as a specialist in Shiraz and Merlot.

My Place

"I'm known as 'The Dirt Man' for my love of viticulture and soil," say Rob. "I'd like to think that this translates into a sense of 'earthiness' about my place as well. It's a free, easy going environment, but we work hard in the vineyards so we don't have to mess around with the fruit too much in the winery. We like to think of ourselves as 'wine growers,' with one foot in the vineyard and the other in the winery."

You wouldn't read about it

"I was operating the crusher at Penfolds in the early '70s when we introduced a new gantry for unloading grape trucks automatically. It was supposed to be revolutionary and speed things up, but there was one legendary grower, Norm Roehr, who insisted on unloading his fruit by himself with a pitchfork. The funny thing was he was so strong he still unloaded his truck faster by hand than we could mechanically!"

Infamous growers

"One of my growers, I'll just call him Will, turned eighty-five years young recently, and was still in the habit of using the old-fashioned method of keeping the birds away from his fruit. The only problem is that his aim isn't quite what it used to be, so I've had to retire his shotgun from active duty!"

Local knowledge

"Autumn is a great time in the Barossa. Everyone starts to relax and has time to stop and chat. If you want to find out any local gossip, get down to the Barossa Farmers Market at this time of year and take the time to chat to the locals."

Wining kids

"We have a toy basket and mat in the cellar door and a Pétanque court and totem tennis pole outside. That

Willows Road Light Pass

Map D13 Winery 17

Ph (08) 8562 3193

www.barossavale.com

anne@barossavale.com

Est 1996

Cellar door tastings open 11-5 daily

Picnic facilities, tours, tutored tastings, crafts, local produce, historical buildings, private lunches by arrangement

Price range $25-$96

Key Wines: Reserve Shiraz, Reserve Merlot, The Dirt Man Shiraz

should keep the kids occupied while you enjoy a tasting!"

Food matches

"I love Merlot and much of our reputation is built around it. With a bit of age, I reckon our Reserve Merlot works perfectly with some good local prosciutto and a block of parmesan."

Rob Gibson seving Trevor March (Heathvale Wines)

65

glaetzer wines

Although Glaetzer wines was only established in the mid-1990s, its heritage runs much deeper. The first Glaetzers settled in the Barossa in 1888 and were among the earliest recorded viticulturists in the region. The name has remained prominent ever since, and today there are no fewer than eight winemakers in the family, working across South Australia and as far afield as Tasmania and New Zealand. Ben Glaetzer took over the winemaking responsibility from his father in 2002. "Behind the scenes, my father Colin and uncle John have had a key influence on a number of significant Barossa labels over more than thirty years," Ben explains. He has already made his own mark, cementing his name among the 'rock star' makers of the region.

Tasting Glaetzer Wines

Ben's lifestyle is perhaps not dissimilar to a travelling rock star.

"I spend six months of the year making wine and six months on the road promoting it internationally and domestically, so this is my focus rather than cellar doors and tourism," he explains. "To find our wines locally, Amon-ra and Anaperenna are available at 1918 and Vintners, and the local pubs have Wallace and Bishop. The full range is available to purchase at Tanunda Cellars."

Infamous growers

"My focus is on making wines that are reflective of their particular regions," Ben says. "Of all the Barossa subregions, Ebenezer is the one where the

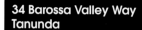

34 Barossa Valley Way
Tanunda

Ph (08) 8563 0288

www.glaetzer.com

glaetzer@glaetzer.com

Est 1995

Price range $20-$90

*Key Wines: Anaperenna
Shiraz Cabernet
Sauvignon, Wallace
Shiraz Grenache*

Glaetzer

BAROSSA VALLEY

wine in barrel looks the most like the fruit in the vineyards. I want my wines to have approachability in their youth but also longevity. And that's what I get from Ebenezer. We source from vines there reputed to be 130 or 140 years old and also young vines — by which I mean 20 or 30 years old. The older vines are not necessarily the best quality but are usually the most consistent.

"We have two great growers in Ebenezer that my father established relationships with during his days at Barossa Valley Estate. Sixth generation grower Adrian Hoffmann runs a vineyard with his father and also their neighbours' vineyard. I take a large majority of their fruit. Adrian is keen to work with me because he understands how keen I am to showcase the best that the

Ben Glaetzer

Adrian Hoffmann (right) with grandfather Gordon, father Jeff and son Byron on their old vine Ebenezer vineyard

subregion can do. He has a real interest in the crop and the fruit but also in the finished product, so we taste together. We have a longstanding association and understanding and we reward him in a good year and we reward him in a bad year. That's the beauty of dealing with guys like him. We both have young sons — five and six years old — and it would be great to think that in ten or twelve generations we can still be sourcing from the same people in the same region.

"Adrian is not doing much dissimilar to what his father, grandfather and great grandfather were doing. And he listens to the older generations, which is critical. He also prides himself on how many committees he's on that are helping the Barossa. I have predicted that he will be Mayor of the Barossa in twenty years' time!"

Wining kids

"I frequently take my son Wilbur up to the numerous national parks for a walk. It's great up there. If you're there between 7:30 and 9 in the morning or at sunset the roos are always out. The Barossa Bowland is a good spot for kids as well. It's just been renovated and it's well run. The Tanunda club has a kids' room at the back, just off the dining room, with a TV and toys and things. Vintners and 1918 have good kids' menus which are interesting and innovative. On Saturday morning the Barossa Farmers Market is good for kids. The kids can buy a bag of cherries or apricots or whatever is in season."

glen eldon wines

Richard Sheedy's impressive resumé lists winemaking stints at leading Barossa cellars including Elderton and St Hallett, as well as being the youngest ever Chairman of the Barossa Winemakers Association. He's currently a board member of the Barossa Grape & Wine Association, a father of four, and still manages to find time for his own brand, Glen Eldon Wines, where he is both General Manager and Winemaker. In little more than a decade, he has established it among the Barossa's more progressive young brands.

My Place

"After nearly twenty years in the Barossa, I've got to know a few of the secrets about its vineyards," says Richard. "It's this understanding of what each area brings to the finished wines that has allowed us to produce regional wines at realistic prices."

Local knowledge

"For great country food and excellent value for money, get over to Buck's Bistro in Springton."

Wining kids

"There are usually enough toys left lying around at cellar door by our children to entertain a bus load of kids!"

Food matches

"Just look at me – I love food and wine! I know Shiraz is the flagship, but we make bloody great Cabernet, too. A favourite would have to be traditional roast lamb with all the trimmings and a bottle of Glen Eldon Cabernet."

Corner Koch & Nitschke Roads Krondorf

Map G10 Winery 18

Ph 1300 653 773

www.gleneldonwines.com.au

info@gleneldonwines.com.au

Est 1997

Cellar door tastings open Mon-Fri 9-5, weekends by appointment

Tutored tastings

Price range $16-$110

Key Wines: Kicking Back Shiraz Mataro Grenache, Black Springs Shiraz, Dry Bore Shiraz, Shiraz Mataro, Eden Valley Riesling

GLEN ELDON
WINES
Barossa

Richard Sheedy

glenburn estate wines

With every wine priced well below $20, Glenburn Estate offers a value proposition for those looking to explore the wines of the Barossa without breaking the bank. Rob and Marg Craigie established the estate on the deep clay soils of Ebenezer in 1998.

My Place

"Our winery is equipped to handle a maximum of seven tonnes of grapes at any one time, so we're the definition of 'boutique'!" says Rob. "This allows us to apply great attention to detail, growing all our own grapes and maintaining full control from vineyard to bottle. We started with the philosophy that we wanted to make wines that we would enjoy drinking ourselves, and nothing has changed."

Local knowledge

"Roaring 40's Café in Angaston is a favourite of ours. It's unpretentious, relaxed and the food is always good."

Food matches

"Try our fortified Chardonnay with a cheese, fruit and nut platter, in front of the fire on a brisk winter night."

Ebenezer Road Ebenezer

Ph 0417 862 574

rob_margcraigie@bigpond.com

Est 2005

Tastings by appointment

Price range $8-$16

Key Wines: Shiraz, Fortified Chardonnay

Rob Craigie with Rusty the dog

god's hill wines

GOD'S HILL

"My grandfather threw me in a vat in Italy when I was about six years old," says Charlie Scalzi. "Making wine has always been a family tradition. We had a little vineyard near Naples with olive trees out the back and he would sell grapes and make wine and olive oil. I migrated to Australia with my father when I was eleven and we've been making wine in Lyndoch ever since. I'm just keeping on the tradition that I've been taught by my father and grandfather. In 2006 I showed my six-year-old grandson how to pick grapes and crush them by foot."

My place

"We wear what our mood tells us to wear, we eat what our mood tells us to eat and we drink what our mood tells us to drink!" says Charlie. "Our wines are influenced by our Italian heritage. The Italian style is more fruit driven so I want the fruit to dictate the flavour of the wine. The fruit is hand-selected exclusively from our single vineyard estate and made into wine with as little interference as possible."

Visiting God's Hill Wines

"My wife and I host our visitors ourselves. Please

Lot 211, Cnr God's Hill Rd and Gilbert St Lyndoch

Map H7 Winery 22

Ph 0412 836 004

www.godshillwines.com

sales@godshillwines.com

Tastings by appointment

Tasting platter or BBQ with Charlie on request

Price range $20-$59

Key Wines: Menzel Shiraz, AMO`ROSSO, III Ros, SELV'AGGIO

phone in advance to make an appointment. We like to host people in small groups, less than twelve, but the smaller the better. We also make an extra virgin olive oil and we pickle our own olives so we put on a bit of Italian antipasto with Italian cheeses, prosciutto and salami (about $10 per person).

Charlie Scalzi

gomersal wines

GOMERSAL WINES
BAROSSA VALLEY

"I went from wrecking things to planting things, and there's a certain irony to that," says Barry White, who traded in his Adelaide-based demolition business to become a vigneron and wine producer. In 2000 he purchased and renovated the run-down Chateau Rosevale building and planted a vineyard the following year.

My Place

"I drink a lot of wine, so I

Gomersal Wines cellar door

thought it would be a good idea to try to get my money back!" Barry laughs. "But pretty soon I worked out that starting a winery was an expensive business! That aside, I've discovered that this is an opportunity to make a lot of friends. When you put people, food and wine together great things happen. And that's what my place has become about: good wine, good people and good times!"

Local knowledge

"Everyone who comes to the Barossa owes it to themselves to pay a visit to Seppeltsfield. It's a magnificent place with a sense of history unlike anywhere else in the Valley."

Lot 137 Lyndoch Road Gomersal

Ph (08) 8563 3611

www.gomersalwines.com.au

info@gomersalwines.com.au

Est 1999

Cellar door tastings open Mon-Sun 10-5

Conferences, functions, coffee, light meals, crafts, local produce, kids' playground

Price range $18-$50

Key Wines: Eden Valley Riesling, Shiraz Rosé, GSM, Shiraz, Fortified Shiraz

Wining kids

"We've always thought it important to be family friendly, so we've set up a fully-equipped kids' playground and plenty of lawn to run around."

the grapes of ross

The Grapes of Ross is the passion of Lyndoch winemaker Ross Virgara and is not to be confused with Ross Estate, also in Lyndoch. Ross Virgara has a particular fondness for the Frontignac grape, from which he crafts a low alcohol Moscato. "It

the GRAPES of ROSS

matches beautifully with cheese, strawberries and paté," he says. Also look out for his subtle and food-friendly rosé.

My Place

"Take a passion for sharing good food, wine and company, add a love of classic books and movies and the Grapes of Ross was born," says Ross. "With a lifelong involvement in the food and wine industry, I've always had the desire to create small volume, hand-crafted fruit-driven wines."

Ph (08) 8524 4214

grapesofross@ihug.com.au

Price range $16-$32

Key Wines: Moscato, Ruby Tuesday Rosé, Black Rose Shiraz

Ross Virgara and his grapes

greenock creek wines

Step through the doors of Michael and Annabelle Waugh's cellar door in the tiny cellar under their 150-year-old stone cottage in the western reaches of the Barossa and you will gain an appreciation for the scale of this little operation. It will come as no surprise that it is only open between the second week of September and the end of November, because by this time the entire vintage has left through those doors. What isn't so obvious, however, is the cult following that this single vineyard red wine specialist has gathered around the world, placing its wines among the most sought-after in the Barossa. Sourced exclusively from estate, dry-grown, low-yielding vines, these are wines of colossal proportions that appeal to those who enjoy more alcoholic styles.

My place

"We're about making wines from what this country will let us make," explains Michael. "It gets very very hot here in the western Barossa, so we make big wines. I don't worry too much about all the controversy about high alcohols. We just make the wines the way we like them.

"Our Roennfeldt vines are our oldest and we're not exactly sure how old they are but they must be getting close to 100 years old. We make five Shirazes, two Cabernets and a Grenache. They're all single vineyard wines because I don't believe in blending. We use predominantly old oak rather than new because our goal is for the big, black fruit to really stand out."

Barossa Character

"My father was in the wine game years ago and he worked for Stonyfell wines up near Penfolds at Magill. I used to go up there and fool around and I thought, 'One day I'd like to do this myself.' The opportunity came in the late 1960s. I was a stonemason by trade and I'd done some work on the cellars at Henschke. I met Robert O'Callaghan at a party. He was looking for someone to help him build a winery and I was looking for someone to help me make wine so that's how we got together and it all started.

Radford Road Seppeltsfield

Map D9 Winery 21

Ph (08) 8562 8103

greenockcreek@ozemail.com.au

Est 1984

Cellar door tastings open Sept-Nov

Price range $29-$190

Key Wines: Roennfeldt Road Shiraz, Creek Block Shiraz

We built his winery in the 1980s and we made my first wine at home in 1984.

"Robert and Chris Ringland contract crushed our wines at Rockford until we built our own winery on Roennfeldt Rd in 1998. One reason I couldn't make wine on our Radford Road property where our cellar door is located was that the electricity supply was very vague. It was a very old cottage on a very old line. One minute it would be on and the next it would be off!

"Robert and Chris have both gone on to bigger things now but we're still the best of mates. They have both been an almighty help to us."

Michael and Annabelle Waugh and their Greenock Creek cellar door

gumpara wines

Looking for a $13 Shiraz made from grapes grown on sixty-five year old vines? Mark Mader left a role at Peter Lehmann Wines in 2000 to establish Gumpara Wines. His value-for-money range is made entirely from grapes sourced from his family's sixth generation estate, with vineyards dating back to the 1920s.

My Place

"Gumpara Wines was started with a simple premise," Mark explains, "to make high quality table wines at a good price, and we'd like it to stay that way. We only sell direct to consumers."

Local knowledge

"You can't beat a bit of yabbying in the local creeks and dams. It's great fun and freshly cooked yabbies are just delicious! Find a local to take you because you need to know where to look!"

Stockwell Road Light Pass

Ph (08) 8562 4559

gumpara@bigpond.net.au

Est 1999

Tastings by appointment

Price range $13-$25

Key Wines: Victor's Old Vine Shiraz, Old Vine Semillon

Food matches

"Marinated, braised rabbit works really well with our Victor's Old Vine Shiraz."

haan wines

"I'm the Austrian Haan variety, not the German variety!" says Hans Haan, who came to the Barossa in 1993 after twenty-six years in Hong Kong as a flight engineer with Ansett and Cathay Pacific. "My work is all about detail, because everything in my previous life was about detail," he says. His splendidly renovated 1850s farmhouse and manicured gardens stand as testimony to his attention to detail.

My place

"All of our fruit is sourced from this property," Hans explains. "All the vineyards visible on all sides are ours, all the way to the tree line at the back. As you drive in, you can see all the varieties labelled on the posts. When people visit, we take them for a look at the vineyards, winery and cellar. During the fruiting season we can show them each of the varieties in the vineyard and then taste the wines.

"We don't do cellar door sales, but we welcome people to visit by appointment. We are very well set up for tastings in the historic homestead. Just give us at least thirty minutes of notice, and preferably twenty-four hours.

"Our primary focus is on Merlot, and in particular our luxury Merlot Prestige. We have also made a name with Viognier and with The Wilhelmus, a blend of five varieties led by Cabernet."

Siegersdorf Road Tanunda

Ph (08) 8562 3788

www.haanwines.com.au

winebiz@ozemail.com.au

Est 1993

Tastings by appointment

Price range $15-$40

Key Wines: Merlot Prestige, Wilhelmus blend, Viognier Prestige

You wouldn't read about it

"We are quite new on the block. We bought the property in 1993 when we came to Australia from Hong Kong. People say that you won't get accepted into the Barossa for about twenty or twenty-five years but that's absolute rubbish! The Barossa has been very good to us."

HAAN

hare's chase

"The more you make wine in the Barossa the more you understand its possibilities," says Peter Taylor. And after thirty years of winemaking in the region, he should know. Following positions as Senior Red Winemaker at Penfolds and Chief Winemaker at Southcorp, he established Hare's Chase in 1997 with neighbour and business partner Mike de la Haye. Their single vineyard Marananga wines are available via mailing list and at selected restaurants.

My Place

"People tend to look back at the 'good old days' and wish for the ways of yesteryear, but for me the Barossa has never been as exciting and vibrant as it is now!" Peter exclaims. "There's so much experimentation and diversity, brought on by new faces with fresh energy and ambition, people who value what the Barossa has to offer. This is just what the Barossa needs, and it keeps a guy like me who has been around for a while on

his toes! I think this shows in the wines of Hare's Chase as well — we're constantly striving to make better wines, and so the brand continues to grow."

Corner Neldner & Jenke Roads Marananga

Ph (08) 8277 3506

www.hareschase.com

info@hareschase.com.au

Est 1997

Tastings by appointment

Price range $14-$25

Key Wines: Shiraz, Tempranillo, The Springer Shiraz Merlot Cabernet

Peter Taylor and Mike de la Haye at work and at play

73

hartz barn wines

Hartz Barn was established in 1997 by New Zealander David Barnett and partner Penny Hart. A subtle tweak of each surname and they had a brand which manages to cleverly capture both the unique German heritage of the Barossa and the international nature of their union.

My Place

"We were told when we started our operation in Moculta that

Hartz Barn Dennistone vineyard

you can't grow grapes here," David says. "Not only have we done so but we've made wines to be proud of. And the best part about it is that it's not a job, it's what we love to do."

Vineyards of significance

"Early in 2007 I transplanted some 112 year old Shiraz vines onto our property. They were about to get bulldozed to make way for a development, and this wonderful heritage would have been lost if someone didn't step up to save them."

Local knowledge

"I think Appellation Restaurant is a real treasure of the Barossa. The service, food and overall quality of the dining experience are outstanding."

1 Truro Road Moculta
Ph 0408857347
www.hartzbarnwines.com.au
penny@hartzbarnwines.com.au
HARTZ BARN WINES
Est 1997
Tastings by appointment
Historical buildings, tours, tutored tastings
Price range $20-$80
Key Wines: General Store Shiraz, Mail Box Merlot, Blackbead Sparkling Lagrein

Food matches

"We were the third producer in Australia to plant Lagrein. Our Sparkling Lagrein is a great match with a slow cooked boned leg of lamb marinated in red wine and garlic."

head wines

After a career in biochemistry, Sydney wine retail and managing Australia's biggest wine auction house, Alex Head established Head Wines in the Barossa in 2006. His two single site Shiraz-based wines, The Blonde and The Brunette, reflect the Stonewell and Moppa subregions of the Barossa. Both are available for tasting by appointment.

My Place

"I've long had a fascination with the wines of Côte Rôtie in the Rhône Valley in France and they are the inspiration for what I do here in the Barossa,"

HEAD
WINES

explains Alex. "I've set out to make Shiraz in a fresher, more drinkable style, but it is crucial to me that they age as well. I like to think of it as a quasi-Old World style with New World attitude."

Local knowledge

"You must put the Barossa Vintage Festival on your list of things to do. It's a wonderful week to get a feel for what the Barossa is all about."

Food matches

"The best lamb in the Barossa is Hutton Vale, and I would simply slow roast it and serve

Nuraip Rd Nuriootpa
Ph 0413 114 233
www.headwines.com.au
alex@headwines.com.au
Est 2006
Tastings by appointment
Price range $20-$40
Key Wines: The Blonde Shiraz Viognier, The Brunette Shiraz

it with pan juices and a glass of 'The Blonde' Shiraz Viognier."

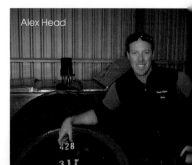

Alex Head

heathvale

'A heritage resumed' is the motto of Heathvale, the name of the original 1850s home of William Heath, one of the first wine producers in the Eden Valley. It was not until 1986 that Trevor and Faye March arrived and replanted the vineyard.

My Place

"When we started Heathvale, the original vineyards were simply stumps held together by mud and termite dust," Trevor recalls. "They were long gone, but you could see that the soil here was something special. We replanted and the quality of the grapes we have grown since has been proof of that."

You wouldn't read about it

"The cooperative and communal nature of the Barossa is a marvellous thing, and somewhat unique to this place. We share our winemaking equipment with our neighbours, Gill and Ben Radford. It's expensive stuff, and we're both crushing small enough volumes that allow us to share it."

Local knowledge

"Buck's Bistro at Springton is a little off the beaten path but a great spot for a casual meal."

Wining kids

"Our cellar door is at Taste

Ph (08) 8564 8248

www.heathvalewines.com.au

trevor.march@heathvalewines.com.au

Est 1986

Tastings at Taste Eden Valley in Angaston or by appointment

Vineyard tours

Price range $18-$52

Key Wines: William Heath Shiraz, Eden Valley Riesling

Eden Valley in the main street of Angaston, a venue that we share with a number of other local producers. There are always a few kids there, and Max the dog will help kids wile the time away."

heidenreich estate

Noel and Cheryl Heidenreich's 'Old School' range of wines commemorates the now defunct Vine Vale school in which Noel and his brothers were educated. When it closed down, Noel became the custodian of the school bell, which still holds pride of place at Heidenreich Estate and accompanies them to tastings and wine shows around the country.

My Place

"As growers, we watched the fruit we grew being turned into wine by others," recalls Noel. "So we thought, 'Why don't we have a go at this ourselves?' We crushed by foot the first year and we've expanded a little every year since. We now make enough to keep us busy, while still leaving time for family, an important priority for both of us."

Local knowledge

"Take a walk down John Street in Tanunda to Goat Square. There are some lovely historic homes in the area, and you'll see a cast iron sculpture in the square that my son-in-law built."

Light Pass Road Tanunda

Ph (08) 8563 2644

www.heidenreich vineyards.com.au

sales@heidenreich vineyards.com.au

Est 1998

Tastings at Chateau Tanunda Small Winemakers Centre

Price range $15-$30

Key Wines: The Old School Principal Shiraz, The Old School Graduates Cabernet, The Old School Chardonnay

henry holmes wines

"Like many family enterprises, we have not been without controversy," says Bill Holmes. "Penny and I have battled for years over the use of their Barossa Valley farm. Penny, an avid breeder of show-winning White Suffolk sheep, has tried to keep the land for the grazing and breeding of her flock. I, on the other hand, believe that the land provides perfect conditions for making world-class wines. The battleground is evenly divided, with one side of the property filled with vibrant, green vines and the other with a mob of ever-hungry sheep eyeing the lush fruit that hangs from the vines. It is this family debate that inspired our logo – a game of tick-tack-toe (noughts & crosses) with the sheep and grapes battling for the use of the land."

My place

"Our Heritage-listed property, 'Woodbridge,' has a unique homestead surrounded by stone and slab outbuildings built by the Henschke family in 1866," explains Bill. "Their original dwelling was a dugout in the side of the creek and can still be seen. We use another cottage on the property as a Bed & Breakfast. It's a beautiful old property with stunning gums and rambling gardens - a great place to immerse yourself in the countryside!"

**Gomersal Road
Gomersal via Tanunda**

Ph (08) 8563 2059

www.woodbridgefarm.
com

henryholmeswines@
yahoo.com

Tastings by appointment

Bed & breakfast
accommodation

Price range $22-$25

*Key Wines: Henry
Holmes Shiraz, Jumbuck
Cabernet Merlot*

Visiting Henry Holmes

"Henry Holmes Wines offers private tastings by appointment in an 1850s cellar. It is small and rustic, but you will be charmed by its hand-hewn native pine beams, rough white washed walls and, of course, the estate grown wines!"

Woodbridge Farm Cottage

Henry Holmes home with original German wood oven visible (left)

Food matches

"As growers of white Suffolk lamb we naturally pair this with our reds. We also spend many summer weekends on the Yorke Peninsula catching scallops, abalone, whiting and snapper. From this evolved our Henry Holmes Blue House Riesling and Grenache Rosé, aptly named 'Shack 68'."

Local knowledge

"The Apex bakery in Tanunda makes my favourite pies. The wood-fired oven has been burning since 1929! It's cash only, the opening hours are not for the benefit of the customer and don't expect a second bake when they run out!

"The local footy is a great day out. Of course, we support Tanunda and if you sit on the rails you might be offered a heart warmer from the famous port keg or find that this is the only footy ground with a five star wine list!

"Historic 'Goat square' in Tanunda has five original settlers' cottages. Two are B&Bs and we like to send our friends to the very authentic Kohlhagen Cottage with its little mixed garden of fruit trees. Our Woodbridge Farm Cottage Bed & Breakfast is a self-contained three-bedroom cottage set amid rolling farmland."

You wouldn't read about it

"In the early 1980s, Gomersal boasted a few dry-grown vineyards. It was back-breaking work to be employed as a hand picker and it would turn into a bit of a blur because it was always Riesling mixed with lemonade for morning smoko, lunch and knock-off. The big question was always whether the grapes ever made it to the winery!"

henschke wines

Henschke Road Keyneton

Map F17 Winery 23

Ph (08) 8564 8223

www.henschke.com.au

info@henschke.com.au

Est 1868

Cellar door tastings open
Mon-Fri 9-4:30, Sat 9-12

Historical buildings, tours

Price range $13-$510

*Key Wines: Hill of Grace
Shiraz, Hill of Roses Shiraz,
Cyril Henschke Cabernet,
Mount Edelstone
Shiraz, Keyneton Estate
Euphonium Shiraz
Cabernet Sauvignon,
Julius Eden Valley Riesling*

If there is one Australian vineyard more famous than any other throughout the world, that vineyard is Hill of Grace. The Henschke family has been the custodian of this precious patch of dirt and its now ancient 'grandfather' vines at Keyneton in the Eden Valley for more than a century and a half. The family first sold wines in the mid to late 1860s from its family home and cellar, built during the 1850s. Today, fifth generation descendent Stephen Henschke takes care of the winery while his wife Prue tends the family vineyards.

My place

"This is the hills side of the Barossa, and it's a fascinating geological landscape," explains Prue. "It's very interesting to go to the edge of the hills and look out over the Murray Plains. Go straight through Keyneton and head east for about five or ten kilometres, toward the edge of the range. You don't really get a good feeling for the altitude here until you see the drop off!

"We're part of an immense mountain range, weathered down to form all the good soils on the Barossa side of the hills. But up here there are only pockets of good dirt, which means that we have to be very careful with our site selection. That's why we're not wall-to-wall vineyards here."

Barossa dirt

"The Hill of Grace is a gorgeous old vineyard," says Stephen, "and it's just amazing to think that that old vineyard and those vines that were planted before 1860 have survived through the Federation drought, the '38 drought and they're still going through drought today. It's just amazing to think what they've lived through, dry grown for all that time, on their own roots, the original vines planted in the ground all that time ago. It's just extraordinary — it's a really special old vineyard.

"It was my ancestor on my grandmother's side, Nicolas Stanitzki, who planted the Hill of Grace vineyard. We don't know exactly when that was but we do know that it was before 1860 because there is a reference to the steeple going on the church overlooking the vineyard. We have no idea how old the vines were at this time, but we suspect somewhere between ten and twenty years old."

Prue explains that one reason that the Hill of Grace vineyard is special is because "it's not a hill at all, it's a valley! It seems to be a collection point for the whole catchment for alluvial soils and for water. Being an unirrigated vineyard, the greenness of the leaf canopy tells us that it's sitting comfortably in the landscape."

Visiting Henschke

"Visitors to the cellar door can usually taste most of our top-end wines," explains Stephen. "Rarely do we taste Hill of Grace, because it is a tiny production and it's precious stuff. There are only a few thousand bottles made for the whole world! It's available for purchase from cellar door for most of the year.

Henschke cellar door

"We are able to offer historical tours of the winery by appointment. Give us a day of notice, or a week if possible. We can show you the old crusher, the old press and the old fermenting tanks. It's a really interesting museum winery. In the old days it was run by steam engines and then diesel engines. We still have the original old basket press that was put in at the turn of the century, although we don't use it very often now."

"If you would like to visit the Mount Edelstone or the Hill of Grace vineyard, make an appointment and come and see us here first."

Local knowledge

"We are members at Gnadenberg Lutheran Church, which means 'Hill of Grace,' and it is opposite the vineyard," says Stephen. "Visitors are always welcome, and you will get the Henschke Tawny Port for communion! It's a three generation blend that I do specially. In 2010, Gnadenberg celebrates its 150th birthday. We're trying to make a Mataro off the Hill of Grace block for the celebration.

Stephen and Prue Henschke in the Hill of Grace vineyard

"We use our old crusher for the Barons of the Barossa declaration of vintage in the middle weekend of February each year. We have a church service in the Tabor Lutheran church in Tanunda. The whole church is decorated out for the thanksgiving and it's quite stunning. The Ambassadors of the Barossa and the Barons, the brass bands and the schools are involved and we all process down the street to the rotunda, where the vigneron and the winemaker of the year are announced and we have the ceremonial crushing. Being a historic, wooden hand crusher, we take it down and use it to crush the grapes from the church and everybody gets a taste. It's a really good event and visitors are welcome to join in. See the Barossa tourism web site for details."

You wouldn't read about it

Stephen recounts a story of a luncheon in Eden Valley some twenty years ago. "Paul Jaboulet came out from the Rhone Valley in France. I put on my '62 Hill of Grace and he put on his '62 La Chapelle. What was amazing was how similar the wines looked and what they had matured into. Our wine was from vines that were over 100 years old and his wine was from vines that were probably only about forty years old. So the Old World was new and the New World was old! An interesting bit of irony that we both enjoyed!"

hentley farm wines

Hentley Farm
Barossa Valley
Wines

In a quaint setting on the banks of Greenock Creek, surrounded by vineyards on all sides, sits a charming 1840s shearing cottage. This is the home of Keith and Alison Hentschke's Hentley Farm, a recently established Barossa boutique winery with a particular focus on Shiraz and Zinfandel. The cottage has been transformed into a cellar door and tasting room while preserving its heritage, including the original shearer's scratchings on the walls.

My place

"This property was the answer to our search for deep red brown soils over limestone in the Western Barossa," says Keith. "Essentially everything you taste here is from this property. The vineyards all around you as you drive in are ours and you can see The Beauty vineyard across the creek from the cellar door. We are a single vineyard Western Barossa Shiraz specialist with nineteen different Shiraz blocks which turn into five different wines that we sell from $19 to $115. We also planted Zinfandel and it's the best thing we ever did!"

Visiting Hentley Farm

Hentley Farm offers the full range for tasting most of the time, until wines have sold out.

"Our focus is on providing more exclusive tasting opportunities for the premium end of the market. We have recently transformed the cottage into a cellar door and a tasting room for structured tastings. It has a lounge bar feel and a wood fire and there's a kitchen from which we can offer high-level catering for our members. Enquire in advance and give us plenty of notice. We're very much looking forward to having intimate lunches and dinners with people here. We want our guests to feel like they're part of the family."

Local knowledge

Hentley Farm is located in the midst of the 'dress circle' of Barossa accommodation. "Seppeltsfield Vineyard Cottage is our neighbour," explains Keith. "The Lodge Country House is a short walk away and up on the hill behind us is The Louise's Atrium property, the most high end accommodation in the Barossa."

Jenke Road Seppeltsfield

Map E9 Winery 24

Ph (08) 8562 8427

www.hentleyfarm.com.au

info@hentleyfarm.com.au

Est 2002

Cellar door tastings open 10-5 daily

Price range $19-$115

Key Wines: Zinfandel, The Beauty Shiraz, The Beast Shiraz, Clos Otto Shiraz

Hentley Farm cellar door

heritage wines

When you visit Heritage Wines, it's the man behind the brand that you'll meet at cellar door. "I'm there most of the time, and otherwise it's my wife, Chris," says Steve Hoff. This small family business is built on providing a personal approach in its homely cellar door. Steve planted the vineyard surrounding the cellar door to Shiraz, Cabernet and Malbec in 1984, and still sources most of his fruit from these vines. "We're absolutely committed to the Barossa and all of our wines are from this area," he says. "This side of the valley grows some bloody good grapes!"

My place

"All of the Barossa is beautiful, but this is a stunning spot with views up to the ranges," says Steve. "There's nothing better than sitting on the back deck with a beer and looking out at the view. You can see Mount Lofty! It's unspoilt and there are no big sheds on the hill."

Visiting Heritage Wines

"The business is about building relationships. There's a lot of good wine around but we've always tried to give people good service as well. It's still a matter of putting your boots on, meeting people and getting to know them. They appreciate that. We notice a difference in people's attitudes

when they come to cellar door and meet me and see that it's my name on the label.

"It's important to us to have a cellar door that isn't intimidating. We want people to feel at home and comfortable here. The whole range is on tasting and this is something I really believe in. It's really important to allow people to taste everything and a lot of people make the comment that the wines are good value."

Local knowledge

"I reckon the Greenock Creek Tavern is great for a local produce meal and they have great specials and a good wine list. I'm always there with a mate on Friday evening. My wife drops us off and his wife picks us up. There's a mad Irishman, Connor, in the kitchen and he knocks out some really good stuff. It's an authentic country pub, unlike many pubs. The Barossa Brewing Company is just across the road and they have their beers on tap at the pub. There's a mishmash of all sorts of people there and sometimes it can be absolutely riotously funny. It has a horseshoe-shaped bar and it's one of those places that you have a good laugh.

"We're so lucky here with butchers and bakers. Thorn's

RSD 106A Seppeltsfield Road Marananga

Map D10 Winery 25

Ph (08) 8562 2880

www.heritagewinery.com.au

enquiries@heritagewinery.com.au

Est 1984

Cellar door tastings open Mon-Fri 10-5 , Sat-Sun 11-5

B&B accommodation

Price range $15-$42

Key Wines: Barossa Shiraz, Rossco's Shiraz

Top Steve Hoff **Middle** Heritage Wines cellar door **Bottom** View to the ranges

butcher shop in Tanunda is brilliant. And Apex bakery for a pie, pasty or bread. It's quite unique to have a wine region

81

with a historical food culture. My dad used to talk about 'steinke caeser' – stinky cheese – and I found it in a shop in Tanunda. The meats and the cheeses and the dill cumbers are really very special. Maggie Beer's daughters, Sas and Elli are doing prosciuttos and all sorts of different styles of stuff. It's a new generation.

"We're particularly fortunate to have The Louise next door. It's probably more than five stars. It really is very smart.

"Our little B&B is a cutesy original 1851 cottage on the property. People enjoy it because it's a really cosy little place for two people in the vineyard. It's right next to our house but we don't know they're there and they don't know we're here. Although we have built some great friendships with people who've stayed here.

"It's all the little touches that make it special for people. I don't like to open the little Qantas-type packs in a hotel, so we make our own soap from our olive trees for our guests. We make olive oil, our chooks lay the eggs and we buy local bacon.

"We grow as much produce as we possibly can. We love scratching around in the vegie patch. We're like a couple of old chooks out there! It's fun and it tastes good! This is the way we live."

Wining kids

"Funnily enough, before we had our own kids we had toys in the cellar door but when we had them they came out. Most kids coming here are from the city and so they love the space to run around, watch the chooks scratching around and find an egg. We're off the road so it's safe for them. I've always lived in the country and that's what I always used to do!"

Food matches

"It was only the other week that I cooked a chicken and rabbit paella and our Cabernet went very well with it."

You wouldn't read about it

"I've got a German name but I'm an Irish citizen!" says Steve. "My grandfather on my Mum's side was Irish, so years ago I paid ten quid to get Irish citizenship."

Vineyard off Steingarten Road, Rowland Flat
Dragan Radocaj Photography

Rowland Flat old vine
Dragan Radocaj Photography

hewitson wines   HEWITSON

The legendary 1853 Old Garden Mourvèdre vineyard in Rowland Flat is the source of Hewitson's wine of the same name, revered as one of Australia's finest examples of the variety. The man behind the brand is Dean Hewitson, who travelled, worked and studied in a range of places as diverse as Oregon, Bordeaux and Beaujolais before establishing Hewitson Wines in 1998. At the time of writing, a new cellar door facility was under construction.

My Place

"The Barossa Valley is the number one recognised Australian wine region in the world," says Dean. "Our winery and vineyard is at No. 1 Seppeltsfield Road, which we consider to be the tourism, spiritual and logistical heart of the Barossa."

Vineyards of significance

"Our 1853 Old Garden Mourvèdre vineyard provides one of the Barossa's best examples of terroir. Completely dry-grown on two-metre-deep sand over limestone, the vine roots delve tens of metres below the surface, keeping the vines healthy, rain or shine."

Local knowledge

"The best place for a relaxing glass of wine is on the peaceful river flats of the Barossa, amongst vines, giant river gums and grazing cattle.

1 Seppeltsfield Road Dorrien

Map E11 Winery 26

Ph (08) 8443 6466

www.hewitson.com.au

dean@hewitson.com.au

Est 1998

Cellar door tastings available soon

Price range $15-$70

Key Wines: Old Garden Mourvèdre, Ned and Henry's, Miss Harry, Gun Metal Riesling

Food matches

"My all time favourite combination is duck breast with our Old Garden Mourvèdre. Chefs and sommeliers from around the world tell me that this would be their key match, too."

hobbs of barossa ranges

Greg Hobbs describes his tiny wine production as "a drop in the ocean by today's standards, but a very fine drop indeed!" The largest volume of any of his Eden Valley wines is just 300 dozen, which allows the family to do just about everything themselves. "We are it!" he says. "We look after the vineyard, we make the wine, we label and we market it."

My place

"The outlook from where we live is sensational!" Greg exclaims. "Our elevation is about 500m, which puts us close to the highest vineyards in the Valley. There are not a lot of vineyards around us, the rest is just sheep grazing on rolling hills. You can get up to the hill behind the barrel shed and see 270 degree views that are just stunning!"

Greg's vineyard includes two-and-a-half acres of vines somewhere between 99 and 106 years old. "It's hard to pin it down exactly," he says. "Our unique point of difference is that we're probably the only place here that makes wines in a semi-dried style. All the dessert wine fruit is put in racks and dried and we also make our Shiraz in this same 'Amarone' style."

Visiting Hobbs

"Visiting us is a family experience. The tasting will be at our house with my wife Allison and myself. What we

Corner of Flaxman's Valley and Randall's Roads Angaston

Ph 0427 177 740

www.hobbsvintners.com.au

cellardoor@hobbsvintners.com.au

Tastings by appointment

Price range $39-$130

Key Wines: Old Vine Hobbs Shiraz, Hobbs Gregor Shiraz, Viognier Dessert Wine

offer is a real small production winery where you meet the people who are the winery. We really enjoy doing this, so give us a call to make an appointment and if we're in South Australia, we'll do it. We'll even change our own events to fit it in!"

hutton vale vineyards

It was in 1843 that the Angas family settled in the rolling countryside of the Barossa Ranges. Over seven generations the family has grown tobacco, apples, pears, apricots, flax, cereal crops, wool, meat and currants on the property, but it was only in 1912 that vines were first planted. Today, Jan and John Angas' Hutton Vale is famous for much more than just wine. This is the home of Hutton Vale lamb, merino sheep for wool, cereal crops and the 'Farm Follies' range of chutneys and pickles. Jan is a leader in the preservation of Barossa Food culture and is active on many committees.

'Hutton Vale' Stone Jar Road Angaston

Ph (08) 8564 8270

www.huttonvale.com

angas@huttonvale.com

Est 1843 (Wines 1990)

Tastings by appointment

Historical buildings, farm produce

Price range $20-$60

Key Wines: Shiraz, Grenache Mataro, Riesling, Cabernet

Hutton Vale

Small volumes of wine are made at Hutton Vale from select parcels of estate grown Shiraz, Riesling, Cabernet and Grenache.

Visiting Hutton Vale

"Hutton Vale's cellar door is for those serious about individual wines," says Jan. "We're only open by appointment, but it's well worth the visit. It's always a personal and private experience with the Angas family. Not only will you experience our wines but also taste our range of Farm Follies chutney followed by a tour of the building and surrounding gardens.

"The vineyard is surrounded by picturesque hills, big gum trees, grazing sheep and cereal crops. Our cellar door is an early 1840s barn, surrounded by walled gardens perfect for soaking up the sun or resting in the shade in summer. It also houses the country kitchen where our Farm Follies range of chutney is cooked. There is an outdoor kitchen with two wood stoves alongside an extensive vegetable garden with rare varieties grown in between whimsical artwork made from farm scrap metal!

"Mail order customers have an opportunity to lunch at Hutton Vale as part of our appreciation for loyalty."

You wouldn't read about it

"Our ancestor John Howard Angas was instrumental in establishing the grape growing industry in South Australia in the 1840s," says Jan. "He nurtured rootstock acquired in France and gave cuttings to his gardener Samuel Smith for propagation. Samuel Smith went on to become the founder of Yalumba!

"Generations later, Ronald Angas planted the Mt Edelstone vineyard in the early 1900s. In the 1970s it was sold to the Henschke family

HUTTON VALE

Walled garden at the Hutton Vale cellar door

after thirty successful vintages of the two families working together. The family friendship continues in harmony, and Mt Edelstone alongside the vineyard remains part of Hutton Vale."

Local knowledge

"We are at The Barossa Farmers Market every Saturday morning with Hutton Vale lamb and sometimes sausages and home grown vegies. You can also find Hutton Vale lamb on the menu at Appellation restaurant and Murdock restaurant."

Wining kids

"Our wide open farm spaces with sheep, kangaroos and even the occasional echidna usually widen the eyes of youngsters!"

Food matches

"Carême pastry tartlets filled with Skordalia, caramelized shallots and a plump fresh oyster on top with a glass of Hutton Vale Riesling usually hits the spot. Slow roasted forequarter of Hutton Vale lamb served on a bed of stirred leafy greens is perfect with Hutton Vale Cabernet Sauvignon. Lamb casserole with fennel, fetta, olives and barley risotto is spot on with rich Hutton Vale Shiraz. The open log fire in the cellar door also goes well with this dish!"

Hutton Vale

irvine wines

IRVINE

Basil Roeslers Road Eden Valley

Map J15 Winery 28

Ph (08) 8564 1110

www.irvinewines.com.au

merlotbiz@irvinewines.com.au

Est 1980

Tastings at Eden Valley Hotel open 11:30-4 daily

Price range $15-$120

Key Wines: Irvine Grand Merlot, The Baroness, Springhill Merlot, "Breughel" Cabernet Franc Rosé

There is one name associated with Australian Merlot more than any other, and that name is Jim Irvine. His Springhill vineyard in the Eden Valley is the home of his iconic 'Grand Merlot' and no less than six other straight and blended versions of his beloved variety. At the budget end of the range, his wines represent some of the best value among the Barossa boutiques.

Barossa Character

"I grew up in a bakehouse," Jim recalls. "My dad taught me about tastes, flavours, smells, colours and textures. He died when I was quite young, but that was the legacy he left me.

"It was in the late '70s that I tasted Petrus (the most revered Merlot in the world) for the first time. I tasted it twice within twelve or eighteen months, and after thirty-odd years in the wine industry, I couldn't believe what I was tasting! It was just so rich and so full, so soft, so velvety, so powerful. 'Where the heck did this come from?' I thought. It was the first real Merlot I'd ever tasted. Prior to that time, Merlot in Australia was basically all blended into Cabernet. And the second time I saw that wine, I said, 'That's it!' It's dumb to think that two tastes of a wine can change your whole life. But it did."

My place

"The Irvines have been settled in the Barossa for longer than most. They settled in Truro in 1851, 158 years ago! We've often been confused as newcomers, but I put that down to the silly Scottish hat that I wear!

"When Marjorie and I bought this property in 1980 there were just two vines and some sheep here. Now, the Merlot that comes off this Springhill block is rated in the top twenty Merlots in the world. It's not me, it's the goddamn block! It's what Merlot loves: a hill with incredible drainage and shattered gravel, so the roots go straight down. There's no soil to speak of on the top, and only 40cm at best at the bottom of the slope."

Tasting Irvine Wines

"The Eden Valley Hotel offers tastings of our wines. We have an arrangement with them whereby they can offer cellar door prices. They're open from 11:30am until 4pm, seven days a week. Give them a call in advance to let them know you're serious. It's a real character experience to go in there. It was built in the 1800s and if you're tall, you'd have to duck your head to get in! You can taste all ten of our wines, right up to Grand Merlot. They pour the wines

Jim Irvine

Springhill vineyard

and then stand back; there's no sales pitch, so you have the opportunity to make up your own mind. And the end of it is a beauty, because you can have a cold Cooper's Ale. Now that's a cellar door!"

Local knowledge

"The Sunrise Bakery in Angaston is the last place you'd expect to go for a snack, but it's the best! It's just something else. The pasties and pies are my favourite, and you might just have to have a sprinkled donut and a slice of honey cake. It's beautiful stuff!

"The greatest meals and the best accommodation in the Barossa are at Appellation. It's beyond anything you can find in any other state. They say they're five star, that's bulls**t – they're six or seven stars! Chef Mark McNamara is something quite out of the box!

"Where would I go for a quiet drink? There's no such thing as a quiet drink in the Barossa! Certainly not in the Eden Valley. I could take you down to the pub, but there's no quiet drink down there! But if you really want an alcoholic quiet drink, the back section of Vintner's Bar and Grill is just great. If you want a non-alcoholic drink, Blond Coffee on the corner opposite the Angaston Hotel is great for relaxing on the weekend."

Food matches

"Grand Merlot with roast duck! You've got to have roast duck. But if you really want to be just sheer decadent, Sparkling Merlot with chocolate mousse or mud cake! Aaah! Merlot with dark chocolate is one of the most sensuous tastes you can get. And they say you can't have chocolate with red wine! Rubbish, absolute rubbish!"

The German heritage of the Barossa has had a strong influence on its food. You don't come to the Barossa for salad, but you do come for meat!

Philip Laffer, Jacob's Creek

Simon Casson
Photography

jacob's creek wines

The vineyard that Johann Gramp planted on the banks of Jacob's Creek in 1847 is believed to be the first commercial vineyard in the Barossa. More than 160 years later, Jacob's Creek is famous around the world as one of Australia's best known wine brands. "What I find fascinating," says Winemaker Philip Laffer, "is that the company today is only a kilometre away from that first vineyard, where it all started."

Barossa Character

Jacob's Creek Winemaker Philip Laffer first lived in the Barossa as a child in 1948 and 1949, returning in 1960 to work as a student at what is now Penfolds. "Even then, the foreman would still speak to the cellar hands in bastard Kaiser, or Barossa Deutsche," he recalls. He now manages a large winemaking team at Jacob's Creek and insists that he doesn't get all the credit. "I've been here twenty years so I'm only a 'Johnny come lately!'" he says.

My place

"The Barossa is a wonderful experience. The two seasons I like most are autumn and summer. Autumn with all of its diversity of colour — the reds and browns and ochres appeal to me. And in summer the contrast between the golden hills, brown paddocks and green vines. It makes for a fascinating drive in the early morning and late afternoon.

"The Barossa is fortunate that its four towns have been well contained and there's no strip of development between them. The towns and rural areas are clearly defined. And despite all of the development with wineries and sheds, most of the new buildings are back off the road so you get a very real impression that this is still a rural area.

"As I've been baching here over the years I've wandered through all the old cemeteries and they are all German names on this side of the range and English on the other side. Angaston was a very English settlement and Tanunda was German. The Barossa has always had strong links with the Lutheran faith, and this has been an important contributor to the community."

Barossa Valley Way Rowland Flat

Map G9 Winery 29

Ph (08) 8521 3111

www.orlandowines.com

JCVC@orlandowines.com

Est 1912

Cellar door tastings open 10-5 daily

Gallery, à la carte restaurant, private facilities for professional functions and specialised tastings

Price range $35-$45

Key Barossa Wines: Steingarten Riesling, Centenary Hill Shiraz

You wouldn't read about it

Jacob's Creek's Steingarten vineyard is one of the most famous Riesling sites in the Eden Valley. Except that it isn't in the Eden Valley at all.

"The fence of the Steingarten vineyard is the border between the Barossa Valley and the Eden Valley," Philip explains. "The boundary runs a dogleg around the Steingarten

Philip Laffer at Jacob's Creek

89

JACOB'S CREEK

vineyard to place it in the Barossa Valley. The wine that is labelled as Steingarten is a blend of this vineyard and another vineyard back in the Eden Valley. Technically, this makes it 'Barossa Ranges,' although it is very much Eden Valley in style.

"Our goal is to get Steingarten back to being just from the Steingarten vineyard. I think we can look to extending the vineyard further. For a viticulturist it is a nightmare and it must be worked by hand. I sat down with Colin Gramp and asked what he had in mind when he planted it. He said it was to create a piece of Germany's Mosel in Australia, producing light, crisp, elegant dry wines. So we went back to this style from 1991 onwards, tidying up the vineyard and doubling its size at the time.

"Stylistically, the wine has been consistent since then. It's very much of the austere Eden Valley style, probably the most consistently austere Eden Valley Riesling. The original style was built to be released at four or five years of age. But most people didn't understand aged Riesling so we now release it as a one-year-old."

Vineyards of significance

"Centenary Hill Shiraz is sourced from vineyards along Jacob's Creek itself, including a large proportion from 1912 vines. We're looking for southern Barossa Shiraz, because it's more elegant, more spicy, more peppery and not as big and bold as typical Barossa Shiraz," says Philip.

Barossa dirt

"You drive over Jacob's Creek as you come into the Jacob's Creek Visitor's Centre. We've done a lot to restore the area and plant native plants. At the moment we're building a walkway from the Visitor's Centre to the creek. It will go down to Johann Minge's cave, but it's become a depression because early settlers cut off slate from the cave for their buildings. You can walk to Minge's island where Gramp planted an early vineyard."

Vineyards opposite Jacob's Creek
Dragan Radocaj Photography

Vineyard opposite Jacob's Creek
Dragan Radocaj Photography

The Jacob's Creek Visitor's Centre

"The Jacob's Creek Visitor's Centre is designed to overlook a spectacular vista of gum trees, hills and grape vines. It's a great opportunity for us to welcome tourists who are looking for an experience but not necessarily to buy wine in quantity, because they can buy at home. The sales counter is very small and you are in no way enticed to buy.

"Visitors can taste the entire range and there is no tasting charge. There's a restaurant in the same room, primarily for lunches, serving dishes designed by our in-house chef to match Jacob's Creek wines. We use Barossa produce wherever possible and when we can't — such as with oysters — we source from elsewhere in South Australia. It's a Barossa experience, it's an Australian experience and it's a Jacob's Creek experience.

"The centre tells the story of the history of Orlando and Jacob's Creek, although the building doesn't attempt to be pseudo-old or pseudo-Germanic. We hear lots of stories from overseas visitors of what a wonderful experience it is.

"We also offer some things that are exclusive, such as old vintages as well as one or two products that aren't available elsewhere. You can do anything by arrangement. You can have a winemaker there to talk you through the wines and you might be able to taste a slightly more interesting range in this way. There is a private room for groups of ten to twenty that can be booked for tastings by prior arrangement. There is no charge unless you are seeking a catered event, which is also available by prior arrangement."

Jacob's Creek Visitor's Centre

jamabro wines

David and Juli Heinze are fifth generation grape growers in the Stonewell area who have been making wines under their own label since 2003. The small family-owned winery uses grapes exclusively from the estate vineyard. "The whole family gets involved in the process in some way or other," says Juli. "We do the picking, crushing and entire wine making process on site, with David as the winemaker."

Visiting Jamabro

"We don't have a cellar door just yet but we do have a tasting area in the winery, so give us a call to arrange a visit," says Juli. "Twenty-four hours'

notice would be preferred so we can put a complimentary cheese platter together for you. But if this much notice isn't possible, give us a call anyway and we'll see what we can do."

Local knowledge

"In our area, walking and bike riding are great for recreation, as is being chauffeur-driven while wine tasting! The Tanunda Club and La Buona Vita in Tanunda are great venues for eating out, and The Novotel at Rowland Flat or the more intimate setting of Seppeltsfield Vineyard Cottage are perfect for accommodation."

Smyth Road Tanunda

Ph 0437 633 575

www.jamabro.com.au

juli_jamabro@
ozemail.com.au

Est 2003

Tastings by appointment

Price range $15-$40

Key Wines: Sunset Rosé, Spiraz Sparkling Shiraz, Bush Vine Grenache, Rough Cut Diamond Moscato

Food matches

"My favourite food match is our 2008 Sunset Rosé teamed with a typical German Barossa platter of cold meats, dijonnaise potato salad and grated cucumber and tomato salad. It's perfect in summer!"

jb wines

"In 1947 I left a pair of pruning shears in a bucket and they went straight through Colin Gramp's crusher. I was three years old at the time – we started young back then!" says Greg Barritt. Today, Greg and business partner Joe Barritt are the team behind JB Wines, a small producer with a focus on Shiraz and Cabernet and recent experimentation with Zinfandel, Clairette and Pinot Blanc.

My Place

"Our vineyard and wine label merge the past with the present," Greg explains. "We are fifth and sixth generation descendents of two of the earliest settlers in the Barossa, but we focus our attention on fresh, new, hand-crafted wines. All of our wines are made from grapes from our estate vineyards with the aim of reflecting the environment

Cnr Rifle Range and Nicolae Roads Bethany

Ph 0408 794389

www.jbwines.com

info@jbwines.com

Tastings by appointment

Price range $15-$20

Key Wines: Clairette, Shiraz, Cabernet Sauvignon

where they are grown. Most importantly, they are produced to be enjoyed in good company."

JB Wines

Jenke Vineyard, Rowland Flat
Dragan Radocaj Photography

jenke vineyards

If the cellar door looks strangely familiar when you visit Jenke Vineyards, there is a good reason. It was featured in the infamous 'Where the bloody hell are you' Australian tourism advertisements. The Jenke family had clocked up five generations of grape growing in the Barossa when winemaker Kym Jenke began making wines under the family name in 1989. A true estate-based brand, Jenke produces all of its wines from its historic Rowland Flat vineyards.

My Place

"When I graduated from college in the 1980s there were no jobs for winemakers," says Kym. My family was getting $190 a tonne for Shiraz from 100-year-old vines, less than the cost of production. This forced me to make a decision about my future. There and then I became the first winemaker in the Jenke family in over a century."

Local knowledge

"For a quick snack you can't beat the pies at the Apex Bakery in Tanunda."

Jenke Road Rowland Flat
Map H9 Winery 74
Ph (08) 8524 4154
www.jenke-vineyards.com
kym@jenke-vineyards.com
Est 1989
Cellar door tastings open 11-4 daily
Picnic facilities
Price range $17-$35
Key Wines: Semillon, Shiraz, Reserve Shiraz

Food matches

"Semillon is a Jenke speciality and it matches perfectly with salt and pepper squid."

Jenke Vineyards cellar door

john duval wines

John Duval has thirty-six vintages of experience making wine in the Barossa, including many years of involvement with some of its world-class old vineyards. "I started at Penfolds in 1974 and I was chief winemaker from 1986 until 2002," he recounts. John Duval Wines commenced in

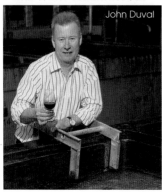
John Duval

2003. This 'one man band' operation is perhaps the antithesis to the magnitude of Penfolds, but what has not changed is that he continues to source Shiraz, Grenache and Mourvèdre from some of the great old vineyards of the Barossa and Eden Valleys.

My place

"I am privileged to deal with a great cross-section of growers in different parts of the Barossa and Eden Valleys," says John. "These span across six generations, like the Hoffmanns out at Ebenezer and Rob Gibson, who was a colleague of mine when he was the viticulturist for Penfolds."

Ph (08) 8563 2591

www.johnduvalwines.com

john@johnduvalwines.com

Est 2003

Available at Tanunda Cellars and Barossa restaurants incl Vintners, Appellation and 1918

Price range $32-$100

Key Wines: Eligo Shiraz, Entity Shiraz, Plexus Shiraz Grenache Mourvèdre

kabminye wines

What do you get when an architect (Richard Glastonbury) and interior designer (Ingrid Glastonbury) put their minds to designing a modern cellar door and café? A building that leaves you feeling as though you are at a picnic, surrounded by vines and sky! In 2001, the couple returned to the property on Krondorf Road where Ingrid's

Kabminye cellar door

great, great, grandparents had settled in 1847. Not only did Richard design the building but he also makes the wines, including a range of unusual varieties such as Carignan, Cinsaut and Kerner. He can be found nearly every day of the year pouring the wines and telling stories at cellar door.

My place

"We designed the building with three-storey high windows to allow visitors to the cellar door and restaurant to comfortably wile away the day with panoramic views of the hills and vineyards,"

Lot 7 & 11 Krondorf Road Krondorf via Tanunda

Map G11 Winery 30

Ph (08) 8563 0889

www.kabminye.com

wine@kabminye.com

Est 2001

Cellar door tastings open 11-5 daily

'Krondorf Road Café', local produce, gallery

Price range: $17.50-$37.50

Key Wines: Kerner, Irma Adeline, Schliebs Block, Carignan, Hubert Shiraz

Kabminye ★ Wines
B a r o s s a   V a l l e y

Krondorf Road scene
with Kaminye wines in the centre
Dragan Radocaj Photography

explains Richard. "The building was designed with ecologically-sustainable and chemical-free principles in mind and has been used as a case study in sustainability by SA Tourism. It includes a gallery space upstairs to showcase contemporary art."

Krondorf Road Café

"The menu in our Krondorf Road Café focuses on dishes from my Barossa German heritage," says Ingrid. "It's based entirely on authentic dishes and local produce that date back to the early Silesian settlers of the mid 1800s.

They came to the Barossa with their own traditions including pickling and smoking, and with the warmer climate have adapted and developed what is now a distinctly Barossa flavour."

You wouldn't read about it

"In winter we have a flock of pregnant merino sheep who keep the weeds down in our vineyard – a cheap and green alternative to pesticides and fertilisers!"

Wining kids

"We have plenty of grassy open space for children to

run around away from traffic, in full view of their parents. Our miniature long-haired Dachshund named Poppy is always patient with young ones and provides hours of free child minding!"

Infamous growers

"Ken Schliebs has spent the last sixty years pruning his forty-eight acre vineyard by hand and is very proud of the wine we've named in his honour. When he and his wife Margaret eat in the café he likes to ask other visitors, 'Do you like that Schliebs Block? That's me!'"

Krondorf Road Café

kaesler wines

Originally established in 1893, the Kaesler brand was reborn in 1997 under the guidance of winemaker Reid Bosward. Since then it has gone on to become recognised internationally as a Shiraz specialist, with its wines now sold in more than twenty countries. Its icon wine, Kaesler Old Bastard Shiraz, is sourced from a single vineyard planted in 1893.

My Place

"My place is about making traditional Barossa wines that are distinctively regional," says Reid. "Before setting up here we looked all over the world for the best place to start, but nowhere offered the unique proposition of the Barossa. It had everything: old vines, a climate conducive to growing high quality grapes, and a predominant wine style that I was really taken with. I really thought that we could take this to the world, so we did."

Barossa Character

"Every year we get two tonnes of Touriga from Mark Jantke, and I get all the kids in my son's class to come down for the afternoon and foot tread it. They have an absolute ball! We all joke that I'm on a winner with the free labour but it costs me twice as much in donuts and soft drink than it would if I simply paid for workers!"

Barossa dirt

"The only problem with the Barossa is that there is too much AFL footy. The people here actually think a Wallaby is an animal."

You wouldn't read about it

"People get confused by our name, walk into cellar door thinking that we're Kaiser Stuhl and ask, 'Where is the cask wine?!'"

Local knowledge

"The thing about the Barossa that always amazes me is the possibility of discovery. Even when you live here, there's always something new to find. I think it's the nature of this 'village' lifestyle that facilitates this continual reinvention."

Barossa Valley Way Nuriootpa

Map D12 Winery 32

Ph (08) 8562 4488

www.kaesler.com.au

mail@kaesler.com.au

Est 1997

Cellar door tastings

Accommodation, restaurant

Price range $12.50-$165

Key Wines: Old Bastard Shiraz, WOMS Shiraz Cabernet, Avignon GSM

KAESLER

ESTD. 1893

Wining kids

"Kids are always welcome at our cellar door. We have lovely gardens with plenty of space and our restaurant is child friendly."

Food matches

"Barossa GSM is a great food wine. Try our Kaesler Avignon GSM with a Seared Eye Fillet and a healthy serve of béarnaise sauce."

Left Kaesler cellar door
Middle 1893 'Old Bastard' Shiraz Vine
Right Reid Bosward

kalleske wines

In a short space of time Kalleske Wines has become world famous as one of the Barossa's rising stars, renowned for the highly-sought after creations of 2008 Barossa Winemaker of the Year, Troy Kalleske. 2002 may have been the first official vintage for Kalleske as a winemaker, but this Moppa-based producer has been growing grapes on its family-owned estate for some of the Barossa's most famous wines since the mid-1800s.

My Place

"Our place is all about our unique patch of dirt at Moppa, a small sub-district of Greenock in the north-west of the Barossa," explains Troy. "In fact, we are the most north-westerly vineyard and winery in the Barossa. We've had this property since 1853, and numerous vineyard blocks over 100 years old are still in production, including our 1875 Shiraz block, so this place is very special to us. Quite simply, the Barossa is the best place in the world to make wine, and we are proud to turn our estate grapes into authentic Kalleske wines – biodynamically grown, vintaged by us, and matured on the family farm. And what a great spot we have for our new tasting room, two doors up from the Greenock Creek Tavern and diagonally opposite The Barossa Brewing Company – does it get any better than that?!"

Barossa Character

"Many people think 2002 was the first vintage for Kalleske, but in 1978 there was a surplus of grapes so John and Clarry Kalleske had those grapes turned into a single vintage tawny port. It's now looking very special, so drop into the Kalleske tasting room and you may be fortunate enough to get a taste!"

Barossa dirt

"Before the 'black gold' we call Shiraz became what defined Moppa, the district was mined for real gold. As kids, we used to have a great time exploring the old mine shafts just over the hill. Now we like to joke

that you can taste the gold in our wines!"

You wouldn't read about it

"Wilbur, my pet pig, was a belated engagement present from my brother Tony. He gave Wilbur as a bit of joke but didn't realise that I'd always wanted a pet pig! He loves it at the winery and particularly

6 Murray Street Greenock

Map C10 Winery 31

Ph 08 8563 4000

www.kalleske.com

wine@kalleske.com

Est 1999

Cellar door tastings from late 2009

Price range $18-$100

Key Wines: Johann Georg Shiraz, Old Vine Grenache, Greenock Shiraz, Moppa Shiraz, Clarry's GSM

Below Brothers Tony and Troy Kalleske
Middle Clarry, son John and grandson Troy Kalleske
Right John Kalleske

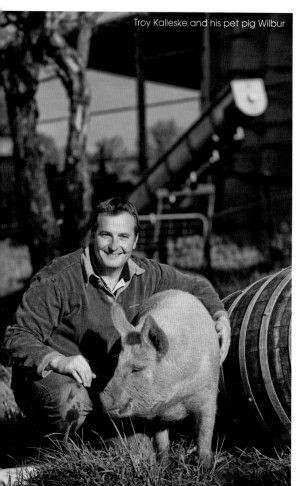

Troy Kalleske and his pet pig Wilbur

enjoys corn, grapes and beer. I'm reasonably sure that half the time he thinks he's a dog and he holds a burning ambition to one day be the centrefold of the Wine Dogs coffee table book!"

Local knowledge

"Our 'local', the Greenock Creek Tavern, is one of the Barossa's best kept secrets. We try to sneak in for a long Friday lunch whenever time allows. Connor the Irishman really knows how to cook, so the food is great. It has great beer, too, made by Daryl Trinne of The Barossa Brewing Company. The Greenock Dark Ale really hits the spot."

Wining kids

"We are in the midst of building a tasting room to open in late 2009. Kids will be welcome as there is a big fenced grass area out the back for them to run around."

Food matches

"Wiltshire is an ancient British breed of sheep that is bred purely for its flavoursome meat. We've been breeding them on the Kalleske farm for many years. Organic Wiltshire lamb slow spit roasted over an oak fire from old barrel wood is a dream with our 1935 planted, dry grown, single vineyard Old Vine Grenache."

Throughout the 1980s and '90s Lorraine Kalleske was Australia's fastest hand grape-picker.

Kalleske was the first certified organic vineyard and winery in the Barossa.

Kalleske was the first grape grower for Penfolds to have their vineyard make Grange three years in a row.

Kalleske farm

karra yerta

The vineyards that produce James and Marie Linke's Karra Yerta old vine Shiraz and Riesling are located high up in the Flaxman Valley. Here they make hand-crafted wines in miniscule quantities. Marie's ancestors were some of the original Barossa settlers in the 1840s and were the third largest landholders in the Flaxman Valley area, after the Angas and Evans families.

My Place

"We have a passion for the heritage of our area," says Marie. "Our tiny winery is a small family business, a ten year hobby of home wine-

making. It operates more for the lifestyle than a massive profit."

Local knowledge

"Schulz's Butchers in Angaston are an outstanding provider of high quality meat."

Wining kids

"A visit to Kathy's Old Fashioned Sweets Shop in Tanunda is always a good idea when you have kids."

Food matches

"Karra Yerta Barossa Shiraz goes very well with lamb shanks, red wine sauce and caramelised onions."

KARRA YERTA WINES
BAROSSA RANGES - SOUTH AUSTRALIA

Ph (08) 8565 3287

www.karrayertawines.com.au

karrayertawines@gmail.com

Tastings by appointment

Restored 1969 Monaro for vineyard tours

Price range $20-$25

Key Wines: Barossa Shiraz, Eden Valley Riesling

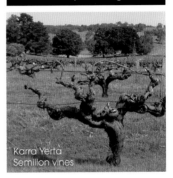

Karra Yerta Semillon vines

kellermeister & trevor jones fine wines

Trevor 'Boots' Jones is renowned throughout the Barossa for his winemaking skill, trademark handlebar moustache and fondness for gumboots. He came on board as Kellermeister winemaker in 1989, taking over from his father Ralph Jones, who established the business in 1976 after a career in sales and marketing at Orlando. Trevor started his own self-titled label in 1995.

My Place

"My place came about when I decided I was going to step away from the family brand and hang out my own shingle,"

Trevor explains. "These days we're a combination of the old and the new. The Black Sash Shiraz Vineyard at the front of the winery is 130 years old and a lot of people retain a great affinity with Kellermeister and its iconic old labels. Trevor Jones wines are more modern in style."

Barossa Character

"Back in the early '70s the wine industry was oblivious to regional tourism as we now know it. But being a marketer at heart, my Dad approached wine from a different angle to most Barossa winemakers. As a result, Kellermeister was the

Barossa Valley Highway Lyndoch

Map H8 Winery 33

Ph (08) 8524 4303

www.kellermeister.com.au

administration@kellermeister.com.au

Est 1976

Cellar door tastings open 9:30-5:30 daily

Tutored tastings, cheese platters, coffee

Price range $10-$75

Key Wines: Trevor Jones Wild Witch Shiraz, Trevor Jones Virgin Chardonnay, Kellermeister Sable Fortified

first cellar door in the Barossa to open its doors seven days a week."

You wouldn't read about it

"Around the Barossa I'm known as 'Boots', for my ever-present and trusty gumboots. When you're a hands-on winemaker, they're an indispensable part of life. Most of the time I can't see a good reason to change out of them, so I tend to wear them out to dinner as well. I even wore them on my wedding day, so I guess I deserve the nick name!"

Local knowledge

"For an outstanding pizza, don't miss Roaring 40's Café in Angaston.

"When I was dating my wife Mandy in the early days, we would climb up to Pewsey Vale peak, sit under the flat top stone pine tree and enjoy a picnic with a cold bottle of Riesling. At 630 metres, it's the highest point in the Barossa and enjoys wonderful views. Technically, though, it's trespassing and there is a huge bull in that paddock that doesn't like people!"

Food matches

"One of my favourite combinations is Kellermeister Tempranillo with home-made lamb and mushroom pie."

Cottage near Angaston
Dragan Radocaj Photography

kies family wines

The Kies family has been growing grapes in Lyndoch since 1857. Today, fifth generation Michael and Tina Kies are joined by their children Bronson, Jesseca and Jordan in managing the business, manning cellar door and serving in their Monkey Nut Café. Their extensive range of wines is sourced exclusively from the family vines behind the cellar door, a restored heritage cottage which was once a chaff mill.

My place

"Kies is staffed by fifth and sixth generation Kies family members," explains Tina, "so it is not surprising that visitors often comment that they feel more like they are being welcomed into the Kies family home than the cellar door! We pride ourselves on a relaxed atmosphere where customers feel like they can relax and enjoy themselves regardless of their level of wine knowledge.

"Nestled below the Lyndoch Ranges, The Monkey Nut Café at Kies enjoys spectacular views of the Ranges, Barista style coffee, homemade cakes and teas, as well as lunches based on local produce. We also have a gourmet tea shop, featuring teas from around the world. The Kies cellar door is situated in a particularly hot part of the Barossa, so in summer customers are invited to try our frozen Bastardo Port, a real treat when it's forty-five degrees outside!"

You wouldn't read about it

"The Monkey Nut Tree is a mushroom-looking pine nut tree at the highest point of the Lyndoch Ranges, so named by the German Settlers of Lyndoch. Ken Kies, the founder of Kies Family Wines, used to fly his light aircraft around the Barossa and Monkey Nut Tree always acted as a beacon for the way home to his small cottage at the back of Lyndoch.

"The Deer Stalker Merlot is one of our strongest brands at Kies. These poor young Merlot vines struggled through the first years of their lives battling Australian wildlife and stock. First it was the hares nibbling on the leaves, then sheep, followed by kangaroos. The vines then battled a beast which is rarely found among Barossa vines. Rogue red deer migrate from adjoining reserves to feast on the delicate vines and to take refuge amongst the foliage on this sheltered hillside. Hence the name 'Deer Stalker'."

Wining kids

"Although the Monkey Nut Café has nothing to do with monkeys, we have received

Barossa Valley Way Lyndoch

Map H7 Winery 34

Ph (08) 8524 4110

www.kieswines.com.au

cellardoor@kieswines.com.au

Est 1969

Cellar door tastings open 9-4 daily

Gallery, picnic facilities, tutored tastings, historical buildings, crafts, local produce, tea shop 9:30-4, café 9-4

Price range $15-$45

Key Wines: Deer Stalker Merlot, Dedication Shiraz, Klauber Block Shiraz

many monkeys as presents over the years which are now hidden throughout the Café. There are monkeys hanging from the ceiling, sitting on the counter and hiding in nooks and crannies. Children are encouraged to count them and if they get it right the prize is a babycino."

View of Heysen Vineyard from Monkey Nut Café

kurtz family vineyards

Steve Kurtz is a fifth generation Barossan committed to making wines that express the character of his family estate in Light Pass. He stepped away from a large company viticultural role in 2006 to focus on Kurtz Family Vineyards, established a decade earlier. "My place is 20 hectares of prime vineyard in Light Pass, with vines dating back to the early 1960s," says Steve. "The Barossa is a special place and the camaraderie and support in the community is like no other."

You wouldn't read about it

"My Mum and Dad bought a vineyard on the same day that man landed on the moon, so they called it the 'Lunar Block'. The grapes from that vineyard now become our flagship wine."

Food matches

"You can't beat roast lamb with our Boundary Row GSM."

Light Pass Road Light Pass via Nuriootpa

Ph 0418 810 982

www.kurtzfamily
vineyards.com.au

kurtzfamilyvineyard@
bigpond.com

Est 1996

Tastings by appointment

Price range $15-$45

Key Wines: Boundary Row GSM, Boundary Row Shiraz, Seven Sleepers, Lunar Block Shiraz

langmeil

To step into Langmeil is to take a trip back to 1842 and into the second German settlement of the Barossa Valley. The old buildings of the original village are still standing, as is the 1843 Freedom vineyard, believed to contain the oldest Shiraz vines in Australia, and perhaps the world. The abandoned property was purchased in 1996 by three local mates, Richard Lindner, Chris Bitter and Carl Lindner, who have since refurbished the winery and restored the village and vineyards to their former glory.

My place

"This is quite a historic little area," Richard points out. "There was a butcher, a baker, a cobbler's shop and a blacksmith named Christian Auricht. It was Auricht who planted the vineyard in 1843."

"We're so lucky that these old buildings are still standing," says Carl. "There was a council order for our old barn to be demolished. So we undemolished it! The walls were bending outwards so, bit by bit, we pulled them inwards with rods and used a bulldozer to push them upright. Eventually we got them square, and it lifted the roof up as well! We had to build a wall to prop it up, so it's back into shape and pretty solid now, even though you can see that the roof isn't quite perfect!"

Barossa dirt

"When we came here in 1996, this place hadn't crushed a grape in eight years," recalls

Corner Langmeil & Para Roads Tanunda

Map E11 Winery 35

Ph (08) 8563 2595

www.langmeilwinery.
com.au

info@langmeilwinery.
com.au

Est 1996

Cellar door tastings open Mon-Sun 10:30-4:30

Crafts, local produce, picnic facilities, daily tours by appt, function areas

Price range $15-100

Key Wines: The Freedom 1843 Shiraz, Orphan Bank Shiraz, Eden Valley Riesling, Valley Floor Shiraz, Blacksmith Cabernet, The Fifth Wave Grenache

Langmeil harvest
Dragan Radocaj Photography

Richard. "Some of the vines had been pulled out, ready to be burnt, but thankfully they left the old vines intact."

"The old Freedom vineyard was pretty derelict," adds Carl. "There were vines and weeds growing wild all over the place. When we first pruned the vines in 1996, we didn't know if they were alive or dead. We had to cut them back quite heavily because they were sprawled out all over the place. It took us a few years to get it up to scratch.

"We love the old vines here. Old vines have been a passion of mine, going back to the days when I was involved with St Hallett. We found

out then about the importance of keeping the old vines, because they had something extra to offer. We started St Hallett Old Block Shiraz in 1980. Soon after that, the vine pull came in and growers were starting to yank out some of their best vineyards, which was a bloody shame. I know I saved four vineyards in that period. It was bloody tragic that our heritage was lost by the government giving cheques to growers."

Visiting Langmeil

"We love the history of this place and we enjoy passing it on to visitors," says Richard. "We take people for tours of the 1843 Freedom vineyard. A coach turns up around midday every

Langmeil cellar door

You wouldn't read about it

"We had old vines on a vineyard near town that was rezoned for housing development," Carl explains. "So we decided to relocate them to the spare land that we have here on the river flat. It's pretty tricky to transport an old vine to another vineyard! We used a machine with three big tapered blades that formed a cone to dig a hole, then drove the same machine half a kilometre to the old vineyard and used it to dig out the vine and put it in the new hole. A day later you could hardly tell that the vine had been shifted! It's been quite successful and those vines now make our 'Orphan Bank' Shiraz. We invited people to adopt a vine and we now have an annual picking day when they come in and pick the grapes from their vine."

day and whoever wants to join the tour can jump on board. There are usually one or two tours a day. We take them out for a walk in the vineyard, show them all of the old historical points around the area and they get a real sense of the history of the Barossa.

"During vintage, visitors watch vintage in action to get a real feel for what happens here. They can stand there, see all of the basket presses going and watch the girls hosing over the open fermenters. This is part of the tour during vintage.

"We've also got a little museum with some old equipment that we show our visitors. It's a good little tour, and people love it. At the end they can taste every wine in our portfolio at cellar door, including The Freedom 1843 Shiraz."

You can view a great little video of the guys digging up, moving and replanting the vines on their web site, www.langmeil.com.au.

Barossa Character

"I collect all sorts of old stuff," says Carl Lindner. "We've got quite a few pieces of old winemaking equipment scattered around the property. All sorts of things, from the old press to old stalk carts and pad filters. But I can't find a spot for my Jags yet! I'm a bit of a Jag buff. I have E-Types, Mk2s and XKs. I've also got the oldest Jaguar in Australia, a 1932 SSI. I've got 35 Jaguars in all, worth about $1.5 million. I have a full-time mechanic to look after them and a full-time body builder and

Winemaker Paul Lindner

Carl Lindner & his Jaguars

Cellar door

Langmeil Freedom vineyard 1843

we're looking at building a new C-Type next year. One day I'd like to start a business with luxury accommodation and luxury tours of the Barossa."

Local knowledge

"Tanunda Cellars is the best wine shop in the Barossa," says Richard. "Trevor Harch has got some interesting stuff there. He's a great guy and we're lucky to have his support. He supports Barossa wineries and the wineries support him, so if they've got back vintages or anything unusual available, they'll supply them to him."

Chris Bitter

Langmeil daily vineyard tour

1840s buildings

105

lanzthomson vineyards

"I drove from Queensland to Brown Brothers in Victoria as a student in 1975 and somehow managed to spend $800, which was a truckload of money back then! That was the start of a long love affair with wine that eventually led me to the Barossa," says Brian Thomson. He is one of four partners in LanzThomson Vineyards, a small producer in Lyndoch.

Phoebe, Anne, Brian, Raf & Nell Thomson

My Place

"When I first came to the Barossa, I clearly remember thinking, 'I could never live here, it's too dry, dusty and desolate,'" Brian recalls. "But I stayed and now see it completely differently - I love the diversity of the region, and watching the way that the seasons change from our place up on the hill."

You wouldn't read about it

"Growing grapes has its share of surprises. We were working in the vineyard one day and looked up to see our old Zetor tractor charging straight at us! Someone had left the brake off and it was careering down the steep slope toward one of the worker's cars. Miraculously, it missed us and the car!"

Local knowledge

"It's worth taking the time to drive randomly along some back roads through the countryside. The landscape is diverse, there's so much to see."

Lot 1 Rosedale Scenic Rd Lyndoch

Ph 0409 693 828

www.lanzthomson.com

brian.thomson@lanzthomson.com

Est 2004

Tastings by appointment

Price range $15-$25

Key Wines: Shattered Rock Shiraz, Shattered Rock Four Friends GSMV, Shattered Rock Viognier

Wining kids

"Kids are welcome at our place. They can run around the vineyard and open spaces to their heart's content. We have 120 acres but we haven't lost anyone yet!"

Food matches

"Deboned Hutton Vale lamb, sealed on a hot BBQ and finished in the oven, is perfect with our Shattered Rock Shiraz."

View from Steingarten Road
Dragan Radocaj Photography

laughing jack wines

"At the age of eight, I grabbed a few bunches of grapes and tried to make wine by forcing them through mum's flour strainer. Mum wasn't particularly excited, but for me it was the start of a lifelong love affair with grapes and wine," says Shawn Kalleske. The dedicated sixth-generation grape grower started Laughing Jack Wines in 1999.

My Place

"Wine has got me hook, line and sinker!" exclaims Shawn. "It's the consuming passion of my life, and I can't imagine a time when that will change. Every year I set out to make the best wines I possibly can, wines that people can appreciate and enjoy. When someone tastes a wine of mine and says to me, 'Wow, that's great', to me that's what this is all about.

"Our vineyard is surrounded by majestic Blue and Red Gum Eucalyptus species which harbour plenty of kookaburras. The nickname of these birds is 'Laughing Jack', hence the name of our brand."

Local knowledge

"The Barossa Brewing Company in Greenock makes wonderful beer, and there are three beers on tasting on the weekends. It's a great place for a palate cleanser to end the day."

Food matches

"My philosophy is to buy the best fresh produce and keep it simple. Fillet Steak from the Mount Pleasant butcher with steamed vegetables is great with a bottle of Laughing Jack Shiraz."

Laughing Jack

Corner Parbs Road and Boundary Road Greenock

Ph 0427 396 928

www.laughingjackwines.com

shawn@laughingjackwines.com

Est 1999

Tastings by appointment

Price range $20-$85

Key Wines: Greenock Shiraz, Jack Shiraz

Shawn Kalleske

Outlook from Laughing Jack Wines

107

View from Steingarten Road
Dragan Radocaj Photography

liebich wein

Clarence 'Darkie' Liebich was a legend of the Barossa, establishing Rovalley Wines in 1919 and building it into one of the powerhouse producers of the region. His nephew Ron established Liebich Wein in 1992 and has since forged a reputation for full-flavoured Shiraz and long-lived fortifieds.

My Place

"I was born into the industry, so wine is in my blood," says Ron. "When you have a history like ours it becomes a part of you and you can't let go. For us, it's not about money; we're driven by a passion for wine."

You wouldn't read about it

"In the old days at Rovalley, pre-booze bus, the place was so much fun. Old Darkie was well known around the place, so everyone used to come down in the afternoon for a drink. It was the hub of social activity. Even the police would drive up from Adelaide, settle in for a few quiet ones, then fill their car up with booze and drive back to town!"

Local knowledge

"People always talk about the views from Mengler's Hill, but I reckon the views from the top of Steingarten Road and Trial Hill Road are just as good. It's nowhere near as busy so it's always peaceful up there."

Wining kids

"We're happy for people to bring kids up here and there's plenty of room outside under trees for them to run around."

Food matches

"I can't think of anything

better than one of our old fortifieds with fried bananas. Simply delicious!"

**Steingarten Road
Rowland Flat**

Map H10 Winery 36

Ph (08) 8524 4543

www.liebichwein.com.au

info@liebichwein.com.au

Est 1992

Cellar door tastings open Wed-Mon 11-5

Crafts and local produce

Price range $20-$40

Key Wines: The Darkie Shiraz, The Leveret Shiraz

Ron Liebich

lienert of mecklenburg

Almost a century and a half after his ancestors first planted vines in the Barossa, John Lienert released a Shiraz from his own patch of vineyard in the western Barossa. Only sixteen barrels are produced under the Lienert of Mecklenburg label each year, with the wines vinified by neighbour and Shiraz specialist Charles Cimicky.

My Place

"Most of the fruit from our 2001 vines was sold to one of the big companies from the outset and it didn't take long before it was going into a label of some renown," says John. "We said, 'Well, for beginners, that'll do us!'"

Barossa Character

"Colonel Light, the founder of the Barossa, is rarely given the credit he deserves. In reference to his journey of exploration, the South Australian Gazette and Colonial Register stated that 'it has accomplished nothing that we have heard of except demolishing three pound twelve shillings worth of pickles.' Who today would not eagerly pay that cost if they could discover another Barossa? The truth is there will only ever be one Barossa, a place discovered and named by a truly great man who deserves to be remembered and honoured."

Local knowledge

"The Melodie Nacht (Melody Night) has long been a traditional event in the Barossa. One of the unique features of this evening of food, wine and music is the serving of the famous Glühwein, the traditional warm Prussian beverage of wine, honey and spice. The king of Barossa Glühwein was Mervyn 'Snowy' Gramp who for many years orchestrated the brew, to great acclaim!"

Food matches

"Our favourite food match with our wine is either roast beef or Kassler (smoked pork loin cutlets) served with cucumber salad a la Barossa (grated cucumber mixed with fresh cream and white wine vinegar or verjuice)."

Section 567 Lienert Road She Oak Log

Ph (08) 85249062

www.lienertof mecklenburg.com.au

lienertjohn@hotmail.com

Est 2001

Tastings by appointment

Price $40

Key Wine: Shiraz

View from Steingarten Road near Rowland Flat
Dragan Radocaj Photography

109

linfield road wines

**65 Victoria Terrace
Williamstown**

Map K7 winery 37

Ph (08) 8524 7355

www.linfieldroadwines.
com.au

sales@linfieldroadwines.
com.au

Est 2002

Cellar door tastings open
10-5 daily

Accommodation, tutored
tastings, light meals on
weekends

Price range $15-$65

*Key Wines: The Stubborn
Patriarch Shiraz, The
Steam Maker Riesling, The
Black Hammer Cabernet*

From left, father Steve, son Daniel and grandfather Arnold Wilson

Linfield Road Wines traces its origins back to 1860, when Edmund Wilson first planted vines in Williamstown. The Wilson family has maintained charge of the property to this day, adding wine production to their grape growing business with the release of their creatively named portfolio of wines in 2002.

My Place

"Our place is about a viticultural tradition that now spans five generations, one hundred and forty-nine vintages, five tractors and at least seven unpatented inventions," says current custodian of the estate, Daniel Wilson. "It's about pruning vines that my great grandpa planted and producing handcrafted, single vineyard wines with my family from the cooler southern Barossa."

Local knowledge

"Schulz's double smoked bacon is the best I've ever tasted. My grandpa still drives up to Angaston from Williamstown just to buy it!"

Wining kids

"We have a lawn area out the front, and we keep a soccer ball and a football out there so that kids can run around to their hearts' content."

Food matches

"We often go fishing up at Streaky Bay, and the whiting are to die for. The crispness of our 'Steam Maker' Riesling suits them perfectly."

Vineyard on Williamstown Road near Cockatoo Valley
Dragan Radocaj Photography

Scene near Tanunda
Dragan Radocaj Photography

linke wines

At the age of nineteen, Scott Linke became one of the youngest brand operators in the Barossa, sourcing grapes from his family's vineyards in the Dorrien and Stonewell districts. "My main aim is to build up a reputation of being a wine producer who makes a quality product that consumers can trust," he says.

My Place

"In my early primary school days I would go out grape picking before my mum took me to school, being careful not to get red grape stains on my uniform," Scott recalls. "The wine industry has been a part of my life for as long as I can recall, and the opportunity to build my own brand at a relatively young age was something too good to pass up."

Local knowledge

"For a great meal The Tanunda Club has always been a winner for me. A chicken 'parmy,' a pint and plenty of local faces - that's about as good as it gets!"

Seppeltsfield Road, Dorrien

Ph 0407 025 363

www.linkewines.com.au

scott@linkewines.com.au

Est 2002

Tastings by appointment

Price range $20-$25

Key Wines: Shiraz, Cabernet Sauvignon, Semillon Sauvignon Blanc

looking glass wines

A common love of wine, family and life brought Kirsty Glaetzer and Jane Osborne together to form Looking Glass Wines. Both had held high profile wine industry roles, Kirsty as Senior White Winemaker with Wolf Blass, and Jane with distribution powerhouse Negociants.

My Place

"Our goal with Looking Glass is to make quality, contemporary wines which are approachable in style and accessible in price," says Kirsty. "The name came about because it bothered us that people were pressured to 'look' for certain things in a wine. We prefer them to taste it for themselves and see in it what they like."

Ph 0431 514 964

www.lookingglasswines.com.au

kirsty@lookingglasswines.com.au

Tastings by appointment

Price range $19-$21

Above Vintage at Loose End Wines

loose end wines

Loose End Wines is a partnership between Rob Gibson and Warren Ward, two veterans of the Australian wine industry with intimate knowledge of the Barossa. The brand focuses on blends and food-friendly styles which can be tasted at the Gibson Wines cellar door.

My Place

"I like to call Loose End 'Gibbo's Wild Child,'" says Rob. "It came about because I needed a new creative outlet beyond our conventional wine styles. I saw this as an opportunity to experiment with flavours and put together interesting wines at good prices. It's a bit of a challenge for me, and a lot of fun!"

Food matches

"Pear, walnut and blue cheese salad is heavenly with our Loose End Barossa White."

Light Pass Rd Barossa

Map D13 Winery 38

Ph (08) 8563 2507

www.looseend.com.au

info@looseend.com.au

Est 2003

Cellar door tastings daily at Gibson Wines

Price range $14-$19

Key Wines: Grenache Shiraz Merlot, Grenache Rosé, Shiraz Viognier

lou miranda estate

After selling Miranda Wines in the Riverina in 1999, Lou Miranda established his eponymous brand in the Barossa in 2004 on the old Rovalley Wines site in Rowland Flat. With a lifetime of wine industry experience and significant vineyard resources dating back to 1889, Lou Miranda has quickly established a large and varied portfolio of wine.

My Place

"In that very Italian way, we're simply about family and trying to make our place as welcoming and homely as possible for everyone," says Lou. "We want people to feel relaxed and unrushed and take the time to get to know us."

You wouldn't read about it

"It is said that our building is haunted by the ghost of 'Darkie' Liebich, the original owner of Rovalley Wines."

Local knowledge

"I'm a huge fan of the meat pies from the Lyndoch bakery. Freshly baked, straight out of the oven, you can't beat them."

Wining kids

"Kids are more than welcome in our cellar door and we've got an area for them to play, equipped with colouring-in books and toys. Just watch out for my wife as she has a habit of stealing babies and taking them to the office to play!"

Food matches

"Our chef makes a great dish of organic chicken breast stuffed with blue cheese and Adel figs. It's an excellent match for the Lou Miranda Leone Pinot Grigio."

Barossa Valley Highway Rowland Flat

Map H9 Winery 39

Ph (08) 8524 4537

www.loumirandaestate.com.au

lisa@loumirandaestate.com.au

Est 2005

Cellar door tastings open 9-5 daily, restaurant for lunch daily

Café, restaurant, crafts, local produce, gallery, historical buildings

Price range $17-$35

Key Wines: Old Vine Shiraz, Leone Pinot Grigio, Leone Botrytis Semillon

Sunrise over the Barossa Ranges,
Dragan Radocaj Photography

lunar wines

Corey Chaplin was so keen to get into wine that he threw in his job as a chef and took up picking grapes for a living. He soon found himself at the iconic Rockford Winery, where he worked for five years under Robert O'Callaghan before launching Lunar Wines. "I'd built a lot of knowledge and needed to do something with it!" he says. The Shiraz and Cabernet Sauvignon that make up his Lunar portfolio are made in tiny quantities.

My Place

"Lunar Wines is my expression of the western Barossa and of traditionalist winemaking," he explains. "For me, Marananga offers a unique opportunity to grow quality grapes and to capture a distinctive flavour."

Local knowledge

"I like to take visitors to the Barossa down to Seppeltsfield to experience the Sherry tastings. These unique wines are world class by any estimation. They're an overlooked treasure of the Barossa."

Food matches

"I like to drink my wines with old-school French-style braises

RSD 108 Seppeltsfield Rd Marananga

Ph 0427 186 295

www.lunarwines.com.au

lunar@lunarwines.com.au

Est 2004

Tastings by appointment

Price range $18-$40

Key Wines: Cabernet Sauvignon, Shiraz

like Beef Bourguignon. These slow-cooked dishes bring out all the intense flavours and are a great match for our Lunar Wines Cabernet Sauvignon."

marschall groom cellars

Winemaker Daryl Groom was the Senior Red Winemaker at Penfolds for five years in the 1980s, during which time he developed a strong affinity for the Penfolds Kalimna vineyard, a key source for Grange. Jeanette and David Marschall independently owned the land next door. A long Barossa wine lunch later, the two were connected and Marschall Groom was born.

My Place

"Our place brings together two very important elements in our lives: family and the Barossa," says Jeanette Marschall. "Groom Wines is a family partnership of two sisters and their husbands, founded on Barossa dirt, the best soil we know of for making world class Shiraz."

Barossa Character

"For us, Peter Lehmann is the Barossa. He is a great mentor, winemaker, and angel to the local wine industry. He has had the most inspirational influence on Daryl's winemaking career, not just in winemaking but in teaching about respect for those around you."

You wouldn't read about it

"My husband David, a fourth generation Barossan, created a bit of stir when he made a TV appearance on Wipeout Australia and became the

28 Langmeil Road Tanunda

Ph (08) 8563 1101

www.groomwines.com

jeanette@groomwines.com

Est 1997

Tastings by appointment

Price range $24-$49

Key Wines: Barossa Valley Shiraz, Barossa Valley Bush Block Zinfandel

only South Australian to win that year (and at forty-nine, possibly also the oldest!)."

Daryl and Lisa Groom (left) and David and Jeanette Marschall

massena vineyards

Dan Standish and Jaysen Collins are close friends who grew up and worked together in the Barossa before creating their Massena brand in 1999. While producing traditional Barossa wine styles, they also enjoy experimenting with alternative varieties.

My Place

Jaysen recalls that "Dan and I were driving to the midnight vintage shift in 1999 in a beat-up Toyota Corolla called 'The Brown Bullet' when we came up with the idea to join forces and make a soft, slurpy wine that would wash down a long night's work. Hence our 'Moonlight Run' Grenache blend, and Massena was born. We're still about making easy-drinking wines in our ancient shearing shed winery in Lyndoch."

Local knowledge

"The best post-hangover coffee in the Barossa is at Blond Coffee in Angaston!"

Food matches

"Slow-cooked Osso Bucco in red wine sauce with mashed potatoes and plenty of butter is ideal with our Massena Barbera."

Lot 100 Barritt Road Lyndoch

Map H8 Winery 40

Ph (08) 8524 5469

www.massena.com.au

jaysen@massena.com.au

Est 2000

Tastings by appointment

Price range $17.50-$35

Key Wines: Moonlight Run GSM, Eleventh Hour Shiraz

maverick wines

Ron Brown holds 100 acres of vineyards across the Barossa and Eden Valleys, with vines up to 150 years old. He produces an array of single vineyard wines that he says "express both their terroir and the diversity of the Barossa region."

My Place

"I made wine in the Languedoc in France for over a decade and then sold up and came to Australia in 1997," Ron explains. "I was fascinated by the diversity of this place, its unique European heritage and the climatic contrasts between the Barossa and Eden Valleys. There appeared to be a wonderful opportunity here to create something special, so I put together four unique vineyard sites and set about trying to make the best wines I could."

You wouldn't read about it

"At our Barossa Ridge vineyard we have a half row of 1860s Riesling, one of the oldest productive Riesling vineyards in the world."

MAVERICK

Lot 141 Light Pass Rd Vine Vale

Ph (08) 8563 3551

www.maverickwines.com.au

ronald@maverickwines.com.au

Est 2004

Tastings by appointment

Price range $15-$75

Key Wines: Twins Barossa Valley Shiraz, Trial Hill Riesling, Trial Hill Shiraz

Maverick Vineyard

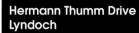

mcguigan barossa valley

Built in 1947 by German winemaker Hermann Thumm, the majestic stone building of Chateau Yaldara sits atop a hill overlooking the North Para River. It provides a view over an estate that has long been regarded as one of the most picturesque in the country. In more recent times, this has become the South Australian home of McGuigan Barossa.

My Place

"In Chateau Yaldara we've found the perfect home for our Barossa winery," says Senior Winemaker James Evers. "It has a wonderful sense of history, complete with some of the oldest vines in the Barossa. We are using this precious resource together with the Chateau's original open top fermenting tanks to craft regionally pure, hand-crafted wines. This is the continuation of a sixty year tradition of small batch winemaking here, combined with four generations of McGuigan wine industry experience."

Food matches

"Our rich and luscious McGuigan The Shortlist GSM is great with a cheese plate in the gardens."

Hermann Thumm Drive Lyndoch

Map G7 Winery 72

Ph (08) 8524 0200

www.mswl.com.au

yaldara@yaldara.com.au

Est 1947

Cellar door tastings open 9-5 daily

Tours, historical buildings, picnic facilities, tutored tastings, conferences, functions, crafts, local produce, café, restaurant

Price range $10-$100

Key Wines: The Shortlist Barossa GSM, The Shortlist Barossa Shiraz, Eden Valley Riesling, Farms Barossa Valley Shiraz

You wouldn't read about it

"Our winery had its first vintage in 1947 when fortified wine was the main focus. We still maintain this tradition, holding over half a million litres of fortifieds, dating back as much as fifty years."

Local knowledge

"Lou Miranda Estate makes Italian-inspired meals for lunch daily. The food is spectacular!"

Wining kids

"At our cellar door there is an enormous garden area and a fountain on the banks of the North Para River. My kids love exploring this area and hanging out with our resident goose, 'Godfrey,' down by the river."

James Evers

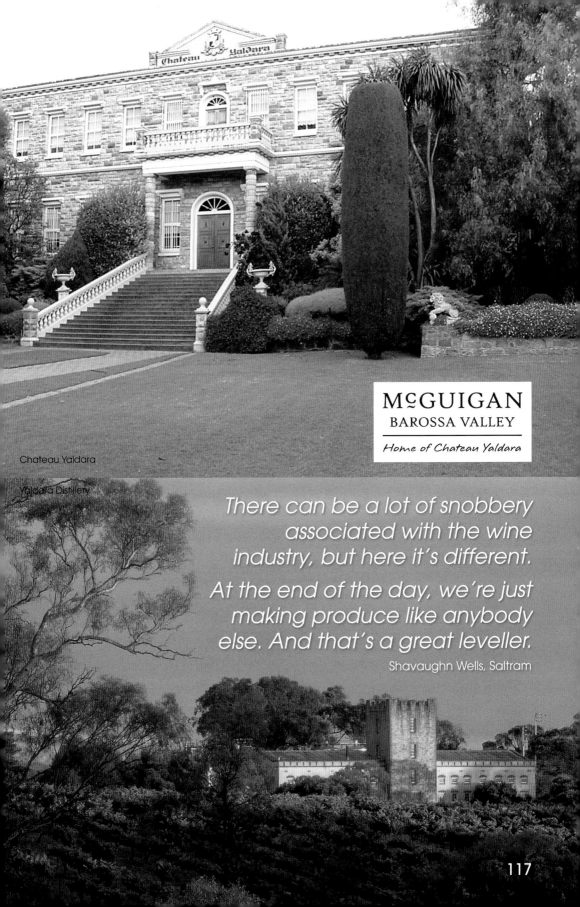

Chateau Yaldara

Yaldara Distillery

McGUIGAN
BAROSSA VALLEY
Home of Chateau Yaldara

There can be a lot of snobbery associated with the wine industry, but here it's different.

At the end of the day, we're just making produce like anybody else. And that's a great leveller.

Shavaughn Wells, Saltram

mclean's farmgate

McLean's Farmgate

Mengler's Hill Road Angaston

Map F13 Winery 41

Ph (08) 8564 3340

www.mcleansfarm.com

bob@mcleansfarm.com

Est 2001

Cellar door tastings on weekends

Price range $20-$35

Key Wines: McLean's Farmgate Riesling, Barr-Eden Riesling, McLean's Farmgate Shiraz Mataro, Barr-Eden Mataro Shiraz Grenache

"I don't need five generations of German ancestors to establish a 100 year old vineyard when I can do it myself!" says industry veteran 'Big' Bob McLean of his 250 acre property high on Mengler's Hill. "Like the forefathers we never had, we planted 6144 dry grown bush vines. And, yes, we do know all their names!" Bob makes Grenache, Shiraz, Mataro and Riesling in such small quantities that he measures production in bottles rather than cases. It's well worth the scenic drive up Mengler's Hill to taste them all and share a laugh with a legend of the Barossa.

Barossa Character

"My thirty year career in wine has spanned public relations roles at Orlando, marketing at Petaluma, Managing Director and half-shareholder at St Hallett, then running Barr-Vinum in Angaston, which was the best restaurant outside of Adelaide right from the day it opened! Now I've come home to my own land on top of Mengler's Hill. Some would call it a sea change but it's nothing like it! I've gone from talking in millions of dollars, sixty or seventy employees, thousands of tonnes crushed and shipping how many containers a year to thinking in kilos of fruit and bottles of wine. I worked out I was actually drinking more than my sales force could sell there for a while! It's true! My accountant was concerned that I was writing off four dozen bottles a week. Mind you, I am a pretty big drinker! But not all for myself, of course! If I came to your place, I'd bring three or four bottles, not just one – we are generous around here! And that's better promotion than any sales force."

My place

"We say we're only open on weekends, but we're really open 24/7 – if the sign's out, you know I'm here! Just give me a call and I'll come straight out of anywhere and have a drink!

"And I always pour enough. I can't stand little tastes! You've got to have enough to get it into your mouth. I don't mind you tipping it out.

"Every year the wines are different here. It's just whatever I make that year. The Big Mac is not into building brands any more. It will be up to you to follow us up the hill! We will always make a GSM blend because I reckon that's where small makers can lay their claim to being great makers. By and large Farmgate wines are only available here. The only other places they will be sold are the odd pub or restaurant

Bob McLean and his cellar door in his barrel hall

McLean's Farmgate vineyard
Dragan Radocaj Photography

where I eat and drink myself!"

Bob's tasting room is between the barrels in his barrel shed. $500 French chairs surround a tasting bench in front of his grand old timber wine rack left over from Barr-vinum days. "It's a great party shed," he says, "where lunches are regular and long," in keeping with a tradition that he has built since 1972. "One of the best parties we had here was a New Year's Eve party. I only had twelve barrels then, so I put six down each side, shut the doors and hung fairy lights everywhere. I put a bar up in the corner and hung the Willie's Wine Bar posters up. It was an absolute blinder of a New Year's Party and it went on for days!"

You wouldn't read about it

"When I was Managing Director at St Hallett in 1993 we made a Reward Cabernet. We got rave reviews! A grower, Feckie, brought the fruit in in five tonne bins, but we couldn't crush five tonne bins! So we had to send it up to Penfolds to crush it, juice it and bring it back. Slingers, a famous Penfolds winemaker, did us a favour on a Sunday morning at 9am and ran ten tonnes through his big crusher. Because he did this, we invited him to our end of year vintage party. There's a story there! We had an amazing booze-up! Anyone who had worked with us during the year was invited. Even Wolfie (Wolf Blass) used to have a driver bring him up. He wouldn't miss it for quids. And she was a ripper! An absolute blinder! We'd start at lunch time and finish the next day! Slingers was there in 1993 so, the next year, he sent down ten tonnes of fruit, just so he'd get an another invite to the party! He did that three years in a row! They were good parties! That's where I broke my knee the first time. I was dancing with Paul Clancy on Stuie Blackwell's terracotta paving. And I was wearing those big snow boot things because it was cold – it was the end of vintage. Clancy and I were both 130kg each and we were rock 'n' rolling at 3am in the morning, to everyone's disdain. I twisted my knee and the boot gave out and I landed on those terracotta bricks! Oh well, I was overweight and drunk – these things happen!"

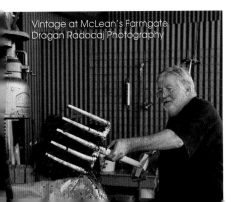

Vintage at McLean's Farmgate
Dragan Radocaj Photography

mengler view wines

Mengler View Wines are produced by the students of Faith Lutheran School as part of their Agricultural Studies program. In 2002 it became the first school in Australia to construct its own purpose-built winery. Stuart Blackwell from St Hallett has mentored the program since its inception and with the support and sponsorship of other Barossa companies, Mengler View Wines has gone on to win medals in the Barossa Wine Show. The wines are sold across South Australia, interstate and are exported to America. "We invite you to visit us, not only to see this magnificent facility but also to enjoy our student-produced wines," says Agricultural Coordinator and Winery Manager, Bob Mitchell.

Magnolia Road Tanunda
Ph (08) 8561 4200
www.faith.sa.edu.au/wine/wineindex.html
rmitchell@faith.sa.edu.au
Est 1995

Faith's school vineyard

Peter Milhinch and his geese

120

milhinch wines

Seize the Day

MILHINCH WINES

Seriously ill with cancer in 2002, Peter Milhinch picked up Lance Armstrong's book, 'It's not about the Bike,' and found both the inspiration to live and the name for his 'Seize the Day' range. His wines are made exclusively from grapes grown on the family estate, which is also the home of Seppeltsfield Vineyard Cottage, a lovingly restored 1860s home that he and his wife run as luxury accommodation.

My Place

"Our first wine was a rosé because I wasn't sure that I would live long enough to drink anything that couldn't be made in a hurry," says Peter. "Thankfully I'm still here, the rosé remains and we've added some other wines to the range. We enjoy sharing them with friends old and new, which is exactly what wine is all about."

You wouldn't read about it

"We've put an enormous amount of effort into the rebuilding of Seppeltsfield Vineyard Cottage, and are very proud of the result. We offer our guests an authentic cottage for two in the countryside overlooking the vineyard. They can even feed the geese in the garden!"

Lot 4 Gerald Roberts Road Seppeltsfield

Ph (08) 8563 4003

www.seizetheday.net.au

wine@seizetheday.net.au

Est 2003

Vineyard tours and tastings by appointment

Accommodation

Price range $20-$38

Key Wines: Seize the Day Shiraz, Seize the Day Cabernet Sauvignon, Seize the Day Rosé

Peter Milhinch & Sharyn Rogers

moorooroo park vineyards

With careers as chefs behind them, it's no surprise that Wyndham and Patricia House craft their Moorooroo Park wines to accompany food. This boutique operation maintains an emphasis on small volume, hand-crafted wines. Beside the vineyard, the couple runs Jacobs Creek Retreat, a luxury accommodation and function venue on the banks of Jacob's Creek.

My Place

"Fifteen years ago we came to this place, and found it run down and in need of some serious care," recalls Wyndham. "With the aid of family and friends, we've built it into what it is today. Along the way we also established our own wine label, which seemed a natural extension of our passion for food and of living and working in the Barossa."

Lot 638 Nitschke Rd Tanunda

Map G10 Winery 42

Ph (08) 8563 1123

www.jacobscreekretreat. com.au

jacobs-creek@bigpond. com

Est 1994

Cellar door tastings open Fri-Mon 10-5

Hotel, restaurant, food and wine classes.

Price range $18-$42

Key Wines: Lotties Shiraz, Samuel Nitschke Cabernets

Local knowledge

"There's a pretty rugged dirt road called Rifle Range Road which runs off Lilly Farm Road. It offers a terrific view of the Barossa — even better than Mengler's Hill."

Wining kids

"We have a few toy boxes and lots of lawn and garden for kids to roam around."

Food matches

"Our passion is food, especially 'slow' food, so we host food master classes, wine education courses and even sausage making classes. Tarragon and chilli pork sausages are a great combination with Sam Nitschke Cabernet Sauvignon."

JACOBS CREEK RETREAT
& MOOROOROO PARK VINEYARDS

Top Moorooroo Park Vineyards cellar door
Middle Tuscan-inspired gardens
Bottom Moorooroo Park Vineyards at night

122

mountadam vineyard

In the far reaches of High Eden lies Australia's first cool climate Chardonnay vineyard. Its name is Mountadam. Between 550 and 600m in altitude, this is one of the highest vineyards in South Australia. "Only the more serious tourists make their way up this far," says owner David Brown. Those who do are greeted with one of the most spectacular vistas in the hills, overlooking a dramatic vineyard with lines of vines winding around the contours of the hills and dodging surreal moonscape-like granite outcrops.

Mountadam vineyard

My place

"I just love the feeling of this place from the moment you drive in the front gate," says David. "It's totally different to the valley floor up here with our altitude and our views. There is a feeling of remoteness even though we're just an hour's drive from Adelaide. I'm a farmer at heart and I love the sheep and the Angas cattle. It's just a great property.

"David Wynn purchased the property in 1970 and planted Chardonnay in 1972. He was visionary enough not to plant in the valleys or on the plains but on the slopes of the hills. Our Chardonnay had almost iconic status in the 1980s and we are now trying to re-establish it as one of the leading Chardonnays in Australia.

"The landscape up here also makes our reds more elegant and refined. The wines are 100 percent estate grown, cool climate and quite different to the Barossa Valley in style."

Visiting Mountadam

"Our tasting area is virtually in the winery so you really get the feel that you're in the middle of things," David explains. "We're open by appointment so give us a call or send an email with at least a few hours' notice."

MOUNTADAM
VINEYARDS

High Eden Road Eden Valley

Map J12 Winery 43

Ph (08) 8564 1900

www.mountadam.com.au

david@mountadam.com.au

Est 1972

Tastings by appointment

Price range $17-$60

Key Wines: Eden Valley Riesling, Eden Valley Pinot Gris, Estate Chardonnay, Patriarch High Eden Shiraz

MURDOCK

murdock wines

Corner of Light Pass and Magnolia Roads Vine Vale

Map F12 Winery 44

Ph (08) 8563 1156

www.murdockwines.com

barossa@murdockwines.com

Est 1998

Cellar door tastings open Wed-Mon 10-5

Tapas restaurant open Wed-Sun 11-late

Conferences, functions, art gallery, café, cooking school, master classes

Price range $18.50-$145

Key Barossa Wines: Barossa Rosé, Barossa Grenache, Barossa Shiraz

To appreciate the success of David Murdock and Kathryn Murray's Murdock Cellar Door and Restaurant, just take a look at the number of winemakers in this book who list it among their favourite haunts. "Our aim was to create a seamless indoor/outdoor dining and tasting experience which was cosmopolitan yet welcoming," explains Kathryn. "Floor to ceiling glass bi-folding doors showcase the best views in the Barossa!" With winemaking under the care of Coonawarra superstar winemaker Pete Bissell, Murdock is worth visiting for more reasons than just the view and the food.

My place

"Murdock restaurant has more than forty Tapas items on the menu, which showcase innovative use of local produce," says Kathryn. "We're open all afternoon and evening from Wednesday through Sunday for casual dining both inside and on our huge deck. The cellar door is integrated into the main restaurant to allow you to taste before deciding which wines to have with your meal.

"Our chefs host two-and-a-half hour Tapas master classes in our private tasting room. We also offer guided tastings and kids' cooking schools. See our web site for dates and details."

Local knowledge

"My other passion is Murdock Indulge in Angaston," says Kathryn. "I source unique jewellery, clothes, home wares and body products from around the corner and around the globe. Indulge is licensed and has a dedicated kids' play room as well as beer and papers in the courtyard for Dad!"

Wining kids

With five- and six-year-old children of their own, David and Kathryn have made it a priority to set up Murdock for kids. "We have crafts, a huge lawn for outdoor games and pod swings," explains Kathryn. "And best of all there are no

Murdock dining

chips, pineapple, pizza, nuggets or anything deep fried or stuffed full of preservatives on our menu. At Murdock, kids enjoy good, wholesome food from our Tapas menu."

Murdock cellar door

murray street vineyards

Andrew Seppelt describes visiting his Murray Street Vineyards as "not just a wine experience but an everything experience! We don't have a traditional tasting bar, we encourage people to sit on lounges and enjoy the wines with food platters. We renovated the 1950s house with the front door to face out over the vineyard so you can sit inside or on the deck and watch the seasons go past."

My place

Murray Street Vineyards is the only cellar door in Greenock at the time of writing. "To find us, keep driving until you're worried that you're out of the Barossa!" Andrew quips. But for him the location means everything. "For us it's all about subregionality. We have Greenock Estate and Gomersal Estate as single subregion wines."

"Our cellar door is open every day except Boxing Day, Christmas Day and New Year's Day. And emergency golf days, of course! Sometimes we put the sign up and go and play golf. We've got a nice bit of lawn out the front and it's great to go out there and smash balls out into the vineyards! It's the best driving range in the Valley!"

You wouldn't read about it

"Cooper is our dog. Like the dog on Footrot Flats he jumps at trees and gets six or seven feet up! He bites at the trees and rounds them up! Visitors love to take photos of him."

Food matches

"We have a regional savoury plate with a focus on things made in the Barossa, including smoked meats, preserves and cheeses – traditional-style nibble foods that match well with our wines. We keep it seasonal, so we change the cheeses according to what's

Lot 723 Murray Street Greenock

Map C10 Winery 45

Ph (08) 8562 8373

www.murraystreet.com.au

wine@murraystreet.com.au

Est 2001

Cellar door tastings

Tours, tutored tastings, coffee, light meals

Price range $17-$75

Key Wines: The Barossa, Gomersal Shiraz, Greenock Shiraz

Andrew Seppelt

in season. During the winter months we offer a soup on the weekends, matched to back-vintage wines from our museum cellar. It's a total food and wine experience, rather than just tasting an old wine at the bar."

Local knowledge

"I've known the guys at Ballycroft Barossa Artisan Cheese for fifteen years. It's just a tiny, artisan cheesery but it's an extraordinary product. They basically know the cows' names that make the cheeses! They've been making an amazingly creamy blue lately, and it's not at all sharp, so it goes well with Barossa wine. We have their cheeses on our menu here. And you can find them at the Barossa Farmers Market every week."

Wining kids

"We've got small kids of our own so we appreciate the importance of having things for them to do. We've got a box of toys for them to play with. A lot of mums pop by for a coffee and let their kids play on the lawn. It's safe and there's a dry creek and trees to climb and you can see it all from the tasting area."

Left Murray Street Vineyards tasting room
Middle Winery building
Right Cooper jumping at a tree

neil hahn wines

Neil Hahn has one of the oldest family names in the Barossa, his descendents having arrived in 1839. As a sixth generation grape grower and winemaker, he draws from 130 acres of family owned and run vineyard, with the majority of fruit being sold to a number of the region's leading brands. The remainder is kept aside for his Neil Hahn Wines, formerly Hahn Barossa Vineyards.

My Place

"At its core, my place is about family and keeping our traditions alive," Neil says. "Heritage, history and community are the lifeblood of this region and give it its distinct identity. My family bought into the Barossa in 1885, and my way of celebrating this tradition is to grow the best possible grapes and to make the best wine I can from them."

You wouldn't read about it

"Starting Neil Hahn Wines gave me the chance to travel and see the world, all while drinking great wine and eating great food. Does it get any

18 Mickan Road Stockwell

Ph (08) 8562 3002

Mob 0408 828 536

www.hahnbarossa.com

neil@hahnbarossa.com

Est 2002

Tastings by appointment

Price range $9-$34

Key Wines: Catharina Shiraz, Yanyarrie Shiraz

better than this?"

Local knowledge

"Linke's bakery in Nuriootpa makes the best pasties that I have ever tasted."

Nuriootpa High School students making wine

nurihannam wines

In 1992 Nuriootpa High School became the first school in Australia to legally operate a commercial winery. Since that time, its wines have won medals at the Barossa Wine Show and have received accolades from international critics. All profits from sales go toward funding agriculture programs and school facilities.

"Our students are involved in every stage of the wine production process," explains Agriculture Coordinator David Bowley. "They grow the grapes, make the wine, bottle it, design the labels and promote and market it. We're particularly proud to have been recognised as the leading school wine program in Australia."

View from Mengler's Hill
Dragan Radocaj Photography

penfolds wines

There is one name more intimately associated with premium Australian red wine around the world than any other. Penfolds had humble beginnings in South Australia in 1844, but it was not until the early 1900s that it established a strong presence in the Barossa. Since that time the Barossa has become the epicentre of operations for Australia's most famous wine company, not only in its tremendous winemaking facility in Nuriootpa but, more significantly, in its historic Barossa vineyards. Names like Kalimna, Koonunga Hill and Block 42 are etched into the list of the great vineyards of the world, and it is these sites that form the backbone of Australia's most iconic wine, Penfolds Grange.

Barossa Character

It's Penfolds Chief Winemaker Peter Gago's aspiration that the company will be "the largest boutique winery in the world." He gets dirty making wine by hand every year at Magill and still completes the winery record sheets by hand for every parcel of fruit. But as the public face of Australia's most famous brand, he spends much of his time travelling the world, waving the flag of Australian wine and entertaining everyone from Prime Ministers and Presidents to billionaires and rock bands. "When I talk about this, people think I'm skiting," he says, "but I just want to remind them that Australian wine continues to attract interest at this level."

Tanunda Road Nuriootpa

Map D12 Winery 46

Ph (08) 8568 9408

www.penfolds.com.au

Barossa.CellarDoor@penfolds.com.au

Est 1911

Cellar door tastings open 10-5 daily

A Taste of Grange Tour $150pp 10am for 2 hours, by request. Tutored tasting of Grange and other Penfolds icons.

Make Your Own Blend Tour $65pp daily 10am & 2pm for 1½ hours or by request.

Price range $50-$600

Key Barossa Wines: Marananga Shiraz, Cellar Reserve Barossa Valley Cabernet, Cellar Reserve Barossa Valley Sangiovese, Bin 138 Grenache Mourvèdre Shiraz, RWT Barossa Shiraz, Great Grandfather Grand Old Liqueur Tawny, Grange Bin 95

The Barossa Vintage Festival *Rare & Distinguished Barossa Wine Auction* is conducted inside Penfold's Red Barrel Cellar in Nuriootpa.
Dragan Radocaj Photography

It's little wonder that so many high-profile people gravitate to Peter Gago. The top winemaker in Australia's most important and influential wine company happens to be one of the most warm and hospitable blokes anywhere in the industry. He is as generous with his time as he is with his cellar. The Australian wine industry needs more spokespeople with Gago-levels of enthusiasm.

My place

"The Barossa offers a collection of activity and engagement that's quite sophisticated and, at the same time, quite real," says Peter. "Dovetailed into this are the Maggie Beers, and everything she's done, from Pheasant Farm days, through to television now. Then there's Angaston – with Angas Park fruits, the bakeries and the cold meats. The Barossa is a big place; there's Lyndoch, Tanunda, Nuriootpa and Angaston – lots of places and lots of regional identities. I was there when the Tour Down Under was on, to catch up with Lance Armstrong, and they finished in Angaston, with every man and his dog in town. It was wonderful!"

Vineyards of significance

"The Barossa is the engine room of Penfolds. The Penfold family bought the Nuriootpa facility in 1911 and the Barossa has been

Penfolds Chief Winemaker
Peter Gago

pivotal to what we've done ever since. I've often said there's a Penfolds triangle and it's Magill, Kalimna and Nuriootpa. Max Schubert said Kalimna was the greatest red wine vineyard in Australia, but, there are other vineyards now, too! We believe that Block 42 has the oldest continuously-producing Cabernet vines in the world. We say mid-1880s, because we're not certain whether it's 1886 or 1888, but either way that's pretty old Cabernet! And we have even older Grenache, Mourvèdre and Shiraz!

"Nowadays, in many vintages the Kalimna vineyard has been superseded by Koonunga Hill for Grange. I think it's a better vineyard.

Kalimna has really old vines – and vine age is very important but it's not the be all and end all. Old vines still need to be in the right soil and the right microclimate. Kalimna varies so much, with different soil types, and we need to pick at different stages there. In Block 42, everything is perfect – microclimate, soil, vine age, and so on. Everything comes together. And at Koonunga Hill, I think we've kind of got it right as well – right soils, right vines, right everything. And the vines are getting older and older and better and better!

"In a semi-humorous way, I talk of putting a beautiful stone wall around Koonunga Hill. Call it Clos de Hill or Clos de Koon or something – ha! And make people take their shoes off when they come in. Like when you visit in Burgundy and see those beautifully walled and gabled vineyards. We just don't do enough of that here. We don't want to make it too ostentatious, but I think we could do more with Koonunga Hill and Kalimna."

Blend your own Penfolds Wine

"The Penfolds Nuriootpa property today has the largest premium red wine barrel hall in the Southern Hemisphere, covering more than five acres. One of the great things that you can do here is to make your own blend. It's been enormously successful, it's just gone berserk! People off the street dress up in lab coats in our tasting room, and pay a bit of money and they get a little certificate and walk away with the bottle that they've blended, with a Penfolds label and their own name on the bottle as Assistant Winemaker. It's incredible! We have Grenache, Shiraz and Mourvèdre which we keep separate, so they're physically making up a blend that is pretty close to Bin 138. If you're very wine-savvy, you can go within a decimal point of the perfect blend – not that there's such thing as a perfect blend, but subjectively what is deemed to be about right. Just ring up the winery and make a booking. You don't need to give much

Max Schubert
Creator of Grange

notice. There are set times each day and if it's not full you can slot in."

Penfolds Grange

"The Barossa has always been a major part of Penfold's wines," says Peter. "Of course, the first two Granges were Magill and Morphett Vale, but, literally, after that they were all Barossa based. Barossa fruit is an integral and usually major portion of most Grange blends. And 1999 and 2000 were entirely Barossa."

Max Schubert

"Max Schubert was born at Moculta, just out of the Barossa," says Peter. "He used to drive a lot of Jeffrey Penfold Hyland cars, which were state-of-the-art sports cars that they drove in those days. The equivalent of the Bentley Continental GTs and Ferraris now. They didn't have red light cameras or speed cameras in his day. He certainly didn't get there slowly, let's just put it that way!"

The unlikely story of Grange
According to Max Schubert in 1979

"Grange is a truly controversial wine, never without interest and always open to debate in one way or another. It was during my initial visit to the major wine-growing areas of Europe in 1950 that the idea of producing an Australian red wine capable of staying alive for a minimum of twenty years and comparable with those produced in Bordeaux first entered my mind.

"As vintage followed vintage, the accumulation of bottles grew and... the time appeared to be ripe to remove the wraps and allow other people to see and evaluate this wondrous thing. Representative bottles from each vintage from 1951 to 1956 were called for and a wine tasting was arranged by the Managing Director. Those invited included well-known wine identities in Sydney, personal friends of the board and top management. The result was absolutely disastrous. Simply, no one liked Grange Hermitage.

"It may be illuminating at this time to record some of the assessments made by experts and critics alike in public and in my presence during the darkest hours of Grange Hermitage. This, by a well-known, respected wine man: 'Schubert, I congratulate you. A very good, dry port, which no one in their right mind will buy — let alone drink.'

"The final blow came just before the 1957 vintage when I received written instructions from head office to stop production of Grange Hermitage. The main reasons given were that I was accumulating large stocks of wine which to all intents and purposes were unsaleable and that the adverse criticism directed at the wine was harmful to the company image as a whole. It appeared to be the end.

"However, with Jeffrey Penfold Hyland's support, I disregarded the written instructions in part and continued to make Grange in reduced quantities. This undercover production continued through to 1959. In all, it was ten years from the time the first experimental Grange was made before the wine gained general acceptance and the prejudices were overcome. Just before the 1960 vintage I was instructed to start making Grange Hermitage officially again.

"Since that time, Grange Hermitage has never looked back. I would like to express the hope that the production and the acceptance of Grange Hermitage as a great Australian wine have proved that we in Australia are capable of producing wines equal to the best in the world."

Over the following decades, the 1955 Grange Hermitage won more than fifty gold medals at Australian wine shows. Bottles of the very earliest vintages, deemed 'unsaleable' in 1957, are now priceless, fetching up to $47 000 at auction.

The Kalimna Homestead, 1896

Penfolds cellar door, Nuriootpa

VIP visits

"Mike Rann, our Premier, was here not long back when we had the Tour Down Under and we hosted a tasting at Penfolds with Lance Armstrong," recalls Peter Gago. It was quite incredible. I pulled out a 70s Grange that we had in the cabinet at the time. It was the '71, which was a fairly highly reputed Grange but I chose it for no reason other than that there was a '71 sitting on the top shelf. Guess what? Guess who was born in 1971? Lance Armstrong! The Premier was like, 'Oh, Peter, we'll get you a knighthood for this!' That just made Lance's trip! Sometimes lady luck is on your side.

"At the very elitist, exclusive end of the tourism business, we fly VIPs into the Kalimna Vineyard for a tasting. We've got a little runway on our golf course block. Or we helicopter them in. We love it because Penfolds Nuriootpa is not your classic, Old World, charming place, it's more a production facility. The Kalimna homestead was originally a manager's residence, built in 1896, and bit by bit we've renovated every room. It's looking terrific!"

You wouldn't read about it

"When we transport wines from Magill in Adelaide to Nuriootpa, we forklift barrels directly on to a truck," explains Peter. "As you can imagine, a full barrel weighs a lot! On one occasion, on a corner in the Barossa coming off the highway, we wrote off ten vines in a vineyard! The barrels came, literally, right off the back of a truck! Now, everything is roped securely, of course! I was called out to have a look at it. I was thankful that it happened on that bend and they went straight into a vineyard!

"I'm tempted to take the Cellar Reserve Barossa Valley Cabernet Sauvignon 2008 to Bordeaux, because I got into a lot of trouble in 2007. I took the 2004 Block 42 Kalimna Cabernet Sauvignon. It was quite theatrical, really. When I opened it the aroma just filled the room! And I got told off, rather humorously, by French winemaking friends, saying, 'You can't bring Cabernet like that to Bordeaux!'"

Penfolds®

Penfolds float in the Barossa Vintage Festival Parade

peter lehmann wines

In all of the Barossa, there is one name that is revered for its contribution to the wine industry above all others. It may come as a surprise that a name that has become a commodity in liquor stores across the planet remains one of the most family-oriented, Barossa-focused companies. Peter Lehmann the man is a Barossa legend and there is hardly a conversation about the Barossa past, present or future in which he is not acknowledged. Peter Lehmann the company is likewise revered and its extensive portfolio encompasses not only some of the Barossa's best value wines but also three of Australia's finest flagships in Stonewell Shiraz, Wigan Riesling and Margaret Semillon. The Lehmann name is prominent in food circles, too, thanks to Peter's wife Margaret, who has worked for decades to raise the profile of the Barossa's food culture. It is no exaggeration to say that the Barossa would not be what it is today without the Lehmann name, and no visit to the Barossa would be complete without a visit to the hallowed turf and beautiful grounds of this vital company.

My place

Chief winemaker Andrew Wigan has been working with Peter Lehmann right from the very beginning in 1976. "The Barossa would be a different place today if Peter Lehmann hadn't done what he's done," he says. "He's a very special man. I couldn't have done it. I often pinch myself and say how lucky I've been to fall into this ride with him.

"We are so lucky to live in the Barossa. Every year I travel around Europe showing people elegantly structured Riesling, refined Semillon and flinty Chenin Blanc and at the same time rich Shiraz, all from within a few kilometres of each other. Where else in the world could you make such a range of wines? You couldn't."

Cellar door

"You can taste our entire range at cellar door and there's no tasting charge," says Andrew. "We do a number of 'cellar door only' wines as something special because we understand

Para Road Tanunda

Map E11 Winery 47

Ph (08) 8563 2100

www.
peterlehmannwines.com

plw@peterlehmannwines.
com

Est 1979

Cellar door tastings open
Mon-Fri 9:30-5, Sat, Sun &
Public Hols 10:30-4:30

Picnic facilities, tutored
tastings, gallery, crafts,
local produce, coffee,
regional produce
platters, light meals,
concerts and festivals,
children's books, wine
path linking Peter
Lehmann Wines to
Langmeil, Stanley
Lambert and Richmond
Grove wineries.

Price range $12-$90

Key Wines: Stonewell
Shiraz, Wigan Riesling,
Margaret Semillon, Eden
Valley Riesling, Barossa
Grenache Rosé, Barossa
Semillon, Barossa Riesling,
Clancy's Rosé

Peter Lehmann Wines
cellar door

Peter
LEHMANN
of the Barossa

that people can buy Peter Lehmann Semillon or Barossa Shiraz virtually anywhere. But when they come here they can taste a range of fortified wines, including a very old tawny and also a spätlese Frontignac that you can't get anywhere else. There are always six or seven of our range of district wines on tasting at any time. And you'll find Wigan Riesling, Margaret Semillon and Black Queen Sparkling Shiraz, all of which are very hard to find elsewhere.

"Platters of local foods are available for $25 from cellar door. You can buy a glass of wine and we won't charge corkage on a bottle to drink. If it's a cold day you can sit in the Eight Songs room, or if it's warm, out on the veranda or in the gardens. There's plenty of space for kids to run around here. It's really a great spot."

Barossa character

The name 'Peter Lehmann' is held in high esteem in the Barossa for many reasons, but perhaps most of all for a remarkable gamble to save Barossa grape growers, ultimately leading to the birth of Peter Lehmann Wines.

"When I left Yalumba and went to work for Saltram in 1960, they were a 400 to 500 tonne winery and grapes were a bit hard to come by in those days," Peter recalls. "With my local knowledge I was able to build it up. It helped that my old man was a Lutheran Pastor and much loved. A hell of a lot of his parishioners

Chief Winemaker
Andrew Wigan

were grape growers, which gave me a little bit of extra leverage to keep wheedling a few extra tonnes out of this one and that one. I call that the God factor!

"By the time 1972 came along, we were a 6000-7000 tonne winery. And the majority of that fruit was from the Barossa. The approach was always, you look after us and we'll look after you. It was a handshake deal. No such thing as a written contract. In 1977, with the full encouragement of the board of the company, I approached Bertie Scholz, who owned The Willows, a fairly big grape grower who had been with Kaiser Stuhl for some time. I talked him into leaving Kaiser Stuhl to sell his fruit to us.

"It was only a fortnight later that I got a letter from Dalgetys, who owned Saltrams. There was no phone call or anything, just a letter came in the post from London instructing me not to buy any grapes for the coming vintage, because Dalgetys had been having a very torrid time. This coincided with a looming oversupply as far as grapes were concerned. So, lo and behold, this letter lobs on my desk in September 1977, saying don't buy any grapes in 1978.

"Well, cripes, a fortnight after I'd done the deal with The Willows I'm supposed to tell them, 'Sorry, we don't want your fruit!' Meanwhile, they'd cut their ties with the previous company. I was told to write a letter to the growers. Which I refused to do! A letter was duly sent out, signed by someone else in the company.

Meanwhile, there was a lot of wheeling and dealing going on, and with the help of friends, relations and some advice, we did a deal with Dalgetys that we could lease the company's facilities to contract crush on behalf of an outside group, which I had to be seen to be at arm's length with. So we made my wife Margaret a joint managing director – I'd hardly call it arm's length! But we raised $180 000, which was a reasonable amount of money back

Margaret and Peter Lehmann

then. And we bought a couple of millions of dollars' worth of grapes with it!

"It worked out beautifully for all concerned. Dalgetys didn't have egg on their faces because the grapes were still seen to be going to Saltrams. They picked up more than a quarter of a million in contract crushing charges. And we saved our integrity and also saved the growers from seeing their grapes rot on the vines. And we made a quid on the side! It was that successful that Dalgetys asked if we'd like to do it again in 1979. We said, 'Certainly!'

"In 1982, after leaving Saltrams, we decided it was time to join what I always term 'the glass jungle' — to go into bottle ourselves. Our majority shareholder said our company name 'Masterson Barossa Vignerons' was too much of a bloody mouthful, so they decided to change it to Peter Lehmann Wines. Which I would never have done in the first place, because everyone would have said, 'Christ, he's up himself!'

"Today, almost thirty years later, Doug Lehmann is Managing Director of the company and Phil Lehmann is in the winemaking team. I toddle over occasionally to help with vintage classification. And Margaret stays actively involved."

You wouldn't read about it

"My favourite story was back in Saltram days," Peter reminisces. "'Tawny,' so named because of his predilection toward the product, loved his drop of Tawny. And in those days it was customary at 10 o'clock for the blokes to have a glass or a couple of glasses at morning tea and a couple at lunch time. These days it's different, they don't drink on the job at all! Anyway, Tawny was drinking a little to excess and one day I came along and he was smashed! I gave him the rounds of the kitchen, most of which, in his foggy state, he didn't comprehend fully. I got one of the blokes to take him home. Next morning he came looking a bit sheepish and he

135

sort of said, 'I've got a bit of an idea that you're sort of not too happy with me, that I blotted the copy book a bit.' And I said, 'Eric,' I said, 'You've been drinking far too much. It's become a worry.' I said, 'I'll tell you what, after yesterday, if I ever catch you pissed on Tawny port again, you're history. You're finished!' And he thanked me. He said I sounded just like his father. He said, 'I needed a good talking to!' And he was terrific for a few weeks. But one day I had to go to Adelaide for a meeting and I came back a bit earlier than expected. I came down and Tawny was a little bit sprung. I said, 'Eric, you're a little bit drunk!' 'Nope.' 'Come on, Christ,' I said, 'I know you well enough.' He said, 'Oh, maybe just a little bit pissed!' I said, 'Oh, God, Tawny, what am I going to do with you?!' He said, 'Well, you can't sack me!' 'What do you mean I can't sack you, why not?' He said, 'I'm pissed on Moselle!' And he was still with us ten years later!

"Another Tawny one I love, too. One day I walked out the back of the winery. Tawny was our sort of Mr Fix it. He could fix anything and wasn't afraid to play with electricity. This day I walked out and he was up a bloody stobie pole! And he's up the top pulling a flagon up on a rope. I said, 'What are you doing?' He said, 'Saving time, boss!'"

The birth of Stonewell Shiraz

"The first years at Lehmann were tough, turbulent years," recalls Andrew. "We were struggling and making a loss. One day in the cellar Peter said, 'It's time that we made a show dry red, because that's what we did best at Saltram.' I replied, 'Well, we have no new

oak and we don't have any money to hold a show wine back for five years. What will the accountants say?' Lehmann looked at me and said, 'Then we just won't tell them!' So we snuck a few American oak hogsheads in past the accountants secretly. And that was how Stonewell was born in 1989."

Food Barossa

Margaret Lehmann was the founding chair of both Food Barossa and the Food South Australia Cooperative. Alongside Maggie Beer and Jan Angas of Huttonvale, there are perhaps few people alive who can be credited more significantly for their support of the transformation of the Barossa into one of the great food regions of the world.

"It all came together in 1995," Margaret explains, "when we saw a need for the food culture of the Barossa to be identified and conserved. Yalumba had the first Harvest Market then, and we had the launch of the Vintage Festival called 'The Winemaker, The Chef, The Butcher, The Baker and The Candlestick Maker.'

"The Barossa is regional in two senses of the word. One is its culinary history and heritage and the other is the simple fact of food being produced in the area. So, you buy your chickens locally, or your eggs or your milk. We developed a system of licensing specification. We got as many producers as we could, and we shoved all the butchers, for instance, on one table and said, 'OK, what is distinctive? What distinguishes what you do from other producers?' And for the butchers it was a wood fire. None of them use painted wood smoke or any of those artificial things. It's natural.

"When I met Peter, I had no idea that I was just living Food Barossa the whole time. Peter had a huge vegie garden and we grew our vegies and swapped them around the Barossa. He used to say, 'Well, that's so-and-so's ducks, that's so-and-

Like Peter Scholz, there are many Barossa folk eager to shout Peter Lehmann a beer so's chooks'. And so, we always knew where all the food on our plate came from. I used to say, 'I want to know whose hands have been in my food.' And that's the thing you can get from the Barossa.

"When we started, we didn't have a cellar door or anything like that. And Peter said, 'I want the weighbridge to be my home during vintage.' Because the waiting times for the growers were quite often long, we'd always have a mettwurst in the fridge, and we still do. We'd have a tea or coffee with the drivers. So the weighbridge was the heart of hospitality.

"Peter looked at what people were eating in 1976 when the first chicken takeaway was opened in the Barossa. They would bring in their cut lunch or takeaway chicken and chips. And he would say, 'No, we'll get lumps of steak and have a proper barbie around the crusher pit.' And we had so much stuff in the garden, we decided to use the vegetables from the garden.

"And the other thing that we started in 1976, which we are still doing to this day, is to feed everyone during vintage. It was crap what the blokes were bringing in to eat, so we put on vintage tea every night and their wives and husbands would come in. It's amazing what you can do. Andrew Wigan's wife Wendy and I cooked dinner for some years, five nights a week. There would be a roast or a barbie, a curry or a stew. There was always fresh fruit, salad, vegetables and whatever else. The growers would bring in bags of carrots or capsicums or watermelons. And we'd feed fifty or sixty people. Sometimes the tanker drivers come in, and the office staff if they're working late. We do a round-up of numbers each day to figure out how many spuds to peel! And even though the night crew only starts at 8pm, they often come in early to join in. At least we know our staff are always being well fed! When they call us a family-oriented winery, this is part of it."

The weighbridge, 'the heart of hospitality' at Peter Lehmann Wines

Local knowledge

"I will go to the various bakers for different sorts of things because each have their own specialities," says Margaret. "If I want rye bread, I'll go to the Lyndoch bakery. If I want special little half-loaves or a floured wholemeal I'll go to Linke's. I love Apex bread because it's so honest and so convenient, so it's our normal staple. But if I'm doing a function or something a bit more elaborate, I'll draw on the others.

"And it's the same with the butchers. Schulz's in Angaston has his smokehouse. And the recipes are all the original ones. The young man who's taken it over is fantastic and he's passionate. And you can have a debate! It's all about keeping the 'personal' in your food. Which is exactly aligned with what we try to do with our wine.

"The Barossa Farmers Market is more than just the market. I don't necessarily go every week because we've got the vegetable garden. But if I need a gossip or if I want to specifically see people, if I've got a bit of a thing running through my head, that's where I go and touch base. It's definitely a must!

"And Zimmy's horseradish is actually the best horseradish in the world!" At this point Peter interjects: "Not as good as mine used to be!"

Golf

"The Barossa has two really good golf courses," says Andrew. "At different ends of the Barossa, they're very different. The Barossa Valley course at Kalimna is more open and Tanunda Pines at the Novotel is more heavily wooded. They're some of the best greens in South Australia, and both are worth playing for a bit of variation."

peter seppelt wines

Fifth generation winemakers Peter and Roz Seppelt continue the tradition of their famous name. Their 'Grand Cru' Estate near Springton in the Eden Valley is the home of their vineyard and range of value-for-money wines.

My Place

"I grew up surrounded by wine," says Peter. "As a kid school holidays meant working in the vineyards. Hence, when we started Peter Seppelt Wines, there were no illusions about what this would involve. We love the challenge of it, and the way of life that our place up here in the hills offers. We grow fruit biologically, with minimum intervention and minimal use of chemicals."

PETER SEPPELT
WINES
GRAND CRU ESTATE

You wouldn't read about it

"I built two wood-fired pizza ovens from scratch. They do such a good job that we decided to open a pizza restaurant on weekends, which has attracted a strong following."

Local knowledge

"The Springton area is one of the most unspoilt and naturally beautiful parts of the Barossa, with massive old red gums and lots of historic buildings. It is a great place for a peaceful, leisurely drive."

Food matches

"A favourite combination of ours is a frozen brandy cream pie with our Peter Seppelt Ratafia dessert wine."

Right Picnic at Peter Seppelt Wines
Below right Grand Cru Tower
Below Peter Seppelt and his pizza ovens

Corner of R. Dewells and Laube Roads Mt. Pleasant

Map M14 Winery 48

Ph (08) 8568 2452

www.peterseppeltwines.com.au

roz@peterseppeltwines.com.au

Est 1981

Cellar door tastings open Thurs-Mon, 10-5

Picnic facilities, conferences, functions, historical buildings, weekend casual dining at Grand Cru Estate

Price range $16-$22

Key Wines: Merlot, Ratafia, Eden Valley Riesling

pindarie

Aboriginal for 'hilly place', Pindarie was established in 2005 by industry veterans Tony Brooks and Wendy Allan. With sustainability as their mantra, the couple have set about personally restoring numerous century-old buildings on the family estate, including 150-year-old stables which will be the home of the Pindarie cellar door from late 2009.

My Place

"Our farm dates back to the 1840s and all of the buildings are well over 100 years old," says Wendy. "In the vineyard, our focus is on managing the soil in the most sustainable way.

"We've planted over 15 000 native seedlings over the past twenty years from the Trees for Life program, and have established a Tawny Frogmouth reserve on the farm as well, all in line with our commitment to sustainability."

Local knowledge

"We're told by many people that we have the best view in the Valley, and who are we to argue? The other great view, of course, is at Mengler's Hill. For a Sunday outing, take your kids up there around 5pm, take a brief walk along the well-signposted path and then just relax and watch the kangaroos come out to feed."

Wining kids

"We've made sure that kids feel welcome at Pindarie. There's a big sandpit under the pepper tree near the cellar door and we have sandpit kits that they can borrow. On cold days they can enjoy toys and books in the kids' corner inside."

Food matches

"Moroccan-style lamb hot pot with couscous is ideally matched with our Bar Rossa Tempranillo Sangiovese blend."

PINDARIE

Wines from the Western Ridge

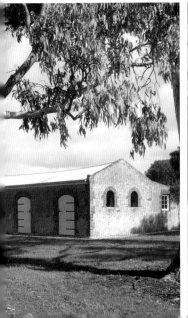

Above left 1890s Pindarie homestead
Below left Pindarie stables, now cellar door
Below Tony Brooks at work on the stables

139

poonawatta estate

Angaston Road Eden Valley

Ph (08) 8565 3248

www.poonawatta.com

info@poonawatta.com

Tastings at Taste Eden Valley in Angaston

Price range $20-$80

Key Wines: The Eden Riesling, The Cuttings Shiraz, The 1880 Shiraz, Monties Block Shiraz

Poonawatta's 1880 vines are thought to be the seventh oldest Shiraz vines in Australia. With more recent plantings of Riesling, this estate focuses on the Eden Valley's two key varietals. "Underpinning this is a sense of family," explains owner Andrew Holt, "with a local family history extending six generations, and three of these actively involved in the vineyard."

Frost on 1880 Shiraz vine

Visiting Poonawatta

"Poonawatta Estate wines can be tasted at Taste Eden Valley in Angaston," Andrew explains. "We are also always happy to accommodate visitors with private tastings and a vineyard tour. Give us a call or send an email. Twenty-four hours notice would be appreciated."

You wouldn't read about it

"The Poonawatta property was purchased by my family in 1966 but we didn't know the age of the Shiraz vines. It was while the vines were being pruned a few years later that Doug Wegener pulled up in front of the vineyard. His first word was '1880'. 'Excuse me?' my father, John Holt, said. '1880,' he said again. 'My grandfather August planted these vines in 1880 and always said I should get some cuttings. So can I?' Doug told us that the vines were planted the year his grandparents were married, hence his assurance of the date."

Local knowledge

"The Barossa Farmers Market in Angaston every Saturday is a wonderful venue for fresh produce and homemade gourmet foods. Gourmet pizza from Roaring 40's Café in Angaston is hard to beat, and the Vindaloo is a favourite. For a local break, we will stay at the Novotel – the facilities allow us a rare escape for twenty-four hours!"

Food matches

"In summer the perfect match to the Poonawatta Riesling is a sunny afternoon with friends. In winter we love it with a Thai Green Curry or roast pork. We love matching our Cuttings Shiraz to roast duck or marinated pork ribs cooked over the coals. The rich concentrated flavour of our 1880 Shiraz pairs beautifully with slow cooked red meats, and we particularly love it with lamb shanks."

Poonawatta Riesling vineyard

poverty hill wines

"We're three good mates with a quirky little brand who love the Eden Valley," says Poverty Hill Wines Operations and Vineyard Manager, Stuart 'Woody' Woodman. Quirky, perhaps, but Poverty Hill crafts its wines from old Eden Valley Riesling and Shiraz vineyards, some of which are well over 100 years old. The wines can be tasted at cellar door, located inside Buck's Bistro in the main street of Springton.

Local Knowledge

"Eden Valley has a vineyard landscape like no other!" exclaims Stuart. "You'll find tiny pockets of ancient Riesling and Shiraz, framed by some of the most majestic gum trees in the world. It's a unique place, and well worth a drive to experience it."

Food and Wine

"Buck's Bistro serves fantastic food. A favourite of mine is the Alaskan crab with one of our aged Rieslings."

Wining Kids

"There's a footy oval right next to the cellar door, where kids can run themselves ragged. Peter at Buck's Bistro makes a mean milkshake, although he doesn't like me to tell anyone!"

14 Miller Street Springton

Ph (08) 8568 2999

www.povertyhillwines.com.au

povertyhillwines@ozemail.com.au

Est 2002

Cellar door tastings open Wed-Mon 10-5

Restaurant

Price range $17-$60

Key Wines: Eden Valley Riesling, Eden Valley Shiraz

POVERTY HILL
HANDCRAFTED WINES
Eden Valley

Left Chris Ringland
Above R Bar

r wines

Chris Ringland's name is synonymous with cult Barossa reds. For more than twenty years, his has been the face behind some of the Barossa's most exclusive (and most expensive) tiny production old vine reds, typically of blockbuster proportions. Today, his bold 'R Wines' label encompasses more than forty different wine brands, including nine Shirazes, five Grenaches and three Cabernets from the Barossa. The branding is as distinctive as the wines, with labels designed by famous names in the design industry, including those who conceived album covers for The Beatles and Madonna. With wine names like Bitch, Evil Incarnate, Suxx, FU and The Wine, it needn't be said that there is little that is conservative about Chris Ringland and his operation.

171 O'Connell St North Adelaide (enter via rear on Fenchurch St and look for R on wall)

Ph (08) 8230 0100

Greggory.hill@rwinery.com

Cellar door tastings in North Adelaide open Wednesday 5pm-10pm, Thurs-Sat 5pm-11pm

Chef available

Price range $14-$1000

Key Barossa Wines: JP Belle Terroir Ebenezer Shiraz, The Wine, Evil Incarnate, FU

Barossa dirt

"We crush a significant amount of fruit from the Barossa," explains Chris. "Everything we do is about tying in the regional and vineyard identities with the wines. We endeavour to give each of our brands a stamp of regional personality. In essence we are a modern 'negociant'. We only own two serious holdings but we deal with more than 100 growers."

My place

"We like to have a bit of fun with conventions and bust the rules. I enjoy challenging the unspoken rules, and some of the labels we've created deliberately poke fun at pretentiousness. 'Chateau Chateau' is a classic example. It's fun to look at it from another perspective.

"One of the things that's always driven us is to challenge conventional models of how people approach things. I've always felt a little bit jaded with the concept that if you have a winery, you have to have it in the middle of the vineyards and people have to come there to experience it. There's nothing wrong with that, but it's by no means the only way of doing it.

"We've developed a tasting and interaction facility in Adelaide instead. R Bar is a juxtaposition of a whole range of styles, just as our brands are. You walk in through the back entrance. There's no front entrance or signage, so you need to know where to go to get there. There is an aisle of barrels from the back entrance and during vintage we'll do ferments there. We've got crushers set up and we've always loved the idea of people walking in off the street to have a wine tasting experience and being able to say, 'This is a ferment. Smell this!'"

Local knowledge

"I go to Ballycroft in Greenock and The Barossa Valley Cheese Company in Angaston for cheese. The antipasti platter at The Branch in Nuriootpa is my favourite quick snack and The Eden Valley Hotel is a good place for a drink. It's worth the experience for the locals alone. I can't abide Cooper's, so any place that serves Little Creatures gets my vote! To really get the best stuff at The Barossa Farmers Market you have to get there at the crack of dawn on Saturday mornings, so I never bother. I suppose I could drop past on my way home from the pub!"

Food matches

"The duck and veal sausages from Schulz's Butchers in Angaston are hard to beat and they are great with Chris Ringland Shiraz."

Lyndoch vineyard
Dragan Radocaj Photography

radford

Ben and Gill Radford are a formidable husband and wife winemaking team. Ben works full time as the winemaker at the iconic Rockford Wines, whilst Gill is one of the region's talented chefs. Together they combine their passion for both pursuits to craft distinctively individual wines from their biodynamically grown old vine Riesling and Shiraz vineyards in the Eden Valley. In recent vintages it has been only women who have made the wines, with Gill and two other girls doing all the work.

My Place

"Our lives revolve around flavour, and that's what Radford is all about," says Gill. "This small corner of the Barossa offers the opportunity to make wines of subtle and specific flavour. The beauty of the Eden Valley is that its wines reflect their site accurately. In growing our vines biodynamically we've found a way to more purely express the characters of Riesling and Shiraz."

Barossa dirt

"The Eden Valley Pub is one of those places you just have to visit. In one of the smallest towns in the area, it's a small pub and a little quirky, but with its own sense of charm."

You wouldn't read about it

"We like to joke that Ben was a mail order husband! We met when he was making wine in my homeland of South Africa. He used some lame excuse about finding a food match for Shiraz to ask me out, so we like to say that Shiraz brought us together. It remains a big part of our lives."

Local knowledge

"Taste Eden Valley is a little shop in the main street of

L Pumpas Road Eden Valley

Ph (08) 8565 3256

www.radfordwines.com

wine@radfordwines.com

Est 2003

Tastings by appointment

Price range $22-$40

Key Wines: Eden Valley Riesling, Eden Valley Shiraz

Angaston that offers an opportunity to taste a wide range of great Eden Valley wines from small producers. There are some wonderful wines there which are otherwise hard to find, so it's well worth a visit."

Wining kids

"Kids are welcome at our place. It's a real farm experience with plenty of space and lots of chooks, peacocks, geese and ducks running around."

Winter mist in the Radford vineyard

richmond grove wines

Para Road Tanunda

Map E11 Winery 50

Ph (08) 8563 7303

www.richmond
grovewines.com

Cellar door tastings open
10:30-4:30 daily

Price range $20-$45

*Key Barossa Wine: Limited
Release Barossa Shiraz*

The chateau that is now Richmond Grove has enjoyed an illustrious life over more than a century, first as Orange Grove Wine Cellars and then Chateau Leonay. As Richmond Grove today, if the splendid, turreted chateau and sprawling grounds are not reason enough to visit, the extensive range of back vintages available exclusively from Cellar Door is certainly enticing. Barossa Valley Shiraz and Rieslings are the local focus here, and vintages right back to 1994 are on sale, with some offered for tasting.

My place

Richmond Grove Winemaker Steve Clarkson lives just a few minutes down the road from the winery in Tanunda.

So close that in the middle of vintage he can hear the refrigeration in the winery starting up at night!

"A lot of visitors enjoy staying in Tanunda and walking between the wineries on Para Road," he explains. "You can walk on the street from Stanley Lambert to Richmond Grove, then along the Para Walk to Peter Lehmann Wines and finally to Langmeil. On the Para Road Wine Path Day on the third Sunday in November each year everyone puts on live music, food, family entertainment and special wines to make a real celebration of it.

"Our Richmond Grove Limited Release Barossa Shiraz is our main focus for this

region. Fruit is sourced from the southern edge of Tanunda, down through to Lyndoch.

"Our cellar door is open every day of the week. We conduct a winery tour at 12:30 and 2:30 each day or by appointment for groups. Visitors can see through The Basket Press Cellar and the original open fermenters, which we still use during vintage. There's also a great little model winery that we use to assist in explaining the winemaking process. We offer tastings out of barrel as part of the 2:30 tour.

"You really need to visit this place to appreciate what we are doing here and get a real feel for the splendour of the chateau and the sprawling grounds. We have picnic tables

Richmond Grove Winemaker
Steve Clarkson

The chateau of Richmond Grove Winery

on the grounds, which visitors are welcome to make use of."

You wouldn't read about it

Richmond Grove began its life as a mixed farm and grove of 100 orange trees. The first wines were released in 1897 under the name 'Orange Grove Wine Cellars.' Orange Grove was sold to Leo Buring in 1945, when it became 'Chateau Leonay.' In 1993 it became Richmond Grove and it was not until 2001 that the spires were added to the turrets, according to Leo Buring's original Flemish Chateau design, completing a 100 year old dream. "Don't ask the cost of the things!" Steve exclaims. "It was a major engineering feat to complete!"

Barossa Character

Recently retired Richmond Grove Master Winemaker John Vickery has a name synonymous with many of the great Rieslings of Australia's history.

"I first came to the Barossa when I graduated from Roseworthy in 1955," John recalls. "Riesling was the pre-eminent white variety at the time — there was really no Chardonnay outside of the Hunter Valley. Gramps planted lovely Barossa Riesling vineyards pre-war and made a style of Riesling which was flavoured and had longevity. We sourced Riesling from the Bethany area and from my property in Greenock. But we really chased the Eden Valley Riesling. When Orlando started producing their fresh, well-made Rieslings in the late '50s, they set the line in the sand. This was the style that we should be making. So that was the challenge for us all.

Richmond Grove
Barrel room

"Leo Buring died in 1961 and Lindemans bought the winery in 1962, which gave us the capital to purchase refrigeration. Our first Riesling made with refrigeration was 1963 and that was when we started winning medals at the Adelaide and Melbourne wine shows, knocking Orlando off its pedestal. We did very well with Rieslings in the '60s and right through to the early '70s. And they're still drinking well to this day.

"Riesling enjoyed great popularity in the '60s and '70s, before Chardonnay came along. It's the Prima Donna of the whites, after all! Chardonnay came along in the early '80s and consumers went to this new, highly-flavoured style of grape and Riesling got lost in the wilderness. There were still a lot of good Rieslings being made but there were too many made that were too sweet, and I think that got a lot of people off-side.

"We're drinking current vintage at the moment as well as 2000s, 2001s and 2002s. The 2002 is still quite youthful. The 1998 is starting to show some development, but it's still fresh, with lovely colour and the honey and lemon butter characters of maturity."

Barossa dirt

"We have always drawn from a big portfolio of Eden Valley growers, all with mature, older vineyards," says John. "We chased the growers that other companies weren't looking after, paid them bonuses and even paid them to plant Riesling.

"Riesling is a variety that really reflects where it's grown better than any other grape. It's the soil and elevation that defines the character of Eden Valley Riesling. The schist, broken down rock of the Eden Valley is similar to the Mosel in Germany. They're not very fertile soils, so we never see vigorous growth or big crops."

Food matches

"I most enjoy Riesling with fish. Garfish is a reasonably priced variety. Whiting if you can afford it. The plainer the better, without too much spice or flavouring. We eat buckets of it!"

John Vickery

rockford wines

Robert 'Rocky' O'Callaghan's Rockford winery is one of Australia's most famous boutique cellar doors. Stepping into the courtyard will transport you back to winemaking as it was 100 years ago. You can watch all the old equipment in action and taste wines made in a traditional style. Robert says that he has built his business on the philosophy of making wine for pleasure and not profit. "If you're a small winemaker the only advantage you can have over the big boys is that you have a personal relationship with your customers," he says. Rockford epitomises this philosophy and its mailing list is among the most sought-after in the country. To join, you literally have to wait until someone leaves!

Barossa Character

"I packed my camper van and did a tour of Australia in 1971," Robert explains. I came back to the Barossa to do a vintage, just to get a bit of cash, then I was going to do another year around Australia. I was offered a job and I stayed in the Barossa and it all developed from there. Unfortunately, the people I worked for went bankrupt, so when I started at Rockford I started with nothing. I had lived in the Combi van for about a year and in 1972 I'd bought the house that is now the cellar door. And it was about the price of a Combi van, $6000. It had a tin bath and a long-drop dunny and one tap, about two lights and one power point! It was pretty basic living."

Krondorf Road Tanunda

Map G10 Winery 51

Ph (08) 8563 2720

www.rockfordwines.com.au

info.contact@rockfordwines.com.au

Est 1984

Cellar door tastings 11-5 daily

Crafts, local produce

Price range $15.50-$56

Key Wines: Basket Press Shiraz, Sparkling Black Shiraz, Alicante Bouchet

My place

"I want people to have the feeling when they come into Rockford that I had when I walked into wineries as a teenager. I want it to have a magic and an aura about it. I set it up as a courtyard because I want to make sure that people are transported from the world that they are in when they get here, to my world. I want people to feel that they are walking into the winery to buy wine, not into a bottle shop. As you walk in, you walk past the crusher and the vintage shed. Everything there is old, 1920 and back. The crusher and the press are

Rockford cellar door

Robert O'Callaghan

probably from the 1890s. As you walk in, on the right-hand side, the vintage shed is exactly as it would have been if you walked into any winery in Australia between about 1910 and 1960. That's what they all looked like.

"When you visit in summer you can smell and hear the vintage, with all of the old machinery cranking away. In the winter on a really cold day we light fires, so when you walk into the courtyard you can smell the burning eucalypt. I

store all the fortified barrels up in the roof of the cellar door, so when you walk in there, it has the smell of old stacks of Sherry and Muscat that I remember as a child from Seppelts at Rutherglen.

"I wanted it to be like the old cellar doors that I went into as a kid. They always had accumulated s**t everywhere. People just stuck things in the roof, and I did that. All the old stuff out of buildings that I found and bits and pieces just get accumulated there. I tried to capture all those things that made an impression on me as a kid and put them in the winery.

"When I built Rockford I had no money. While everybody else was throwing their old equipment out, I went and picked it up. I had presses and crushers and pumps and slate fermenting tanks that I'd scrounged. So, I had a shed full of hundred-year-old winemaking equipment. I knew how it all worked, and it was free! I set the whole vintage shed up and I physically built a lot of it myself. I didn't have many customers when I started at Rockford,

Rockford cellar door courtyard in autumn

so I'd go and lay some stones and if someone turned up they'd just wait until I finished the barrow load and I'd give them some wine and then go back and put some more stones on the wall. That went on for bloody years!"

The Vine Pull

In 1986, soon after Robert O'Callaghan established Rockford, the Barossa was under threat from a government subsidy encouraging growers to pull out their vines. "It really set off the alarm bells," he recalls. "S**t! All of a sudden there were big heaps of vines everywhere, burning every weekend. The Barossa was on fire and we were under a huge threat! The vine pull said to the state government, 'The Barossa as a viticultural region is finished!' Their development plan was to bring the boundaries of Adelaide out further and turn all of the Barossa into five acre blocks for rural living. We responded by forming the residents' association and I was the founding chairman.

"I had a very powerful emotional commitment to old vineyards because my grandparents on both sides of my family were grape growers in the Riverland. I grew up in vineyards and I knew what it felt like when you can't sell your grapes. So, I personally appealed to growers not to pull out their old vines. I had growers who sent their cheques back. I talked them out of taking the vine pull subsidy!

"I was convinced that these old vines would one day be the most valuable asset in the region and I saw this as an enormous opportunity for Rockford to get five or ten great vineyards. And all we had to do was to guarantee to take the grapes and pay the growers $600 per tonne. The going rate for Shiraz in the Barossa was $200. And so I went and signed up my long-term growers on that basis. And I've still got them all today."

As chair of the residents' association, Robert appealed to the state government and the zoning of the Barossa was permanently changed to protect it from residential development. "It was a massive success," he says.

Rockford cellar door courtyard in winter

Golf

"I've been a member of the Tanunda Pines Club since 1971. A few years back when the club got into trouble they sold it to the members, so there are a few of us who now own shares in the club. We sponsor it every year because it doesn't make any money! I've been very lucky through meeting Australia's premier golf writer Tom Ramsey at cellar door to have been able to travel the world and play all of the great golf courses. Tanunda Pines is on a really beautiful piece of land, quite hilly, heavily wooded country and it's a beautiful walk. With elevated tees, you can look out across the valley. My favourite hole is the 13th. It's a classic hole – the big carry from an elevated tee, across open country then across a creek on to a slight dog leg, but you can see the whole hole from the tee. And it's got giant gum trees down both sides. It's fantastic – a beautiful old-fashioned golf hole where you can see everything, nice little undulating greens with hollows on either side. It's a real tester course, it can really test good players."

Drinking

"I don't like bad drunks. I'd always like to think that the people who drink my wine don't abuse it or the people around them. It seems like a funny thing to say when you're in the business of selling wine, but you don't want to be selling things that are causing a lot of bloody drama! It's nice to make something that people can sit down and really enjoy."

Local Knowledge

"You can go up to the Kaiser Stuhl National Park any evening or any morning and go for a beautiful walk through the bushland, as the Barossa would have been before it was settled. Without exception, the kangaroos come through and there's goannas and it's really neat. It's a tiny little park and, because it's tiny, you're into it in five minutes. It's a lovely little excursion for a traveller here – rather than just eating and drinking all day!"

Historic crusher atop Rockford's old Bedford
in the Barossa Vintage Festival Parade
Dragan Radocaj Photography

rocland estate wines

"I've always wanted to be involved with wine," says Franc Rocca, whose father migrated to Australia from Italy in 1945. His business began as a wine storage business before morphing into Rocland Estate Wines. There's no lack of imagination in the wine names, with labels including 'Ass Kisser', 'Kilroy was Here', and 'Duck Duck Goose.'

My Place

"We're just easy-going people who make easy-going wines," Franc sums up the operation. "It's a family company, and we all love good food and wine."

Local knowledge

"There are a number of outstanding local artists in the Barossa and the Old Mill Gallery Café in Tanunda is a great place to see their work exhibited."

Wining kids

"Kids are welcome at our place. Our own kids are usually playing out the back and we have plenty of open space and a bocce area."

Food matches

"Our Lot 147 Shiraz is a great match for braised pork with wild mushrooms and blackberries."

Lot 147 Sturt Highway Nuriootpa

Ph (08) 8562 2142

www.roclandestate.com

info@rocland.com.au

Est 1999

Cellar door tastings open 10-4 daily

Price range $17-$28

Key Wines: Shiraz, Lot 147 Shiraz, Kilroy was Here Cabernet Sauvignon

Lucy, Seth, Franc & Isaac Rocca

rohrlach family wines

Rohrlach
Family Wines

With only fifty cases of wine made each year, Rohrlach Family Wines ranks among the Barossa's most exclusive producers. Grape growers Graham, Kevin and Wayne Rohrlach share responsibility for the management of a large vineyard estate that has been in the family for three generations.

My Place

"We grow grapes for a number of different wineries in the Barossa," explains Graham, "but it was always in the back of our minds that we would one day like to drink the fruits of our labours. There was no grand plan, just to make a wine that we would be proud to put our name on."

Local knowledge

"It's a well-worn path, but a visit to the Rockford cellar door is a must. It's one of the great institutions of the Barossa."

Kalimna Road Nuriootpa

Ph (08) 8562 4121

www.rohrlachfamily wines.com.au

rohrlach@esc.net.au

Est 2000

Tastings by appointment

Price $20

Key Wines: Barossa Cabernet Merlot, Barossa Shiraz

Grape vine budburst
Dragan Radocaj Photography

151

rolf binder veritas wines

Brother and sister Rolf Binder and Christa Deans might be the only brother and sister winemaking team in the country, with Rolf overseeing red winemaking, and Christa white. Previously under the banner of 'Veritas Winery' the estate has established a worldwide following for its extensive portfolio of wines, and most notably its Heysen and Hanisch Shirazes.

My place

"We tend to source most of our red fruit from the northern end of the Barossa, Koonunga Hill and Kalimna," explains Rolf. "I call this area the 'Marananga bowl' or the 'Western strip' and it's always been known for good Shiraz. I'm a 'dirt man', when it comes to looking at vineyards and there seems to be a vein that runs from here to Seppeltsfield. The wine that it produces is distinctive, it's full-bodied and it's rich.

"The Hanisch vineyard is just up the hill from the winery and the vines were planted in 1972. It's a unique vineyard of just twelve rows, 500m long, and it moves through four distinctive soil types. Since 1988 we've kept this fruit separate and it's always stood out. It's always deeper in colour and more fragrant. We have no idea why, it just seems to be the patch of dirt. Our white fruit comes from Christa's property, which is the highest vineyard in Eden Valley."

Visiting Rolf Binder

"In our cellar door our aim is to present interesting wines and not mainstream wines to the public. At busy times of the year we'll open interesting wines like the Heysen or something from our Magpie Estate range. The Hanisch is our premium release, our only single vineyard wine, and we always have it on tasting in cellar door for the month of October, when we release it. There's no tasting charge, because I get to take the bottle home at the end of the day!

"We're a relaxed and

Corner Seppeltsfield & Stelzer Roads Dorrien

Map E11 Winery 52

Ph (08) 8562 3300

www.rolfbinder.com

cellar@rolfbinder.com

Est 1955

Cellar door tastings open Mon-Sat 10-4:30

Tutored tastings, crafts, local produce, concerts, festivals, gallery, picnic facilities, tours

Price range $15-$150

Key Wines: Rolf Binder Heinrich Shiraz Mataro Grenache, Veritas Winery Binder's Bull's Blood Shiraz Mataro Pressings, Rolf Binder Heysen Shiraz, Rolf Binder Hanisch Barossa Valley Shiraz, Magpie Estate The Fakir Grenache

unpretentious place to come and taste wines. Our cellar door is about education, to teach people about wine and make them feel confident. It's not about selling. You'll see me doing cellar door once a month on a Saturday, because I like to keep in touch with the public. The good thing is that

Left Christa, Rolf and Oma
Below Rolf Binder Veritas Winery and vineyard

Moorooroo vineyard
Dragan Radocaj Photography

a lot of people don't know who I am, so I'm able to hear so much from the public. They tell me what they want and what their tastes are like, which has allowed us to respond and tweak a few cellar door styles."

You wouldn't read about it

"The great surviving story of our winery was my Dad, Rolf Heinrich. He just had an unbelievably infectious laugh. People had such a great time in the old winery that they'd get there at three o'clock and leave at seven o'clock with a car full of wine and not remember anything! He always had a great saying that three bottles of our Bull's Blood Shiraz Mataro would produce a son. One guy looked up at my Dad once and said, 'Three bottles will produce a bloody miracle!' And as a joke one day, somebody came into the winery with a baby and put it into Dad's hands and said, 'Well, here's your three bottles of Bull's Blood!'

"My mother had her own style in the cellar door, very European and very direct. She would tell people what they would and wouldn't taste! Somebody once told me, 'Only the wind gets past your mother!'"

Local knowledge

"Christa has a B&B on her vineyard, named Naimanya cottage. It's the most sensational place! We love to sit and watch sunsets. It's cool and clear at night and you can sit there sipping a few drinks. It's got two rooms and caters for four. It's a beautiful spot and the Kaiser Stuhl National Park is nearby, so you can go for a lovely walk and step on snakes and so on!

"I had a group of Americans who I took in there and they were desperate – they'd never seen kangaroos. We walked around a couple of trees and there were about fifty kangaroos just lying there. They were sensational! A week later I took four Japanese people up there. We walked for an hour and a half and only saw one kangaroo in the distance!"

rosenvale wines

Old Rosenvale cane cart

The Rosenzweig family settled in the Barossa in 1850 but it was not until 1999 that it produced its first wines, when James Rosenzweig make the jump from grape grower to wine producer. Rosenvale Wines now utilises a diverse range of vineyards to craft its small portfolio of wines.

My Place

"My place is still a work in progress despite the fact that my family has been here for over 150 years," James says. "It is the perseverance and hard work of the generations who have gone before us that have given us both outstanding sites and old vines, crucial components for any brand aspiring to make great wine."

Local knowledge

"Take a short trek out to Greenock and try some of the great beers brewed by Daryl Trinne at The Barossa Brewing Company."

Lot 385 Railway Terrace Nuriootpa

Ph 0407 390 788

www.rosenvale.com.au

info@rosenvale.com.au

Est 1999

Tastings by appointment

Price range $20-$40

Key Wines: Estate Semillon, Reserve Cabernet Sauvignon

Wining kids

"Kids are welcome here. If our kids are around they love to share their playground and kick the footy around the yard."

ross estate wines

Former engineer Darius Ross fell in love with the Barossa and bought 100 acres of vines in Lyndoch in 1993. After renovating the vineyards he established Ross Estate in 1999.

My Place

Darius describes himself as "an engineer by trade but a wine lover at heart. We aim to cater to both classic and modern tastes and I like to think that we make creative and thoughtful wines."

Local knowledge

"Sunset, Champagne and Mengler's Hill Lookout are a great combination!"

Food matches

"A thick beef fillet with brandy cream sauce, field mushrooms and caramelised onions is great with our Ross Estate Reserve Shiraz."

Barossa Valley Way Lyndoch

Map H8 Winery 53

Ph (08) 8524 4033

www.rossestate.com.au

rossestate@rossestate.com.au

Est 1999

Cellar door tastings open 10-4

Tours, tutored tastings

Price range $15-$50

Key Wines: Lynedoch Cabernet Sauvignon Cabernet Franc Merlot, Reserve Shiraz

Ross Estate cellar door

We were doing a big tasting in Hampshire in the UK with a group of Barossa winemakers a few years ago when a guy approached me and asked, 'Are you all from the Barossa?' I said, 'Yes,' and he replied, 'But aren't you in competition with each other?' I explained that that's never seemed to matter in the Barossa because it's a place where everyone helps each other. He said, 'Wow, you'd never find Bordeaux doing that!' It made me proud to be a Barossan.

Dennis Canute, Rusden Wines

Rowland Flat vineyard
Dragan Radocaj Photography

rusden wines

RUSDEN
BAROSSA VALLEY
Single Vineyard Wines

"We need to put the Barossa back on the world stage, to reinvent its identity and to change how this region is perceived globally," suggests Rusden owner Dennis Canute. "Rusden is our vehicle to go about doing that." This family-run business prides itself on individuality and strong family involvement. Son Christian is the winemaker and wife and mother Chris has been the hands-on vineyard manager for more than thirty years.

My Place

"We want people to have a bloody good time when they are drinking Rusden!" says Dennis. "Our little corner of the Barossa isn't the most fashionable, but we feel that the wines from Vine Vale have their own distinct character, and this is something to be celebrated."

You wouldn't read about it

"My wife Chris has pruned all of our vineyards herself for more than thirty years. When the kids were young she would just take them out with her into the vineyard. One day our four-year-old son Christian disappeared. She looked everywhere for him, but he was nowhere to be found. She was about to jump in the car when she saw a blanket on the roof and there he was, wrapped up, sound asleep and dead to the world on top of the car!"

Local knowledge

"Get your weekend started with a bacon and egg roll at the Barossa Farmers Markets on Saturday. Arrive early, though, because they've become an institution and the line starts at 7:30am and gets longer by the hour!"

155

russell wines

Classical musician John Russell came to the Barossa in 1990 to establish the Barossa Music

Russell vineyard, Greenock

Festival. Three years later he returned to build a house but instead planted vines. With his wife Rosalind, he now holds a substantial and varied cross-section of premium Barossa vineyards.

My Place

"I wasn't deeply into wine when I first came to the Barossa," John recalls. "That soon changed when I got to know the place and its unique personalities. I met people who helped me to understand the vinous treasures that can be unearthed here by those who are passionate about the process of making great wine. From then on I was hooked."

St Vincent House, 45 Murray Street Angaston

Ph (08) 8564 2511

www.russellwines.com.au

wine@russellwines.com.au

Est 2001

Tastings by appointment

Concerts, festivals, tutored tastings

Price range $15-$85

Key Wines: Greenock Farm The Fenceline, St Vincent Shiraz, Augusta Shiraz

saltram wine estate

With more than 150 years of heritage, Saltram ranks among the oldest wineries in the Barossa. It balances a focus on its traditional wine styles with the addition of newly emerging varieties like Tempranillo and Sangiovese. While its 150 years of winemaking tradition has been largely under the Salter and Dolan families, it is now in the hands of two young winemakers who "want to keep the heritage but at the same time establish the new and emerging in order to keep in front of the times."

My place

To Saltram Winemaker Shavaughn Wells, "the Barossa is about great food and wine flavours, and people with lots of character as well."

Richard Mattner oversees Saltram's second label, Pepperjack. "I was born and bred just down the road here, at Light Pass. I haven't moved, haven't shifted and haven't seen the need to. You can get everything here, and I just love it. Fourth or fifth generation – I can't even remember what I am now! But I can't think of anywhere that I'd rather move

Nuriootpa Road Angaston

Map E13 Winery 54

Ph (08) 8561 0200

www.saltramwines.com.au

cellardoor@saltramestate.com.au

Est 1859

Cellar door tastings open 10-5 daily

Restaurant

Price range $18-$75

Key Wines: No 1 Shiraz, Mamre Brook Cabernet Sauvignon, Mamre Brook Shiraz, Pepperjack Stylus

Left Salters Restaurant
Right Saltram Mamre Brook House

to. I have opportunity to work with any variety that I would ever want to, and I just love it!"

Food matches

"We've got a great restaurant," says Richard. "Salters uses as much Barossa produce as it can. I love the wood oven pizzas — they're just fantastic. When it's a cold day outside, there's a real warmth seeing a guy standing in front of a wood oven, making it for you. I like having a crisp Semillon with pizza. The mix of flavours is something quite refreshing. The kangaroo dish is really nice but I'm fairly traditional and I love my steaks! I love coming in here and having a rib eye, with a glass of No 1 Shiraz. But we cover virtually every wine style here, and people can try different things over a meal rather than simply having a big Shiraz."

You wouldn't read about it

"We make a beer here, Pepperjack Ale, with Shiraz from Eden Valley!" Richard exclaims.

"I don't think that's done anywhere else in the world. It's a bit quirky having Shiraz in a beer, but it's no different to having a lemon infusion or anything else that's being done these days. We concentrate the Shiraz and use it as part of the sugar source at the beginning of ferment. It's only a really small percentage, but it gives the beer a red tint and it looks fantastic! You can see some of the aromatics that come out of the grapes, rather than just tasting beer and hops. I'm a big beer drinker and it's one of those beers that I can sit down and drink with a meal and really enjoy. You can buy it at cellar door and at restaurants."

Local knowledge

"The Barossa Farmers Market in Angaston is my favourite place," says Shavaughn. "I find it hard not to walk out with a 'pain au chocolat' — that's my standard Saturday morning breakfast! It's packed every Saturday morning. I find it hard to keep up with everyone during vintage,

Saltram vineyard

so I enjoy going there to bump into everybody throughout the morning. A lot of locals volunteer time to cook bacon and egg sangers for breakfast."

"It's fantastic the way that the whole of the Barossa promotes Barossa food and wine, and all of the butchers and bakers have their own specialties," adds Richard. "I go to Schulz's up in Angaston for my Bung Fritz, Linke's for their mettwurst and Jaegerbraten and Apex bakery for pasties. The quality is just fantastic!"

Wining kids

Both bringing up kids in the Barossa, Shavaughn and Richard are well familiar with the best haunts for entertaining littlies.

"There are toys in the restaurant at Salters and kids are welcome to play out in the gardens," suggests Shavaughn.

"There are mountains of things to do for kids in the Barossa. At the libraries in Nuri on Monday and Tanunda on Friday they have a free

reading session at 11am. And I've taken Tom to that since he was three or four months old, and he claps his hands and gets all excited!"

"There are great parks in the Barossa," adds Richard. "Centennial Park in Angaston has been redone, and the oval in Nuri is great. The train park has swing sets and all. If you venture out to Kapunda, there's another train park with the old-style steamers up on rails."

schild estate wines

Mick Schild left school at fifteen to immerse himself in the family grape growing business, and to get 'his education on the land' in the same way his father did before him. Not yet forty years of age, he now controls over 400 acres of vineyard and is one of the Barossa's largest landowners.

My Place

"We are a family of grape growers who evolved into winegrowers when we decided to start putting our name onto a label," explains Mick. "Right from the beginning our philosophy has been about crafting distinctive Barossa wines from the wonderful vineyard resources at our disposal. It is a rewarding business and the pride that we feel when we see someone drinking and enjoying our wine never goes away."

Local knowledge

"The Tanunda Club is one of the great institutions of the Barossa. It has a wonderful atmosphere and it's a place where everyone in the Valley meets to exchanges tales and advice.

Corner Barossa Valley Highway & Lyndoch Valley Road Lyndoch

Map H8 Winery 55

Ph (08) 8524 5560

www.schildestate.com.au

purebarossa@schildestate.com.au

Est 1998

Cellar door tastings open 10-5 daily

Coffee and light meals

Price range $15-$85

Key Wines: Moorooroo Shiraz, Barossa Riesling, Ben Schild Shiraz

"There's a bike track all the way from Tanunda to Nuriootpa. It's flat and you can just cruise along at your own pace and enjoy the view."

MOOROOROO VINEYARD

Kids are part of the Barossa. Everywhere you go, no one will ever turn up their nose if you rock up with your 'attachments.'

— Shavaughn Wells, Saltram

Yalumba gardens
Dragan Radocaj
Photography

Wining kids

"There's a secure courtyard at our cellar door with a shaded area for kids. We have to make kids welcome as I've got three of my own under three!"

Food matches

"I'm almost neurotic about fresh Riesling. I love the zesty drive of it and as soon as the new vintage of our Barossa Riesling is released I am finished with the previous one! I love it with fresh whiting, seasoned with cumin, pan fried and served with a green salad."

Schild Estate bush vine grenache vineyard

schutz barossa

Young businesswoman Tammy Schutz hit the ground running when she established Red Nectar Vineyards (now Schutz Barossa) in 1997. Taking advantage of premium vineyard sites in the Stonewell and Ebenezer districts and the considerable talents of cousin Troy Kalleske as winemaker, she has established a comfortable niche at the boutique end of the market.

My Place

"My husband Stuart and I are fifth and sixth generation vignerons," says Tammy. "It's a great legacy, and we have been fortunate that the traditions and skills of those who have come before us have been passed down over time.

Through experience we've built the belief that the best wines are created in the vineyard, and we grow our grapes to reflect the classic richness of the western Barossa."

Infamous growers

"My husband Stuart remembers his grandfather telling stories about his time as a foreman at a Barossa winery. In the time of horses and carts an 'innovative' grower added a few solid logs to the underside of the wagon on the way in to the weighbridge. A short detour after unloading ensured that the wagon was significantly lighter when it weighed off. The old timers weren't always so squeaky clean after all!"

Stonewell Road Tanunda

Ph 0409 547 478

www.schutzbarossa.com

wine@schutzbarossa.com

Est 1997

Tastings by appointment

Accommodation

Price range 25

Key Wines: Red Nectar Shiraz, Red Nectar Cabernet Sauvignon

SCHUTZ
BAROSSA

Local knowledge

"If you're looking for a quick snack, the Tanunda Bakery has beautiful baked goods and great lemon gelato."

Wining kids

"A great thing to do with kids is to put together a picnic basket at the Barossa Farmers Market, put on your walking shoes and spend some time at Kaiser Stuhl National Park. It's a lovely opportunity to see kangaroos, birds and other wildlife in their natural habitat."

Food matches

"Spiced lamb shanks with couscous and pistachios are great with our Schutz Barossa Red Nectar Shiraz."

Tammy Schutz in her Shiraz vineyard

schwarz wine company

Biscay Road Bethany
Ph 0417 881 923
www.schwarzwineco.
com.au
jason@schwarzwineco.
com.au
Est 2001
Tastings by appointment
Price range $20-$32
*Key Wines: Nitschke
Block Shiraz, Thiele Rd
Grenache*

As the son and grandson of state pruning champions, Jason Schwarz has a lot to live up to. After experimenting with various vocations around the world he returned to the Barossa to start the Schwarz Wine Company in 2001. He draws on over 100 acres of family-owned vineyards in the Bethany subregion.

My Place

"The Schwarz Wine Company has always been about making wines that are accessible to everyday drinkers," Jason says. "They're about expressing the fruit flavour of the Bethany subregion, where my family has grown grapes for four generations."

You wouldn't read about it

"I once ended up with a winemaking job in South Africa. The only problem was that I wasn't a winemaker at the time! It's just as well I'm a quick learner!"

Local knowledge

"One of the great places for a sunset drink is Presser Road, at the end of Schwarz Road on the other side of Tanunda. Everyone tends to head up to the Eden Valley side, but this gives a whole new perspective."

Food matches

"The Greenock Creek Tavern makes an awesome rabbit stew that's ideal with the spiciness of my Thiele Road Grenache."

Jason Schwarz

seabrook wines

Lot 350 Light Pass Road Tanunda
Ph 0427 224 353
www.seabrookwines.
com.au
hjseabrook@bigpond.
com
Est 2005
Tastings by appointment
Price range $20-$38
Key Wine: Barossa Shiraz

Descended from a renowned wine merchant family, Hamish Seabrook carries a famous Australian wine industry surname. After gaining winemaking experience under legendary winemaker Viv Thomson at Best's Great Western winery and as senior winemaker at Brown Brothers in Victoria, he established his own brand in the Barossa. From one of the smallest working wineries in the region, Seabrook Wines specialises in Shiraz, with a focus on structure and ageability.

My Place

"My family's been in the wine game for over a century, and the Seabrook philosophy has always been to source the best grapes wherever they're grown," explains Hamish. "We've continued this practice and we love what the Barossa gives us to work with. We produce Shirazes from three regions – the best of each world made in the best part of the world!"

You wouldn't read about it

"I'm the fifth successive generation of my family to judge at the Royal Melbourne Wine Show."

Local knowledge

"Jo and I love visiting some of the Barossa's smaller wineries like Gibson and Whistler. We relax with the people there and enjoy good food, wine and company."

seppeltsfield wines

Seppeltsfield is much more than just a historic cellar door and winery. It is a fully self-contained, heritage listed wine village with a tremendous history that dates back to 1851. This history remains alive because sealed in its vaults are some 24 000 barrels containing more than seven million litres of fortified wines dating from 1878. These stocks represent some of the most extensive in Australia and perhaps in the world. Fortified winemaker James Godfrey describes them as "a living museum of the fortified industry." Visitors have the privilege of not only visiting this remarkable and unique collection but also of tasting and even purchasing these historic treasures.

Barossa Characters

James Godfrey has completed every vintage at Seppeltsfield since 1978 and says he can't think of anywhere else he'd rather be working. "These old fortifieds are irreplaceable," he says. "Many are older than me!"

Seppeltsfield Director Nathan Waks describes himself as a "Cellist turned wine man." A musical director and composer, he says his office is the stage of the Concert Hall of the Sydney Opera House, where until recently he was the Principal Cellist with the Sydney Symphony Orchestra.

Seppeltsfield Road Seppeltsfield

Map D9 Winery 56

Ph (08) 8568 6217

www.seppeltsfield.com.au

cellarsales@seppeltsfield.com.au

Est 1851

Cellar door tastings open 10:30am-5pm daily

Benno's Kiosk in the picnic grounds open Sept-Apr Sat, Sun and Public Holidays 11am-4:30pm.

Tours, tutored tastings, café, concerts, festivals, historical buildings, picnic facilities

Price range $15-$975

Key Barossa Wines: Show Vintage Touriga, Paramount XO Tawny, Para 100 Year Old Vintage Tawny

Seppeltsfield fortified barrels containing every vintage since 1878
Dragan Radocaj Photography

Seppeltsfield panorama
Dragan Radocaj Photography

My place

"Visitors can come to Seppeltsfield and experience one of the most complete collections of historic buildings in their original form in the Barossa," says Nathan. "If you are to see anything in the Barossa that will give you a snapshot of its history, Seppeltsfield is a good place to start.

"And our heritage is contained not only in our buildings, but in the oldest continuous collection of living wines in the world. Seppeltsfield is the history of Australian fortifieds. This country has developed its own unique way of making fortifieds and I don't think there's anywhere else that has a range as complete as Seppeltsfield, from our Barossa

sherries and ports through to Rutherglen muscats and tokays."

James reflects that "in all its former life, the site was huge. In the very early days they had everything happening here. It was the oldest working gravity feed winery in Australia. They even had a distillery, vinegar house, stables, chicken coops, they bred pigs and had smoke houses. But with the decline of fortifieds from the '40s through to the '60s many of these beautiful old buildings were mothballed. They have been sitting here for decades doing very little. But Nathan and his team have a strategy to use them again."

Nathan explains that "the village has been around for 150 years and we are trying to make

STACK 2

163

it more and more alive by reviving each part of it to provide more things to do and see. We now have a picnic area where people can bring their own food and buy wine. We've named it Benno's and set it up with a kiosk with snacks and simple things to eat.

"We've also pouring the only German-style beers made in the Barossa, a 'Barossa Blonde' Pilsner style and full-strength 'Barossa Bock'. Our director of operations was a brewer, although not brewing when I first came here. I mentioned in passing that I wanted to make a beer and he said, very politely, 'Well, that's what I used to do.' So I said, 'Right, Mike, you've got another job!'"

You wouldn't read about it

Seppeltsfield 100 Year Old Para Vintage Tawny was first made in 1878 and is released exactly 100 years after vintage. It represents the only unbroken collection of wines spanning more than 130 vintages in the world, and is the only wine in the world to be released at 100 years of age.

"We start with more than 1000L in several barrels each year," explains Nathan. "As it ages it slowly evaporates and concentrates so we progressively transfer it into one barrel. After a century it ends up as just 200-250L. We still have every vintage so if someone comes in and asks for a vintage between 1878 and 1909 we can usually bottle that for them out of barrel.

"The 1878 is now all in glass as we only have 12L left, and when it's finished, that's in a sense the end of the dream. How can you keep the dream alive?"

James tells the story behind a new wine called Paramount XO Tawny. "For the past thirty years I've been quietly sneaking away something very special. When the 100 Year Old Para is finally released and the level in the barrel diminishes such that we need to transfer it into a smaller barrel, there are about thirty-five litres of solid lees in the bottom. I mix it up with twenty-year-old tawny and some Para and collect the stuff. We now have a reasonable supply across 30 vintages — a large base of great old wine! So we've put a blend together of those bases. The wine inherently contains something from every vintage from 1878 through to 1908. And every year we take a small portion of the new 100 Year Old Para vintage and put that

into the blend to make sure that every vintage is represented. We have created a continuous solera which will always contain a little of every vintage ever released of the 100 year old. It will become a sort of living history of 100 year old Para — a way of sustaining its memory forever."

Paramount XO Tawny has an average age of probably forty years, but it's remarkably fresh, balanced and drinkable. By comparison, the hundred year old is more of an essence of wine; a curio; an amazing thing to look at and understand and examine."

Paramount XO Tawny is the flagship of a range of Paramount fortifieds that James describes as "the very best of what we do across the range."

Seppeltsfield spirit

"When we bought Seppeltsfield we knew that there was a shed holding the old fortified spirit," explains Nathan. "It turns out that it also holds another Seppeltsfield treasure, which is extremely old Seppeltsfield brandy, going right back to 1935. We're going to release the 1935 as a single vintage brandy in 2010 with 75 years of barrel age. It's truly unique in the world of spirits."

SEPPELTSFIELD
~ EST 1851 ~

Barrels of entertainment

"We've reinstated a cooperage in the old Seppeltsfield stables, where we're making small barrels out of old fortified barrels, so they're properly seasoned already," Nathan says. "We bring tourists here as part of our tours to see the cooperage in action. They can see the firing of the barrels, which is particularly spectacular!

"The idea of the cooperage is that you can take home not just a souvenir but a barrel that you can fill. They're not decorative, these are working barrels. If you like good fortified wine and you like to have it in barrel because you know that it continues to age, you can buy a 10L, 20L, 40L or whatever barrel and have it filled with any quality — we have absolutely every level here. It's not just going to be for those who want cheap sherry or port — we've certainly got that — but we also offer Rare Muscat or a Rare Tokay. And why wouldn't you have a Rare or Grand wine in there?!"

1850s Seppeltsfield buildings
Dragan Radocaj Photography

Tour Down Under 2009 passes Seppeltsfield

PARA TAWNY

Nathan Waks with his wife, Candice Williams

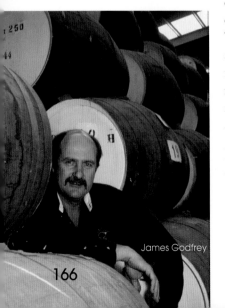
James Godfrey

Drinking fortified wines

Fortified wines may be out of vogue these days, but Seppeltsfield has some clever ways to make them more versatile. "Our new Ruby Lightly Fortified Grenache Rosé is lower in alcohol than our other fortifieds," James points out. "It's fresh and vibrant and the spirit integrates beautifully, so it's great to drink on ice. We encourage people to drink all of our fortifieds really chilled. This knocks the alcohol down a bit without suppressing the fruit or the complexity too much. They take on a whole new complexion this way."

Wining kids

It's not all about wine at Seppeltsfield. Seppeltsfield's famous Raspberry Cordial is made according to the old recipe by the Seppeltsfield team. It can be found at the cellar door.

Visiting Seppeltsfield

"We have various tours at different times of the day, mixing heritage, history and wine samples together," Nathan explains. "We offer a Private Tasting ($8), a Cooperage Tour ($15), a simple Heritage Tour ($15), a Grand Insight Tour and Tasting ($18), a Journey into Fortifieds ($29) and a Legend of Seppeltsfield Tour including a taste of 100 Year Old Para Vintage Tawny ($79)."

Tours range in duration from thirty minutes to two hours. Enquire at Cellar Door or see www.seppeltsfield.com.au for times and details. Bookings are necessary for some tours.

The full range is available for tasting at cellar door, and a refundable tasting fee applies.

sieber wines

The Barossa has always had a strong sense of family heritage, but few wine producers can boast the level of family commitment of Sieber Wines. With both parents and three sons actively involved in the estate, the Siebers are deeply invested in the future of their business. A new winery is set to be completed in 2010, and with experienced viticulturist Ben Sieber back on board, Sieber Wines are set to make big strides in the years ahead.

"The Barossa can't be beaten," says Ben. "In terms of the lifestyle and community spirit, this place is second to none."

My Place

"Our place is about a family-orientated, broad acre farming business that turned to viticulture in 1998," explains Ben. "We're third-generation Barossans with a goal to make wines that are true to style, authentic representations of the Barossa, the best place in the world to make wine!"

Sieber Wines cellar door

You wouldn't read about it

"My grandad bought this farm in the 1930s and decided to pull out all the vines on the property - he had no time for vineyards at all. And no, we don't like to talk about what we could do with them now!"

Sieber Road via Seppeltsfield

Map E8 Winery 57

Ph (08) 8562 8038

www.sieberwines.com

sieberwines@bigpond.com

Est 1998

Cellar door tastings open 11-4 daily

Price range $18-$28

Key Wines: Special Release Shiraz, Ernest Shiraz, GSM, Shiraz Viognier, Viognier

SIEBER RD

Clockwise from top Tom, Jarrod, Ben and Daniel Sieber enjoying a beer on the harvester

small fry wines

Wayne Ahrens bought his first vineyard when he was just seventeen years old. With a family grape growing tradition of five generations behind him, perhaps that's not such a surprise. In 2005 he took up winemaking and established Small Fry. Based in Angaston, he specialises in hand-crafted, food-friendly wines and personal service.

My Place

"My place is all about making people feel at home," Wayne says. "That's a good thing as our home is also our cellar door in the main street of Angaston. Either myself or my partner Suzi pours the wine, and there's a good chance the cat, the dog and the kids will also lend a hand from time to time. We're small, so we open when we can or when we know someone is coming. We love meeting new people, so just give us a call."

Vineyards of significance

"We were lucky enough to purchase one of the few remaining vineyards that had the character of the place where I grew up. It has lovely old bush vines interspersed with citrus trees."

Wining kids

"Kids are no problem at our place. Our back yard is always available to any kids who want somewhere to run, and our children always want to take them out to see the peacock. Most of the time they don't want to leave!"

13 Murray Street Angaston

Map E14 Winery 58

Ph (08) 8564 2182

www.smallfrywines.com.au

wayneandsuzi@smartchat.net.au

Est 2005

Cellar door tastings most weekends and by appointment. Phone ahead to confirm.

Historical buildings

Price range $15-$28

Key Wines: Eden Valley Riesling, Eden Valley Cabernet Sauvignon, Eden Valley Shiraz

Food matches

"We never miss a week at the Barossa Farmers Market in Angaston! And you can't beat Linke's Bakery in Nuriootpa for the best bread and pastry."

Wayne Ahrens, Henry and the 2008 reds outside the Small Fry Wines cellar door

smallfry

small gully wines

"I was good at Maths, Chemistry and Physics at school and I grew up in a family that drank beer and expected me to study Geology. Somehow, I ended up in wine!" says Stephen Black, who left a successful career in the pharmaceutical industry to pursue winemaking. In 2000 he formed Small Gully Wines with business partners Robert Bader and Darren Zimmermann. Their distinctive and creative labels commemorate Black's links to his former vocation.

My Place

"We've always been quite hard to find, so we would give long-winded directions that ended, 'you'll find us on the right as you come into a small gully,' says Stephen. "We said it so many times that 'Small Gully' stuck. From the start the wines have always been our priority. We are fortunate to have superb vineyards and we are particularly meticulous with fruit selection and attention to detail in the winery."

You wouldn't read about it

"We had no mains power or water at Small Gully until 2008. For the first six years we operated using a generator and collected rainwater for all of our winery operations!"

Roennfeldt Road Marananga

Ph 0411 690 047

www.smallgullywines.com.au

smallgully@ozemail.com.au

Est 2000

Tastings by appointment

Price range $15-$80

Key Wines: The Formula Robert Shiraz, Mr Blacks Concoction Shiraz Viognier, Small Gully Marananga Shiraz

Local knowledge

"For a fantastic meal, stay at Jacob's Creek Retreat. The proprietors are both chefs and they turn out some of the best food in the Barossa."

smythe road vintners

"I love the mystique of wine," says Grahame Tonkin. "The intriguing thing is that no one knows everything about it and everyone who drinks wine has the right to decide what they like." Having spent a long career in wine distribution, Grahame understands the nature of consumer preference. After being encouraged by friend and winemaker Jim Irvine to plant Shiraz on his Stonewell property, he released his first wine under the Smythe Road label in 2003.

My Place

"The legendary Peter Lehmann once said, 'The Barossa is the real Garden of Eden,' and I can't agree with him more," says Grahame. "A unique heritage, proud history and unsurpassed food and wine culture make this a very special place to live and make wine. In its wines, the Barossa gives intensity of flavour and elegance of structure at the same time. We like to call these qualities 'pure Barossa' and we strive for them in our wines at Smythe Road."

Lot 9 Smyth Road Tanunda

Ph 0417 303 965

info@smytheroad.com

www.smytheroad.com

Tastings by appointment (email or phone)

Price range $19.50-$27.50

Key Wines: Pure Barossa Shiraz, Eden Valley Pinot Gris

Local knowledge

"Get out and see three or four smaller Barossa wineries. The personal attention and traditional, warm Barossa welcome is good for the soul!"

sons of eden

Simon Cowham created Sons of Eden with friend and winemaker Corey Ryan to "make the best wine we can from unique sites." The versatile pair came to Sons of Eden after variously trying viticulture, microbiology, aeronautics and sales before finding the inspiration for their brand in the cool climes of the Eden Valley.

Simon Cowham

My Place

"Both Corey and I are passionate about wine and about finding ways to maximise both creativity and quality," says Simon. "We look for small parcels of fruit with a difference and we take full control of the process from vineyard to bottle, which allows us to refine the personality of our wines. As a result, they have a sense of individuality."

Barossa dirt

"I think the best thing about the Barossa is the sense of pride that people have about living here. There is a real identification with community and when you combine this with the great wines and the flow of people through the place it just makes for a great place to live."

Local knowledge

"I'm an ex-captain of the Tanunda Football Club, and still a passionate supporter.

Penrice Road Angaston

Ph (08) 8564 2363

www.sonsofeden.com

info@sonsofeden.com

Est 2000

Tastings by appointment

Price range $22-$52

Key Wines: Romulus Barossa Shiraz, Remus Eden Valley Shiraz

Unfortunately we never won the flag while I was playing. Perhaps that's the reason that I'm still hanging around! If you're here in winter, head to the local footy ground on the weekend and have a friendly yell at the ref with the rest of us! Then join us all afterwards for a beer at the Tanunda Club."

Food matches

"Osso Bucco with sweet potato mash and some crusty Apex bakery bread to mop up the gravy is ideal served with a glass of our Remus Shiraz."

SONS OF EDEN

The view of Light Pass from Sons of Eden winery

sorby adams wines

"In the Barossa Valley the octane junkies call us the girls up on the hill because we make lighter-bodied wines, but we're proud of that!" says Eden Valley winemaker Simon Adams. "We try to make wines with cooler climate aromatics rather than alcohol and oak, because this is what the Eden Valley does best." In keeping with his family name, his range of wines includes 'The Morticia' and 'The Thing.'

My place

"I'm passionate about this place," says Simon. "I live in the Barossa but I think of Eden Valley as my home. It's a prettier place up here and it's more interesting, with its hills, unique rocky outcrops, massive gum trees and small pockets of Riesling and old vine Shiraz. There are surprises around every corner. We tell people just to pick a road in the northern Eden Valley and explore and they'll find great old vineyards and historic churches. We've had people come back three hours later and say, 'We didn't know where we were but it was just sensational and we loved it!'"

Barossa Character

"When I finished school in Adelaide in 1979 I got out the yellow pages and wrote to ten wineries. The first to reply was Yalumba so I worked for them and they offered to pay my way through uni. I left Yalumba twenty years later, having worked there during the years that 'Octavius' and 'The Menzies' were developed and 'The Signature' was established as a benchmark style."

Tasting Sorby Adams Wines

"Visitors can make an appointment for a tasting by calling my mobile or they can go to Taste Eden Valley, our communal cellar door in Angaston. That's a great place to taste eight small Eden Valley growers. I'm happy to go down there to meet people and talk them through the wines. Or if they're staying at our B&B I can take them through a tasting there."

Local knowledge

"My favourite place to eat is at Murdock. They run a full tapas menu and it's a great place to kick back on Sunday afternoon with a glass of wine. Blond coffee shop in Angaston also has great food.

"My wife Helen and I run a B&B accommodation named 'Jellicoe House' in the middle of a vineyard. We bought the vineyard and fully renovated the historic bluestone homestead in 2007. It has self-contained accommodation for up to eight guests, a full cook's kitchen and seasonally laden fruit trees. Helen runs

Angaston Appetisers and offers meals and local produce to our guests, including provisions for a full cooked breakfast."

Wining kids

"I have three kids between ten and seventeen and I can recommend the skate parks in Nuriootpa and Angaston. There are bike tracks that link Tanunda and Nuriootpa and there are bikes available for hire from the Tourist Information Centre in Tanunda. There are also public tennis courts at the Angas Recreation Park, Moculta Park and Tanunda Recreation Park. "

Simon Adams

soul growers

"Soul Growers is a coming together of four mates who share their passion and philosophies from many years in the wine industry," says Managing Director and Winemaker, Paul Heinicke. "Soul Growers is about the simple things that are good for the soul – wine, food, family, music, mates and fun." The company makes four wines, Shiraz, Cabernet, Shiraz Cabernet and Shiraz Grenache Mourvèdre.

My place

"The Soul Growers vineyard at Seppeltsfield was hand planted by our families and like-minded mates," explains

SOUL GROWERS
It's a quality of life

BAROSSA VALLEY

Paul, "many of whom required a little enticement at the end of each row. I guess that's why some of the rows are not exactly the straightest!"

Tasting Soul Growers

"We are happy to conduct private tastings and/or a vineyard tour. Give me a call or send me an email at least a day before your visit."

**5 Second Avenue
Tanunda**

Ph 0439 026 727

www.soulgrowers.com

paulh@soulgrowers.com

Tastings by appointment

Price range $25-$50

Key Wines: Shiraz, Cabernet, Shiraz Cabernet, Shiraz Grenache Mourvèdre

Local knowledge

"Apart from a bite to eat and a couple of drinks at our implement shed overlooking the Valley, you're most likely to catch us having a beer or dinner at the Greenock Creek Hotel or the Tanunda Club."

Sunset over Seppeltsfield
Dragan Radocaj Photography

Sunrise over Barossa Valley Way
Dragan Radocaj Photography

spinifex wines

"Great terroir is inimitable," says Peter Schell. "Our job is simply not to get in its way." It's a philosophy that Peter and his wife Magali Gely explored while making wines in the Languedoc in southern France before establishing Spinifex Wines in 2001. It's no coincidence that the Spinifex style shows a strong leaning toward the red blends of southern France, with Shiraz Viognier, Grenache and Mataro a particular focus. Spinifex has quickly etched its name on the list of the Barossa's most impressive wine names.

My Place

"In an abstract way, our place is about self indulgence," says Peter. "We started Spinifex to do what we wanted to do, which was to make wines that we like to drink. This means wines of character that express the uniqueness of the place where they are grown."

Barossa Character

"The Barossa is so different to anywhere else I've ever lived in that its mindset, tradition and social culture are still very much shaped by its historical roots. I still get a kick out of dealing with the Barossan culture on a day-to-day basis, however unusual and challenging it may be!"

You wouldn't read about it

"I grew up in New Zealand and only discovered a few years after moving to the Barossa that my great, great, great grandfather actually lived in Langmeil near Tanunda in the mid-1800s. We thought that was an amazing coincidence until we also discovered that one of the first winemakers at Chateau Tanunda was a Frenchman named Gely, and related to my wife! I guess we were destined to end up here."

Food matches

"Lachsschinken (cold smoked pork fillet) is something of a Barossa speciality and a great match for the savoury lightness of Spinifex Rosé."

Biscay Road Bethany

Ph (08) 8564 2059

www.spinifexwines.com.au

info@spinifexwines.com.au

Est 2001

Tastings by appointment

Price range $20-$60

Key Wines: Shiraz Viognier, Indigene Shiraz Mataro, Esprit Grenache Mataro Carignan Cinsault, Rosé, Lola white blend

st hallett wines

When you walk into the cellar door at St Hallett and say hello to Stewy, the Eclectus Parrot, you will immediately feel that this is an easy-going, friendly place to visit, completely devoid of pretence. The focus here is on Barossa wines across a spectrum of styles and price points. St Hallett produces some of the Barossa's best budget wines as well as one of its most outstanding icons, Old Block Shiraz.

Barossa Character

This down-to-earth approach comes right from the top. Senior Winemaker for more than thirty-five years, Stuart Blackwell brings his love of wine, love of food, love of people and sense of humour to all that he does. These days Toby Barlow has taken over the reins as winemaker and brings a contagious energy into the winery. Stuart describes him as 'the hip-hop man' and himself as fast looking at being 'the hip-replacement guy'!

"What I like about this place is the tenure of the people that are here," says Stuart. "Meredith Goers has been in cellar door every weekend for twenty-nine years now because she loves it! Everybody knows her as 'Merry'. We even produced a wine for her, because she demanded she have something sweet in cellar door. We made a sweet Spätlese Fronti and called it 'Sweet Meredith'. That really annoyed her! But, at the end of the day I think she loves it. And now we've made her a Moscato. That's all her doing."

St Hallett Road Tanunda

Map G10 Winery 59

Ph (08) 8563 7000

www.sthallett.com.au

sthallett@sthallett.com.au

Est 1944

Cellar door tastings open 10-5 daily

Picnic facilities, tours, tutored tastings, concerts, festivals

Price range $15-$80

Key Wines: Old Block Shiraz, Blackwell Shiraz, Faith Shiraz, Eden Valley Riesling, Poacher's, Gamekeeper's Shiraz Cabernet

Toby Barlow and Stuart Blackwell

My place

"Cellar door is purposely not ritzy, it's not glass and polished stainless steel," explains Stuart Blackwell. "It's warm, it's folksy and it's comfortable, somewhere that people feel they can relax, where they can feel comfortable to ask the dumb questions that they may not have been able to ask in other places."

Wining kids

"We've got a great lawn and it's totally safe out there. It's a great place to kick a soccer ball or a football. And there is a chipping and putting area for any would-be golfers. People are very welcome to bring their picnics and put a cloth down on the lawn. We can supply some Pétanque and they can make a bit of an afternoon of it. We have all our functions on the lawn as well. We're here to share the Barossa.

"Kids can run around out on the lawn. We should give them hard hats during the magpie season, because we have a pair of magpies that nest here every year, and it's right at the time of our football grand final. Tanunda North is in it and we can't get rid of any magpies because our team colours are black and white! So we have to put up with it for about two-and-a-half weeks."

Visiting St Hallett

"The point of difference with St Hallett is that we keep every single block separate in the winery," explains Stuart. "And we keep the bottom, middle and top of each vineyard separate. So, we might have anything up to 200 different parcels of Shiraz kept separate in any vintage!

"For people with a real passion for wine, with an interest in the area or who are looking for more than just a quick taste, the opportunity is here for a tour through the winery and a barrel tasting. And for those who want to go further, we can do barrel samples and go to a vineyard and taste the different wines in their own vineyard. People are blown away when we take

Stewy, the Eclectus Parrot, greeting visitors at St Hallett

barrel samples out and show them the different tastes of different parts of a vineyard. To make an appointment for a tutored tasting, phone cellar door to set it up in advance."

You wouldn't read about it

"Our bird, Stewy the Eclectus parrot, is well known. I suspect he might be named after me, but he and I don't have the warmest relationship. Perhaps because I'm the first one to get here in the morning and I undo the alarm and wake him up? I think I've pissed him off over the years, so he really doesn't like me! But if you're a female visiting St Hallett and you've got a bit of time to talk to him in his cage, he will chat to you. And he does talk quite a lot. But if you're a male you tend to get ignored. He's quite entertaining — unless you put your finger inside his cage!

"I had an amusing moment when Miss Japan was visiting one day and leaning over and having a bit of a chat with him. And he got down and started humping his doll! Half way through she said, 'What's going on?' Then she looked at me and said, 'He needs a girlfriend, doesn't he?!' Miss Japan was right on the money!"

Local knowledge

"The Keg Factory across the road is a great place to visit for a barrel for fortifieds – it's quite a unique thing. And you can have it filled with bulk port at places like Lehmann's, Grant Burge and Yaldara.

"When I take friends for a tour, I always take them to Schulz's at Angaston to show them the smokehouse. If you're here on Mondays or Tuesdays the smokehouse is operating and if they're given a bit of warning and they're not crazy busy they're quite happy to open it up and show people. The smoking is an amazing thing to see. It's very traditional and similar to smokehouses that have been operating here for decades, using very high quality red gum chips."

Golf

"Tanunda Pines Golf Course is a favourite haunt of mine! There is a very unfair story going around that anyone who works here is chosen on their golf handicap. It's not true, but it does help! We like to have a strong golf team between our winery staff and some of our growers. It's something that's a real passion for a few of us here. If I've just got back from overseas and I arrive in time to get out there on Saturday morning I'll still be there on Saturday afternoon. It's always a great way to get over being cooped up in a plane!"

Food matches

"Food and wine in the Barossa is strong, and getting stronger," says Stuart. "People are taking a lot of interest in the great food that we've got in the district. And every winemaker thinks they're a cook, so there's a lot of fun sharing a table and hosting at home.

"We can get the freshest calamari. I've got a great little dish where I'll do salt and pepper calamari in semolina and cornflour with aioli and rocket. We'll do this as a kick-off with chopsticks and it always breaks the ice, and away you go! With the aioli, you can't beat Eden Valley Riesling. It's a killer wine pairing!"

st john's road wine co.

"We're just three guys who love the wine game," says St Johns Road Director, Alister Mibus. "From the time we could sniff, the three of us have dreamt of being wine men." The family-owned business produces an Eden Valley Riesling and a range of competitively-priced old vine and single vineyard reds from Greenock on the north-west slopes of the Barossa.

St Johns Road Greenock
Ph (08) 8432 0272
www.stjohnsroad.com
info@stjohnsroad.com
Est 2002
Price range $18-$22
Key Wines: Blood 'n' Courage Shiraz, Peace of Eden Riesling

Vineyard opposite Jacob's Creek.
Dragan Radocaj Photography

Standish 1855 cellar
Inset Dan Standish

standish wine company

"I am simply trying to convey what the vineyard has seen during the past year with a message in a bottle," says Dan Standish. After growing up in the Barossa, Dan left to earn a Chemical Engineering degree and then found his way back to his birthplace as a winemaker. He gained experience with leading Barossa producer Torbreck before establishing The Standish Wine Company in 1999. His focus is on producing small quantities of hand-crafted wines from single vineyard old vine Shiraz.

My Place

"I'm a sixth generation winegrower who started pruning with my grandpa at the age of six," Dan recalls. "That connection to the vineyards is maintained today in my philosophy of crafting wines to find the most innate expression of each site."

Barossa dirt

"Some of the Barossa's greatest vineyards are in the most obscure, far out places. I love the mystery and the sense of possibility that comes with this."

100 Barritt Road Lyndoch

Ph (08) 8564 3634

www.standishwineco.
com

info@standishwineco.
com

Est 1999

Tastings by appointment

Historic cellars built in 1855

All wines priced at $95

Key Wines: The Standish Shiraz, The Relic Shiraz Viognier, Andelmonde Shiraz, Borne Bollene Shiraz

The Standish Wine Company

stanley lambert wines

Veteran winemaker Lindsay Stanley and American business partner Jim Lambert are the names behind Stanley Lambert. Previously known as Stanley Brothers, this family-orientated business operates its cellar door off the main street in Tanunda seven days a week.

My Place

"Wine makes you silly!" exclaims Lindsay "It must, for no sane person would get into this industry for any other reason! We love wine, and the wine business. It's a family affair and everyone works in the old-fashioned, hands-on way. I've been making wine since my Kaiser Stuhl days in the Riverland in the '70s, and I'm still making wines the same way today. That's one of the reasons people keep coming back to us - they know what we stand for, and what they'll get."

Barossa dirt

"The Barossa has seen a lot of change but the memories of the old weighbridge days at Peter Lehmann are still fresh.

Everyone would tell jokes, have a laugh, munch on mettwurst and have a quiet glass of wine while waiting to unload. They were great, uncomplicated times."

You wouldn't read about it

"I've been fortunate enough to know most of the Barossa legends for some time and I've enjoyed Doug Lehmann's company on many occasions. I would say, however, that going duck hunting with him when he has a hangover and can't see properly is not particularly recommended!"

Local knowledge

"If you want to learn about the Barossa, head to the nearest pub and strike up a conversation with some of the square heads, the old German lads who still talk to each other in Barossa Deutsche. Some of them have been here for the best part of a century and half of them have never been to school. Buy them a boy's raspberry (port and lemonade) and just sit back and listen."

Barossa Valley Way Tanunda

Map E11 Winery 60
Ph (08) 8563 3375
www.stanleylambert.com.au
sales@stanleylambert.com.au
Est 1994
Cellar door tastings open 9-5 daily
Crafts and local produce
Price range $15-$65
Key Wines: Chardonnay Pristine, Three's Company GSM, The Thoroughbred Cabernet Sauvignon

Wining kids

"We have a play area for kids in the cellar door, and also serve soft drinks."

Below right Jim Lambert in the vineyard
Below left Raymond & Lindsay Stanley enjoying a beer in the crusher

178

steinborner family vineyards

91 Siegersdorf Road Tanunda

Ph 0414 474 708

www.sfvineyards.com.au

steinbornerwine@
optusnet.com.au

Est 2003

Tastings by appointment

Price range $15-$35

*Key Wines: Barossa
Deutsche Shiraz, Barossa
Ancestry Shiraz Viognier,
Caroliene Semillon*

The Steinborner family ancestry in the Barossa dates back to 1865. Today, winemaker David Reynolds and father-in-law Michael Steinborner produce a small amount of wine under the Steinborner Family Vineyards label from grapes grown on its old vine vineyards in the Vine Vale subregion.

My Place

"I'm fairly certain that I'm the only Liverpool (UK) born winemaker in the Southern Hemisphere," says David. "People hear my accent and ask me what I'm doing here. I'm tempted to say, 'hiding from the police!' In truth, what I'm doing is stepping into the heritage of a family-based business with more than a century of Barossa Deutsche tradition and wonderful old vine resources. From a winemaking point of view it's everything I could hope for."

tait wines

Yaldara Drive Lyndoch

Map H7 Winery 61

Ph (08) 8524 5000

www.taitwines.com.au

tait@taitwines.com.au

Est 1994

Tastings by appointment

Price range $18-$40

*Key Wines: Ball Buster
Shiraz Blend, Basket
Pressed Shiraz, Basket
Pressed Cabernet
Sauvignon*

Bruno Tait's distinctively named Ball Buster Shiraz encapsulates the Tait Wines philosophy of bold wines with a big personality made from old vine grapes. This value-for-money label has led the brand to develop a strong following in the United States and Canada.

My Place

"Tait Wines is simply about making wines that speak of the Barossa," explains Bruno. "They're made in the traditional, handcrafted way and are unapologetically ripe and full-flavoured. That's what the Barossa does best, and what Tait Wines is best known for."

Local knowledge

"People often overlook Bethany Reserve as a place to have a picnic, but the fact that it's lesser known just makes it a quieter and more relaxing spot."

Food matches

"A well hung T-bone cooked medium rare and served with the Tait Basket Pressed Shiraz is a great thing to share with friends."

Bruno Tait praying
for a good vintage

179

tearo estate wines

"It takes great characters to make great wines," suggests TeAro's Business Development Manager Todd Rowett. If you're in Williamstown at the right time you might be able to meet a few of the people he's referring to. TeAro's Fromm family has a habit of inviting guests to share a glass or two at their Sugarloaf Homestead. This late 1800s part-restored stone cottage is a relaxing place to have a chat with second, third and fourth generation family members, all of whom are still actively involved in the business.

My Place

"We got caught up in the romance of wine," says Todd. "It was a long courtship as our forebears started planting vines on our land back in 1919 when great grandfather Charlie Fromm used a crow bar to part the soil for our first plantings of Shiraz. Today we're all very much unified in the pursuit of a common goal – to make great wine and share it with as many people as possible."

You wouldn't read about it

"Our grandfather Charlie was working cattle in the 1930s

Lot 501 Fromm Square Road Williamstown

Ph (08) 8524 6116

www.TeAroestate.com

trevorf@TeAroestate.com

Est 2001

Tastings by appointment

Tutored tastings

Price range $18-$30

Key Wines: Two Charlies GSM, Pump Jack Cabernet Sauvignon, Charred Door Shiraz

Ryan Fromm & Todd Rowett

when a bull took offence to him and gored him badly in the leg. His wife Minnie stemmed the blood flow and, lacking anything else to disinfect the wound, poured a bottle of wine over it. We will soon be releasing a Tempranillo called the 'Charging Bull' in honour of the moment!"

Local knowledge

"The Corner Store Bakery in Williamstown serves coffee as good as anywhere and their vanilla custard slice is to die for!"

Food matches

"A 300 gram Wagyu steak with chilli jam at The Lord Lyndoch is perfect with the richness of our Charred Door Shiraz."

Dragan Radocaj Photography

teusner wines

Of the growing band of talented 'young gun' winemakers in the Barossa, the wines of Kym Teusner are among the most impressive. His passion for old vine Grenache, Shiraz and Mataro from the Ebenezer and Moppa districts may not be unique, but the skill with which he preserves the definition of this fruit in his wines is without parallel. Oak is a lower priority for Kym than it is, perhaps, for any other Barossa maker, and it is this that frees his old vine fruit to express the full depth of its character. Every wine in his range is eminently drinkable in its youth and many also mature beautifully. Competitive pricing places these wines among the best value old vine reds in the Barossa and, indeed, the world.

My place

"I was in Adelaide studying winemaking and working in restaurants," says Kym. "At one of the Christmas shows in 2001 I met the Riebke brothers, who had been farming vineyards in Ebenezer in the Barossa for five generations. They were discussing an eighty-year-old Grenache vineyard and they were pretty dark on the fact that they would have to rip it out because it wasn't paying enough to make it viable. The big companies weren't too concerned about eighty-year-old Grenache and had suggested that it be pulled

Corner of Railway Terrace and Research Road Nuriootpa

Ph (08) 8563 0898

www.teusner.com.au

info@teusner.com.au

Est 2002

Tastings by appointment

Price range $18-$130

*Key Barossa Wines:
Joshua Grenache Mataro Shiraz, Avatar Grenache Shiraz Mataro, The Riebke Shiraz, Albert Shiraz, The Salsa Rosé*

out to plant Chardonnay. Nowadays you can't sell Chardonnay in the Barossa Valley for love or money! I was aghast and couldn't believe what I was hearing. As soon as I got out of there I got in touch with my mate Michael Page and we scratched together some cash to buy enough of the fruit to allow the vines to

Kym Teusner in the Riebke Brothers' old vine Grenache vineyard

181

stay in the ground. We had no idea about wine marketing, we had no grand vision, it was just blindly leaping in.

"The first wine came up trumps. It was a 2002 unoaked Grenache that we called 'Joshua.' All our mates told us that we were idiots because no one drank Grenache and no one drank unoaked reds so we were sure to go broke. That unoaked Grenache has now gained the biggest following out of any wine we make! And that first vintage is still looking fabulous to this day.

"What's wine about? It's not about what you put it into to mature it. The oak vessel was originally there to transport it, not to flavour it. For us, oak is a maturation vessel, not there to give it flavour. The wine is about the wine. I hate seeing wines where you can't see the fruit for the oak."

Infamous growers

"Without the Riebke brothers' fruit we wouldn't be here. The Grenache was eighty years old when we first made it and they've got Shiraz right up to 135 years old. It's all from Ebenezer and Moppa, my favourite parts of the Barossa. The Riebke brothers are as passionate as we are about growing good fruit to make good wine. We started off buying five tonnes of fruit from the Riebkes in 2002 and now we buy 250 tonnes!"

You wouldn't read about it

"Just after the 2008 vintage we were all at fairly high stress levels and not really in the mood for anything. We had builders working on our offices. And an old guy pulled up in a little Suzuki. He was pretty hunched over and he looked like he was about 95. When someone comes on to a building site in the Barossa it's usually to complain about something. I was dragging hoses and I wasn't in the mood for this today so I kept my head down, hoping he would talk to someone else. He asked the builders, 'Who runs this joint?' And they pointed over to me. So I wandered over and said, 'G'day mate.' He said, 'Do you run this place?' I said, 'Yep.' He said, 'I've lived here all my bloody life. It's about time someone did something with this bloody place.' And he shook my hand and said, 'Good on ya'!'"

Local knowledge

"For us, Sunday lunches are almost always at either The Valley Hotel or The Club in Tanunda. Chicken 'Parma' is my choice at The Club. How do you go past a Chicken Parma? And the mixed grill is pretty good at The Valley.

"There are three restaurants that we frequent in the Barossa. I think Appellation is one of the best restaurants in South Australia. They do a fantastic job with the atmosphere; the food is A-grade and the staff are knowledgeable about wines and service – you don't even know they're there waiting. That's real service! 1918 is a good fun place. We know all the staff there well and we often rock in at 8:30 at night after a few drinks. And, of course, Vintners is just up the road."

Visiting Teusner

"We do tastings by appointment here and we're working on renovating one of the buildings as a cellar door. At the moment our tasting room is the kitchen in the office. It's pretty rudimentary but people seem to like it! It's real!"

Riebke Brothers' old vines

thorn-clarke wines

THORN·CLARKE
Barossa Wines · Australia

Gawler Park Road Angaston

Map E15 Winery 63

Ph (08) 8564 3036

www.thornclarkewines.
com.au

thornclarke@thornclarke.
com.au

Est 1998

Cellar door tastings open
Mon-Fri 9-5, Sat-Sun 12-4

Price range $15-$50

*Key Wines: Sandpiper
Riesling, Shotfire
Quartage, William
Randell Shiraz*

Thorn-Clarke Wines is one of the modern success stories of the Barossa, growing to an 80 000 case production in just seven years of its first vintage. With a focus on exploring the influence of site on wine style and quality, Thorn-Clarke sources grapes from four distinct districts within the Barossa. This is a family-run operation owned by fifth generation Barossans David and Cheryl Clarke, with son Sam managing the business and daughter Nicole actively involved.

My Place

"The heritage of the Barossa is the heart and soul of this region," says Sam. "Like most Barossa wine businesses, family is at the core of Thorn-Clarke. We have our name out the front, we work in the business and we strive together to manage our vineyards to get the best out of each site."

Barossa Character

"I reckon the mayor of the Barossa, Brian Hurn, is a very interesting character. He has great community spirit, is tirelessly promoting the Barossa and has a 'no BS' policy! A natural sportsman, he's about two axe handles wide across the shoulders and has a grandson, Shannon, who is playing for the Eagles in the AFL."

Barossa dirt

"It isn't widely known, but there was plane crash up on the other side of the Kaiser Stuhl mountain in the 1940s and you can visit a cairn erected by the locals at the site. There's also a pretty good view from the top of the hill if you're feeling fit!"

You wouldn't read about it

"Our family has stronger links to an English heritage rather than German, but there is a Prussian Baron in our family tree. He allegedly killed someone in a fight in Prussia and had to leave in a hurry. He made it to Australia but tragically drowned in the River Murray trying to save someone."

Grape stomping

Wining kids

"Most of the kids who visit us seem to keep themselves amused by running around on the lawn at the front of our cellar door. If they get bored we can always throw them in the vineyard - there's plenty of work for everyone there!"

Thorn-Clarke vineyard at Mount Crawford

183

tim smith wines

"I can't think of a better place than the Barossa to live and make wine," says Tim Smith. It's an assessment that carries some weight because this widely travelled winemaker has worked extensively overseas and for a number of Australia's big names including St Hallett, Tatachilla and Yalumba. Alongside his own self-titled wines he holds down the winemaking duties at Chateau Tanunda. When he's not up to his armpits in grapes, he spends his time exploring the local countryside on a restored 1981 Triumph Bonneville motorcycle.

My Place

"I was sitting near the Chapel on the hill of Hermitage in France some years back," Tim reminisces. "It was a magnificent day, I'd opened a bottle of Condrieu and I had one of those moments of clarity. I realised that what I was doing making wines purely for other people just wasn't for me anymore and I needed to get out and make wines of my own. That's when Tim Smith Wines was born."

You wouldn't read about it

"I was a flying winemaker for many years, making wines in Portugal, France and New

Ph (08) 8563 0939
www.timsmithwines.com.au
tjsmith@chariot.net.au
Est 2002
Tastings by appointment
Price range $28-$60
Key Wines: Viognier, Barossa Shiraz, Mourvèdre Grenache Shiraz

Zealand. Now my son is following the same path and spent the 2009 vintage in Marlborough, New Zealand."

Local knowledge

"For me, Hutton Vale lamb is one of the great revelations of the Barossa. It has a flavour and tenderness that sets it apart."

Hutton Vale

Eden Valley vineyards
Tyson Stelzer Photography

tin shed wines

Peter Clarke is a busy man. When the ex-commercial airline pilot isn't busy with Tin Shed Wines, he's behind the stoves as head chef at Vintners. His Angaston-based restaurant is one of the Barossa's most popular and acclaimed dining destinations.

My Place

"I started Tin Shed because I like wine," says Peter. "That sounds a bit simple but I get a lot of enjoyment out of drinking it, and I've always been fascinated with the idea of making it. Being in the restaurant game it seemed a natural extension of my life. I chose Eden Valley for its softer, food-friendly wine styles."

Barossa Character

"The Barossa is a wonderful place to live. There's a great sense of camaraderie here and a strong identification with the region among those who call it home."

Infamous growers

"One grower we work with has a great Shiraz vineyard that just happens to have a number of white grape vines planted variously through every row. Of course, we don't want these grapes in our wine, but somehow they always seem to end up at the very bottom of the grape bin when the grapes are delivered. It's become a standing joke between us!"

Local knowledge

"Go out for the day and visit a few smaller wineries. You'll meet a whole raft of really passionate, hands-

Light Pass Road Tanunda

Ph (08) 8563 3669

www.tinshedwines.com

info@tinshedwines.com

Est 1997

Tastings by appointment

Price range $16-$50

Key Wines: Single Wire Shiraz, MSG, Wild Bunch Riesling

on winemakers who make wonderful wine. Then buy a bottle and bring it to one of the good restaurants in the Valley for dinner. BYO is always welcome at Vintners."

Food matches

"Mushroom risotto with squab, Linke's bacon (the best in the Barossa) and fresh beetroot is perfectly matched with the earthy flavours of Tin Shed MSG."

torbreck vintners

In just fifteen years, David Powell's Torbreck has transformed from nothing into one of the Barossa's big success stories, and his wines can now be found all over the planet. Only ever using Barossa fruit, he has a focus on Rhone varieties, reds in particular, and most notably the blend of Shiraz and Viognier, led by his flagship cult wine, RunRig. In David's words, "We aim to make big, powerful wines that still have a sense of elegance to them." From his winery in Marananga he says, "This side of the Barossa is like the dress circle but at the same time I think that the Barossa is reflected best through blends of different areas." It is this blending philosophy that defines his flagship wines, of which he has five priced above $120.

Infamous growers

"One of the great strengths of the Barossa is that we have the longest unbroken heritage of grape growing of anywhere in the world in some of the oldest vines on the planet that are still in production," says David.

Lot 51 Roennfeldt Road
Marananga

Map D10 Winery 64

Ph (08) 8568 8123

www.torbreck.com

cellardoor@torbreck.com

Est 1994

Cellar door tastings open 10-6 daily $5pp

Picnic facilities, tutored tastings

Price range $17.50-$225

Key Wines: RunRig Shiraz Viognier, The Gask Eden Valley Shiraz, Woodcutter's Shiraz

"Our growers are one of our great strengths. People like Adrian Hoffmann, a sixth generation professional grape grower who deals with most of the top makers in the Barossa. Marcus Schultz and Roger Mattschoss often come over to the cellar door for a drink after work when they're sick of pruning. When they do, our cellar door staff shut up and let them talk our visitors through the wines.

"It took me a long time to build the loyalty of growers, and rightly so. But once you get their trust they are fiercely loyal people. And that's what makes the Barossa so special. We have more than thirty growers on our list, and more than fifty vineyards between them."

David Powell

Torbreck winery

Visiting Torbreck

"Our cellar door cottage is over 150 years old. We keep it open later than everyone else, until 6pm. A lot of people come by at the end of the day and they enjoy the fact that they can go somewhere between their last tasting at 4:30 and dinner at 7pm.

"All of our wines are on tasting. It astounds most people that RunRig is available every day of the week. We believe that if people are good enough to buy wine then they're good enough to taste it. Everything is available to taste until it sells out.

"We charge a $5 tasting fee at Cellar Door so people don't feel obliged to buy a bottle at the end of the tasting. Of course, if they do, they don't pay the fee. Come to think of it, I don't remember the last time we actually charged someone the fee!

"We're a farming community and our cellar door people are friendly and authentic. They don't speak Queen's English. Our staff like to be able to spend a good amount of time with visitors to give them a real insight into the wines. It's possible to do a sit-down tasting in our tasting room, but you should call to book in advance.

"Visiting Torbreck is not just about tasting wine but about getting a feel for the place. We have a lovely garden setting with table and chairs and people are most welcome to bring their own picnic. Our goal is to give people more than just a tasting experience."

Local knowledge

"Maggie Beer's Farm Shop is just over the hill and we often go over for a quick bite with a glass of wine," says David. "I often pop into the Greenock Creek Hotel after work. Cellar door shuts at 6 so we'll be there by 6:20. It's a small pub and they do pretty good meals on weekends.

"There are only really three really good restaurants in the Barossa. 1918, Vintners and Appellation. But I also like going to the beer garden at the Tanunda. That's my pub. It's just fabulous, and it has a good wine list. If I'm going to make a night of it, that's where I'll go. The Torbreck crew is very well known there – I'm not sure if that's a good thing or a bad thing!"

torzi matthews vintners

Domenic Torzi leads a double life as both an innovative grape grower and winemaker and as a producer of Barossa extra virgin olive oils with partner Tracy Matthews. Their Una Wild 1880 Extra Virgin Olive Oil is made from a unique resource of ancient, wild olive trees scattered throughout the region, with origins dating back to the 1880s. The couple also runs the Angaston Tudor Bed & Breakfast.

My Place

"Some people were sceptical when we planted our small pocket of frost-prone vineyard in the Eden Valley," explains Domenic. "The vines went in, the frosts came, the yields were low and our Frost Dodger range was created! The goal was to grow grapes here that would produce a distinctive, flavoursome, Italian style wine, the type that would suit the sort of Mediterranean food that we love."

TORZI
MATTHEWS

You wouldn't read about it

"During the 1970s my family was able to secure access to many magnificent wild olive trees throughout the Barossa by offering to prune them for their owners so that they would provide better shelter for stock. No one really cared much about olives back then, but that foresight has meant that we are now able to source exceptional fruit to make oils with character and personality."

Local knowledge

"Get out onto the back roads and dirt tracks around the Valley and up into the ranges. Watch out for the local guys working their fences and paddocks, and get out of the car and say hello. You'll discover the real Barossa and meet approachable people who'll happily give you the time of day if you make the effort."

Food matches

"A favourite of ours are new

**96 Eden Valley Road
Mount McKenzie**

Ph 0412 323 486

www.torzimatthews.com.
au

domenic.torzi@bigpond.
com.au

Est 2002

Tastings at Taste Eden
Valley in Angaston

Bed & breakfast, olive oil

Price range $15-$30

*Key Wines: Frost Dodger
Shiraz, Schist Rock Shiraz,
Schist Rock Riesling, Vigna
Cantina Sangiovese*

Domenic Torzi

season field mushrooms, picked late, with a touch of earthiness about them. We sauté them with a dash of shiraz reduction, new season extra virgin olive oil, lemon juice, pepper and rock salt. Served with a side of ripe tomato, Provolone cheese and wood-fired bread, it's perfect with our Vigna Cantina Sangiovese."

Tyson Stelzer Photography

travis earth

Travis Earth O'Callaghan, son of Rockford's Robert O'Callaghan, made his first vintage under his Travis Earth label in 2008 in a handful of barrels under his house in Marananga. He has two wines, a Mataro Shiraz blend off his Dad's Krondorf farm vineyard and an Eden Valley Shiraz sourced from one of the highest vineyards in the region.

Barossa character

"Earth is my middle name," explains Travis. "I was born in 1973, so, crazy times and crazy name! But it kind of suits the way I've been all my life, growing up in vineyards and wineries. I have been lucky enough to get this ten acre block and my goal here is to be self-sufficient by growing biodynamic food and to make a small quantity of really premium wines."

My place

"The Barossa is home for me.

Ph 0458 233 065

Est 2008

Key Wines: Mataro Shiraz, Eden Valley Shiraz

It's a nurturing community, a community where if you have a rough time they'll support you. If you get out of line they'll kick you in the arse, like a proper small community should. And I've had that many times! As a community it's diverse and there's a real focus on the quality of life, without being greedy or excessive."

troll creek

"There's an ancient, German-made, red gum bridge on our property that survives despite the best efforts of time," says James Hage. "We always told the kids that a troll lived under it!" James and wife Jo operate Troll Creek Wines, producing small quantities of hand-crafted wines exclusively from their fifth generation family estate.

My Place

"Our family have been growers in Bethany for more than 100 years and we have been in the vineyards all our lives," explains James. "Vines remain our passion, so it seemed natural that we should make our own wines. We have purposely kept our production small and quality-focused."

Local knowledge

"The hills at the back of Bethany offer great views over the whole valley and we enjoy taking visitors there for a tour."

Food matches

"Steamed blue swimmer crab with chilli and black pepper is great with our Troll Creek Rosé."

Troll Creek

Lot 362 Bethany Road Bethany

Ph 0408 821 641

www.trollcreek.com

jjhage@bigpond.com

Est 1998

Tastings by appointment

Price range $18-$55

Key Wines: Shiraz, Cabernet Sauvignon, Cabernet Sauvignon Shiraz, Cabernet Franc Rosé

James Hage

tscharke and glaymond wines

Damien Tscharke

Sixth generation vigneron Damien Tscharke doesn't seem old enough to have worked on his family's vineyards for more than twenty years. A leader among the Barossa's new generation of winemakers, Damien has distinguished himself through his passion

for alternative varieties. He was the first producer of Montepulciano in Australia and also the first to plant the variety thought to be Albariño. At the time of writing it is not clear what this variety will be named in Australia. What is certain, however, that Damien's 'Girl Talk' is one of its best expressions in the country.

My Place

"All of my wines are an expression of our terroir," explains Damien. "I make my wines only from our estate vineyards in Marananga and Seppeltsfield and my goal is to express these unique subregions and all of their subtleties. My wines are very

Seppeltsfield Road, Marananga

Ph 08 8562 1044

www.tscharke.com.au

damien@tscharke.com.au

Tastings by appointment

Price range $21-$90

Key Wines: Girl Talk, The Master Montepulciano, Distinction Shiraz

much made in the vineyard.

"For me, what makes the Barossa special is the combination of its people, its history and its capacity to produce premium wines year in and year out."

Alternative varieties

"I have really enjoyed the chance to pioneer Albariño and Montepulciano in Australia. What excites me most about these varieties are not only the unique styles of wine that they produce but also their suitability to our environment. They really flourish in Marananga and seem to cope with extreme weather conditions and heatwaves better than most other varieties. In our harsh Australian climate, I can see these varieties being planted more widely in the future. Perhaps they won't be considered 'alternative' for much longer!"

Seppeltsfield
Dragan Radocaj Photography

The bride arriving for a garden
wedding at Peter Seppelt Wines

turkey flat vineyards

Bethany Road Tanunda

Map F10 Winery 65

Ph (08) 8563 2851

www.turkeyflat.com.au

info@turkeyflat.com.au

Est 1992

Cellar door tastings open 11-5 daily

Picnic facilities

Price range $18-$42

Key Wines: Rosé, Shiraz, Pedro Ximenez

At Turkey Flat, the vineyards come first. Pulling into the driveway you'll make your way past 1920s Grenache vines before you see the 1847 Shiraz. At the end of the driveway is a quaint 1860s butcher's shop which is now the cellar door. Here you'll find one of Australia's best rosés alongside a range of wines crafted from traditional Rhone varieties.

My place

"This property was called Turkey Flat right from the time that the first settlers arrived here," recalls proprietor Peter Schulz. "There were bush turkeys all over southern Australia, but these flats were very fertile and there were plenty of things for the turkeys to eat here, so there were plenty of them here. There was a Turkey Flat brass band and a bit of a community in the area so the name has always stuck. It was the obvious choice for us, and more memorable than Schulz & Co, which was the name of the butcher's business.

"Christie and I are proud to have been able to buy back the farm that has been in our family since 1860. It was on the brink of being either share farmed or pulled out and turned to housing in 1987, so we saved it from a fate worse than death! We believe that we are custodians of the property and we will hand it on to our children and they will hand it on to their children.

"We started making wine here in 1990 and we ran cellar door ourselves between 1993 and 1998, developing a substantial mailing list, which is still a very important part of our business. I don't get into cellar door myself any more. I was thrown out years ago!"

Visiting Turkey Flat

"The wine sales building was an old butcher's shop, on one of the earliest land divisions in the Barossa. It was a big business from 1860 until about 1922. Twenty-four butcher's carts used to leave here every day!

"Christie and I have deliberately focused our cellar door on being a place where you come to taste wine and buy it, and not a coffee shop or a souvenir shop. When people walk in there, they're in the middle of a vineyard and they see pictures of grape vines on the walls so they're under no illusions as to where they are. Underneath there is a cellar, where our museum stock is kept.

"Winemaking happens right here. If you're lucky enough a tractor will drive past and

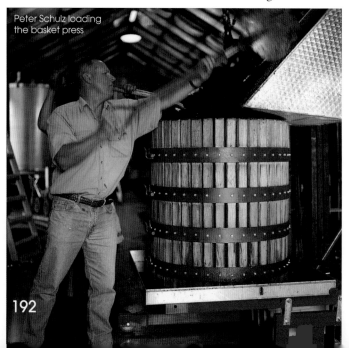
Peter Schulz loading the basket press

you'll see a trailer with grapes on it or someone filling barrels because it's a living, working business. We often work in the winery with the doors open and we'll see people stop and look and think, 'Wow, there's a winery in there! I can see stainless steel tanks and barrels and the floor's wet and someone's playing dreadful music on the radio!'"

Local knowledge

"You have to be a cyclist to work for Turkey Flat or you don't get a job!" jokes Peter. "That's not true, but there are quite a few of us in the company who are cyclists. We cycle to Keyneton via Mengler's Hill and Eden Valley. The Kapunda run is fun, and Eudunda is a good ride. We often go to Mount Pleasant via Williamstown. There are about twenty runs that we do regularly. It's a very good area for cycling and the weather is always good. "

Variety of varieties

"We're really passionate about Rhone varieties. Shiraz, obviously, and also Grenache. In 1992, we were one of the first to make a Grenache in the Barossa. And we make a straight Mourvèdre and a Rhone red blend from Shiraz, Grenache and Mourvèdre. I have always been of the view that this area is too hot for Semillon but our Marsanne, Roussanne and Viognier handle the heat remarkably well. I think there is a great future for these varieties on the valley floor.

"Of course, we love rosé – it should be Australia's beverage of choice! Our Rosé is hand-made from the vineyard. It's a complex assemblage process, blended from fifteen or sixteen cuvées."

Food matches

"Our Marsanne Viognier Roussanne blend is a pretty big wine. It's really a red wine drinker's white, as are the white wines out of the Rhone, they're not delicate styles. And so they go with anything that's oily and has some power. The white can even handle chorizo. The reds like something that's got some sort of oil or fat and they even go with cheeses. The Mourvèdre goes well with cassoulet or game, because it is quite a gamey wine. Rabbit and pork work well. You can throw a fair bit of spice at our wines and they can handle it. Our Pedro Ximenez is magic with blue cheese."

two hands wines

TWO HANDS WINES

"To us the Barossa is number one," say the 'two hands,' Michael Twelftree and Richard Mintz. "We sell wines from many regions, and the Barossa always sells first." In just a decade, the company has established an enviable international reputation for its large portfolio of red wines, with a particular focus on regional Shiraz. These can be tasted at the quaint cellar door. "It's quintessentially South Australian," says Richard, "an old stone building, surrounded by vineyards and gumtrees on a creek." Immaculately renovated, the beautiful heritage façade of the building has been maintained, and a contemporary feel has been created inside.

My place

"The Barossa is the best wine region because the quality of the fruit always shines," says Richard. "It's also a beautiful place. No matter what the season is, there's always something that makes you sit up and have a look when you're driving in."

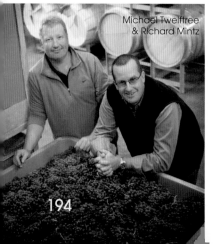

Michael Twelftree & Richard Mintz

"I always think it's the light," adds Michael. "I enjoy getting up first thing in the morning and driving through Eden Valley at first light. It's the garden of Eden – we've always said that."

You wouldn't read about it

"The last thing we ever want is to have the road here bituminised," says Richard. "We want people who drive up from the city to feel like they're in the country. To us, it's that feel of getting away from it all. We transplanted a 100-year-old Shiraz vineyard from Greenock to the paddock next door.

"When we were looking for a home for our cellar door, Michael was driving around one day and found this place. All that was here was a ruin of a shell, nothing else. No power and no plumbing. It was just muck and trees and paddock. The old building hadn't been lived in for 50 years. The last guy who lived here turned up one day and said, 'I lived here when I was ten years old.' And he was sixty. There wasn't one bit of graffiti or vandalism or damage to the place. And that's always stuck with me, because that's the kind of place that the Barossa is.

"When we redug and restored the cellar in the bakehouse we found 98 dead pigeons!" recounts Michael. "That was

a disgusting day! Originally it would have been a food cellar, not a wine cellar, and they would have done all of their cooking above it. We've restored the oven so you can see the original brickwork. And we've added a glass floor so you can see the cellar below. It's triple-laminated, shatter-proof and it weighs a tonne! To replace a panel you've got to take the entire roof and ceiling out, get a crane in, cut the piece out, lift it out and bring another one in. It's an absolute monster of a job – thankfully we've only ever had to do it once!"

Visiting Two Hands

"We wanted to create a really

Neldner Road Marananga

Map D10 Winery 66

Ph (08) 8568 7900

www.twohandswines. com

cellardoor@ twohandswines.com

Est 2000

Cellar door tastings $5pp open Mon-Sun 10-5

Bakehouse Master class $25pp Thurs-Sun 11-12. Book in advance on 08 8562 4566

Picnic facilities, tutored tastings, coffee, light meals

Price range $18-$165

Key Barossa Wines: Aphrodite Cabernet Sauvignon, Ares Shiraz, Aerope Grenache

Two Hands cellar door cottage and bakehouse

intimate space, for those customers who want a special experience, so we conduct master classes in the bakehouse," says Richard. "You'll come in and the girls will pour and talk you through the wines and then leave you for a few minutes and come back in to do the next flight. It's a nice experience that isn't rushed — the last thing that we want is someone standing at the end of the table pushing you through it.

"You can book a master class tasting in the bakehouse for Thursday to Sunday, 11am-12pm. There is a table in there for eight people, so we make it quite intimate. We need a minimum of four people, but you can make a tentative booking for fewer, in the hope that others will book also. Call cellar door in advance to book."

Tastings at cellar door are $5 per person. "You can either stand up at the front or sit down for a structured tasting at a specially-designed bench," says Richard.

Wining kids

"I've got three kids and Michael's got four and they're all young," says Richard, "so we're very sympathetic about children here."

"We've created an area in our cellar door with leather couches and a fireplace," says Michael, "so if you have a designated driver or children, there's an area where they can go and hang out, read a magazine and relax. We've got colouring in for kids, a box of crayons and other stuff, and a bit of lemonade in the fridge, so they can feel included in the experience.

"When we bought the property we were about to knock the pond in out the back. It was all covered in sheets of iron, with an old stone wall around it; an underground water tank that had been hand-dug and the wall built by stone masons. 'But,' we thought, 'this was built over 100 years ago, so let's make a feature out of it!' It was just magnificent, far too good to push in, so we made it into a fish pond. I've gotta say, if there's one place where every kid ends up it's — no, not in the pond, we put a very nice rail around it — but standing up on the rail looking at the fish. Kids just adore it!

"We also have a big grassed area. It's all about including the family. I also like to take my kids to Salters at Saltram, and they love the wood oven pizzas. And they always want to go to the Whispering Wall!"

veronique wines

As well as managing the well-priced range of Veronique wines, Peter and Vicki Manning run the Meadow Springs Bed & Breakfast in a restored 1890s cottage in the Eden Valley township of Mt Mackenzie. Built for the spinster sister of South Australia founder, George Fife Angas, the building has previously operating as the local post office and a Cobb & Co outpost.

VÉRONIQUE

My Place

"Veronique Wines came about as a result of numerous chats over a glass of wine or two with our neighbour Dom Torzi, who encouraged us to pursue our dream," explains Peter. "I've always enjoyed a ballsy Barossa red and, like most people in this part of the world, I wanted to make my own. Dom helped us to source the grapes and he makes the wines. Our focus has been on making quality wines at affordable prices."

You wouldn't read about it

"We have a wonderful

Sugarloaf Hill Road Mt McKenzie

Ph (08) 8565 3214

www.veroniquewines.com.au

petkiptyltd@bigpond.com

Est 2004

Tastings by appointment

Meadow Springs Bed & Breakfast

Price range $15-$19

Key Wines: Regions Barossa Shiraz, Old Vine Grenache Mataro Shiraz, Sauvignon Blanc

100-year-old hedge which hides a secret sculpted garden. Come and have a look!"

Outlook from Mengler's Hill
Dragan Radocaj Photography

villa tinto

Spain in the Barossa? 'Villa Tinto' may sound a little out of place on Krondorf Road in Tanunda, but Albert Di Palma and his wife Dianne are very much at home here. The Argentinean born winemaker has transplanted a touch of trans-continental flavour in the Barossa and when he's not growing grapes or making and selling wine he can usually be found in his backyard, his Argentinean BBQ firing, entertaining all and sundry in a manner for which Villa Tinto has become renowned.

Albert Di Palma

My Place

"My husband says that this is a hobby that he's just kept doing for years," says Dianne. "He's extremely passionate about making wine and we both love living on Krondorf Road, growing grapes and enjoying this small but close-knit community."

Villa Tinto cellar door

Villa Tinto grounds

Krondorf Road Tanunda

Map G10 Winery 67

Ph 08 8563 3044

Mob 0414 349 999

www.villatinto.com.au

villatinto@ozemail.com.au

Est 2001

Cellar door tastings open 11-5 daily

Tours available

Price range $12-$33

Key Wines: Cabernet Sauvignon, Shiraz Mercedes Blend Cabernet Semillon

Villa Tinto

DI PALMA FAMILY
VINEYARD / WINERY

You wouldn't read about it

"I speak Spanish and English and my wife speaks Spanish, English, German and Italian," says Albert. "As a result, we tend to have a lot of overseas visitors coming to us, which makes for a wonderful opportunity to meet new people and make new friends."

Food matches

"Being an Argentine, I love 'asado,' a special cut of beef like a spare rib charcoal-grilled on the BBQ. Eat it with plenty of chimichurri sauce and a glass of our Villa Tinto Cabernet Sauvignon."

vinecrest fine barossa wine

VineCrest has one of the most accessible and visible cellar doors in the Barossa Valley, just north of Tanunda on Barossa Valley Way. A change of ownership in recent years has seen a youthful and enthusiastic team taking up the reins.

My Place

"I've been working with VineCrest in one way or another for about ten years, long enough to watch it grow from a small family business to one with national and international distribution for our extensive range of wines," says Manager Matt Dunning.

Food matches

"Our favourite food match for the VineCrest Cabernet Sauvignon is a rack of mustard-encrusted lamb with smashed potato and garden salad."

Corner Barossa Valley Way & Vine Vale Road Tanunda

Map E11 Winery 68

Ph (08) 8563 0111

www.vinecrest.com.au

finewine@vinecrest.com.au

Est 1998

Cellar door tastings open 11-5 daily

Picnic facilities, crafts, local produce

Price range $15-$115

Key Wines: Merlot, Sparkling Shiraz, White Port

waky mute

This Monty Pythonesque brand name finds its genesis in the first letters of the names of business partners Kym Teusner and Warwick Murray. The winemaker and viticulturist respectively started Waky Mute in 2007. All wines are priced under $20 and are available for tasting by contacting Kym Teusner.

My Place

"Like many great ideas, Waky Mute was born over a beer or two," explains Kym. "Warwick and I wanted to get ourselves into a good piece of dirt and make some quality wine at a decent price. We were both of the opinion that the Barossa is the easiest place in the world to grow premium wine grapes, so it was then just a matter of finding a suitable vineyard that fitted our needs. Fortunately, we found a good one, and the positive response to the wines seems to suggest that we made the right choice."

Barossa dirt

"Everyone needs to take a trip up Steingarten Road. It has the best view in the Barossa!"

You wouldn't read about it

"Warwick and I came from sheep farming backgrounds with little to no interest in wine. Once hooked, though, the idea of making a bit of wine in the back shed suddenly seemed very attractive!"

Local knowledge

"For a quick snack, drop into the Angaston Mobil

147 Murray Street Tanunda

Ph 0409 351 166

info@themutevintners.com.au

Est 2007

Tastings by appointment

Price range $10-$20

Key Wines: Round 2 Shiraz, Cabernet Sauvignon, Chardonnay

Roadhouse. It's only 300m from the Waky Mute vineyard and it serves great bacon and egg burgers!"

Food matches

"The Waky Mute Round 2 Chardonnay is not your typical Chardonnay. It's more zesty and steely than most expect, which makes it perfect with oysters or freshly caught, vinegared yabbies."

westlake vineyards

Winter at Westlake Vineyards

Sixth generation Barossa grape growers Darren and Suz Westlake manage a vineyard nestled among the rolling hills of Koonunga and Moppa that has been in their Kalleske family for three generations. "We believe it is important to be involved with all aspects of the vineyard and winery, and aim to do most of the work ourselves," says Darren.

My place

"What makes our place so special is its location! We can go to the top of our hill and enjoy the most amazing views overlooking the beautiful Barossa ranges or we can go down to the creek and feel like we're tucked away from it all. We're out of sight from our neighbours and rarely get any traffic. We can peacefully tend to our vineyard and contemplate on how lucky we are to be part of an iconic grape growing region."

Visiting Westlake Vineyards

"We love to meet the people who buy our wines and we will attempt to show them as much of 'our little piece of the world' as their hearts desire. You can make an appointment to have tastings and/or book intimate tours where we can take you through the vineyard and even to the

Diagonal Road Tanunda
Ph (08) 8565 6208
www.westlakevineyards.
com.au
info@westlakevineyards.
com.au
Tastings by appointment
Price range $27.50-$55
Key Wines: Albert's Block Shiraz, Eleazar Shiraz, 717 Convicts The Warden Shiraz

winery in Greenock. The earlier you phone the easier it is to accommodate your needs. Our wines are also available for tasting on weekends at the Greenock Tasting Room, Adelaide Road Greenock."

Wining Kids

"As we have young children, we enjoy more laid-back venues like The Company Kitchen in Angaston rather than the more sophisticated places. We go to the Angas Park Hotel in Nuriootpa for a great pub meal."

WESTLAKE
Vineyards

Autumn at Westlake Vineyards

Steve and Mark, the locals at Westlake Vineyards

whistler wines

At Whistler Wines, the focus is on family. You'll always meet one of the family at cellar door because every one of the nine employees is family, led by brothers Chris and Martin Pfeiffer. "There's rarely a day that goes by when we don't sit down at the end of the day with our cellar door guests and finish the last of the open bottles and chat about the wine and the day," says Chris. This focus on family extends across the facilities, and there is no cellar door in the Barossa that is better set up for families with children of all ages.

Whistler Wines

You wouldn't read about it

'Pfeiffer' is German for 'Whistler.'

Barossa dirt

"Our cellar door is in a wonderful bush setting away from the traffic, just off Seppeltsfield Road," explains Martin. "You have to drive through the vineyard to get here." Martin's focus is in

Seppeltsfield Road Marananga

Map E11 Winery 69

Ph (08) 8562 4942

www.whistlerwines.com

sales@whistlerwines.com

Est 1999

Cellar door tastings open 10:30-5 daily

Picnic facilities, crafts, local produce

Price range $18-$60

Key Wines: Riesling, Semillon, Cabernet Merlot, Cabernet, Shiraz, Reserve Shiraz

the vineyard. "I managed Penfolds vineyards for twenty-eight years, including the Kalimna vineyard," he says. "Now I look after everything that you can see from our cellar door – thirty-five acres with seven varieties."

Visiting Whistler

"Everything in our range that hasn't sold out is available for tasting at our cellar door," says Martin. "You can order a cheese platter at any time. Or if you'd like to arrange a full meal, call a month in advance and we'll arrange catering for as little as eight or ten people. Otherwise, you can book in to use the BBQ for free. Call us to book it a few days in advance. A lot of people bring their own picnic lunch and have a picnic on the lawn or at the outside tables."

Wining kids

The range of activities for kids at Whistler is the most extensive of any cellar door in the Barossa. "We have kids of our own and we want to ensure that we always cater for families," Chris explains. "We've set up a great play area for little ones who are three or four, and we have plenty of activities for five- to ten-year-olds."

"We've just built a kangaroo enclosure in front of the cellar door," says Martin. "It's a two-and-a-half acre space with a dam and a shelter. The kangaroos have been hand-reared so it's quite safe for people to buy a bag of feed from cellar door and go in there and feed them. We've often had kangaroos hopping around in the middle of

Martin and Chris Pfeiffer

our functions, but the enclosure guarantees that locals and internationals can come and be sure to see a kangaroo."

"But that's not all," adds Chris. "When kids visit they can play on the swings in the play area, use the slippery dip, climb trees, use the Pétanque pitch for Pétanque or cricket, kick the footy, play with the skipping ropes or other outdoor games, read a book or, for the very young, play with the toys in the toy basket inside. There's plenty of space for kids to run around and we're away from the road so it's quite safe.

"All of our events include a separate area for children with their own marquee which includes face painters, Clumsy the clown, craft activities, painting, colouring in, storytelling and sometimes old-fashioned games. At our Australia Day celebration we have a thong throwing competition for the children and adults and at the Pfeiffer Fest we have a whistling competition."

Whistler Wines cellar door

An eventful Whistler

"When you come to the Barossa for a week you sometimes run out of will to taste wines and need something else to do," says Martin, "so we run twelve events each year that each attract between 500 and 1500 people."

"We have 'Shiraz & Stew', 'Australia Day', 'Easter Sunday', 'Twilight Concerts', 'Barrel Shed Concerts', 'Gourmet Weekend', 'Pfeiffer Fest', 'Shakespeare in the vines,' 'Festival of Food, Wine and Music' and 'Wine Down at Whistler.' We have food from local caters, local live bands and all sorts of activities. In winter we get camp fires going throughout the lawns. At every event, all of the profits from food and raffles goes toward a charity. We support a number of charities and last year we raised $35 000 for childhood cancer.

See www.whistlerwines.com for the program of events.

My place

"The Barossa community still values family, church, sport and food and wine culture," says Chris. "We have worked very hard at keeping these things alive. There are not many old butchers and bakers that go back five generations anywhere else!"

"There are at least sixteen Lutherans who own wineries in the Barossa. It's an important part of the culture of the place that there are so many people who are committed Christians. The church is an integral part of the community here and I don't see that elsewhere. Every week someone comes through and we end up talking about the role of Lutherans in the Barossa."

Local knowledge

"Blond Coffee in Angaston has the best coffee in the Valley, as well as great snacks," suggests Martin. "And Mick Schluter's Greenock Creek Hotel is our favourite spot for a quiet drink."

"Whistler Farm B&B at my place is the Barossa's newest B&B," says Chris. "We have two contemporary units, each with a kitchenette, courtyard and BBQ on our farm just around the corner from the cellar door, on Samuel Road toward Maggie Beer's Farm Shop. It's very much a farm atmosphere as we're on forty-two acres, with olive trees, sheep, chooks and a horse. From the rooms you can look out over the neighbouring vineyards. We have an underground cellar and you can go and select your own bottle of Whistler wine. Each evening we sit down and have a drink with our guests and we can bring them to the cellar door to do a tasting."

Martin chatting with visitors at Whistler Wines cellar door

the willows vineyard

Light Pass Road Light Pass

Map D13 Winery 62

Ph (08) 8562 1080

www.thewillowsvineyard.com.au

enquiries@thewillowsvineyard.com.au

Est 1989

Cellar door tastings open
Wed-Mon 10:30-4:30.
Tues by appointment.
Bookings for 10 or more.

Price range $14-$50

*Key Wines: Shiraz, Single
Vineyard Semillon, The
Doctor Sparkling Red*

"I was never naturally entranced by wine," admits Peter Scholz, "but I grew to love it because of this area and the people in it." Scholz's roots run deep, with a family history in the Barossa that dates back to 1845. His early ancestors were doctors who ran one of the first hospitals in the region, an association commemorated today in The Willows' flagship 'Bonesetter' Shiraz.

My Place

"We were getting $180 a tonne for great Shiraz in 1987, which was less than it cost us to grow it, so Dad said, 'Let's make some wine,'" Peter recalls. "That was the start of The Willows Vineyard as a brand. We've grown a little year by year but have kept to the fundamentals of being family-owned, estate-grown and single vineyard. Family involvement has become more important as the years have passed. We hope that what we've created can pass on to the next generation, for them to retain its heritage and identity."

You wouldn't read about it

"The Barossa is an inclusive place. It accepts people, and allows them to be a part of what history has built. It is important that this essential character of the Valley is protected."

Infamous growers

"I worked for Peter Lehmann on the weighbridge for many years. A guy turned up one day with a truckload of grapes and told me he'd just started working for a new boss. We got the truck ready to unload and he asked me, 'Aren't you going to hose the grapes down first?' I asked why, and he said, 'My old boss always gave the grapes a good hose before I drove off to deliver them.' It seems he never caught on that the previous employer was just trying to add a bit of weight to the load before it hit the scales!"

Local knowledge

"It's worth a stop in the township of Light Pass to have a look at Luhr's cottage, the original schoolmaster's residence. There's also an old saying that there are more churches than people in Light Pass, and I don't think it's an exaggeration, either!"

Wining kids

"Kids are welcome here and our dog Archie the Boxer is quite good company."

Food matches

"We love egg and bacon pie with The Willows The Doctor Sparkling Red. For breakfast, of course!"

Peter Scholz

wolf blass wines

Wolf Blass is such a household name that it might come as a surprise that the brand originated with just one man, Wolfgang Franz Otto Blass. Fresh out of Germany, Wolf arrived in the Barossa with little money and a diploma in winemaking in 1961. Within fifteen years he had won The Jimmy Watson Trophy in three consecutive years with the first three vintages he produced under his own name. The Barossa has been the home of Wolf Blass Wines ever since, and the winery has grown to rank among the largest in the country.

Barossa Character: Wolf Blass

"History has been kind to me, but it wasn't an easy time initially," Wolf says. "Things didn't fall into line. I started right at the bottom, earning $2.50 an hour. I first made my own wine in 1966 and I used other people's equipment because I didn't have my own. They helped me out with crushing and bottling and everything. I started with a $2000 overdraft and an old army shed outside of Nuriootpa.

"My focus when I came to Australia was on women, and women weren't allowed into bars then. How the bloody hell do I get close to beautiful women if they're all sitting somewhere in front of the television set? I wanted to know how I could make a product that women could enjoy. Len Evans started screaming that everyone should drink red wine, but you had

97 Sturt Highway Nuriootpa

Map C14 Winery 71

Ph (08) 8568 7311

www.wolfblass.com.au

visitor.centre@wolfblass.com

Est 1966

Cellar door tastings open Mon-Fri 9:15-5

Tours, tutored tastings, gallery

Ultra Premium Experience $30pp by appointment. Tutored tasting of ultra premium wines in private room

Blend it Like Blass $40pp by appointment. Make your own blend.

Price range $10-$158

Key Barossa Wines: Platinum Label Shiraz, White Label Eden Valley Riesling

Wolf Blass

Chris Hatcher

to put it away in the cellar for a few years first. So I started making a style that could be drunk immediately. We did everything that we could in the cellar to make the wines more drinkable. When I started producing my style of red and white wines I said they would 'make strong women weak and weak men strong'. And I still believe that today, after all these years.

"I'll always remember Orlando and Lindemans and Leo Buring going up there and picking up all these trophies. And I was sitting there, going, 'S**t, one day I am going to be part of this bloody deal!' And eventually we turned the tables and gave them a bloody hiding at every bloody wine show!"

Barossa Character: Chris Hatcher

Foster's Australia Chief Winemaker Chris Hatcher can be seen zipping around the Barossa in his Black BMW Z4. "Two things I love are Champagne and cars," he says. "The great Champagnes have the stamp of the house style. The greatest cars are the ones that have maintained the same styling throughout the years. And that's what Wolf Blass wines are about. Maintaining the style but evolving the elements. They should be recognisable as Wolf Blass but refined in style over the years."

My place

Chris Hatcher celebrated his 21st vintage with the company in 2009. "I first went to the Barossa at the end of 1974," he recalls. "In those days there were very few restaurants, mainly pubs, and the style of food was very German. There was a lot of sauerkraut and Jaegerbraten and things like that. The transition in the Barossa from the mid-'70s until now has been quite phenomenal, and it reflects the societal changes that have occurred right across

Wolf Blass Wines Visitor Centre

the country, from basic food and a very basic way of living, to a very sophisticated way. It reflects in many ways how the wine industry has changed as well, from a very basic farming industry with people who were passionate about wine, to a world standard industry.

"People like Wolf Blass and Peter Lehmann were instrumental in pulling the whole thing forward. The industry was very conservative and elitist before Wolf. And I think his great success was because he had a completely different approach to marketing and making wine fun.

"I think if you look back on it, the backbone of the Barossa is its Germanic heritage. They were always very strong through their church and the Lutheran tradition. If anything ever goes wrong in the Barossa, everyone chips in and helps out. Other farming communities certainly do the same, but it's one of the few wine communities where most of the winemakers live in the region and it has become a part of their lifestyle.

"Other than Adelaide, I've never lived anywhere other than the Barossa. I went back to Adelaide and commuted for a couple of years when my kids went to school, but I found it harder to enjoy the Barossa when I had to drive back to the city. There's just something very good about the sense of community in the Barossa, and wine is at the centre of it. There are very few communities that are driven around one thing.

"Out of all the wine districts around Australia, the Barossa stands out for its regional food, its tourism and its concentration of vineyards. Just before I came, the South Australian government imposed a moratorium on building within the

WOLF BLASS®

Valley. You could only build in the townships. That added to the flavour of the Valley, and now when you drive around you don't see houses and developments all over the shop. It's a much more European approach to a wine district, rather than the Aussie way of banging a house here, there and everywhere. This keeps the vineyards as the focus of the Valley.

"The Barossa has a lot of smaller makers that are interesting from a tourist's perspective. It's a really good combination to have the big, the small and the mid-sized all in one region. You can go and see a Wolf Blass and then a Rockford, a Charlie Melton, Orlando and Yalumba. Wine quality is high across all of those, and that's one of the interesting things about the Barossa, unlike many other regions where there's a huge variation from the professionals to the hobbyists. There's a strong regional flavour in the small producers and also at Lehmann and Yalumba. At Blass we have a sort of modern regional flavour."

You wouldn't read about it

"The Vintage Festival was a really big thing every second year," recalls Wolf. "It was community driven and winemakers participated in a big way. But then new laws came in and, for various reasons, the Festival fell away and virtually died. So in 1972 one of the executives from Yalumba and I came up with an idea! We selected $3000 worth of wines from all over the Barossa, put them on an old horse wagon and chained them all up. We got a golden key and sent it to all the media around Australia to entice them to come to the Festival. And this revived the Festival again. But what happened, on the first day, some bastard came and opened the thing and took all the bloody wine! It was just the beginning of the Festival, so we had to immediately organise another bloody load of wine!"

Local knowledge

"In the early days there wasn't a lot to do in the Barossa apart from wine, but now there are plenty of other things going on — things that are associated with wine but provide alternative things to do," says Chris. "Blond Coffee in Angaston has a very cosmopolitan approach to food and coffee in a wine district, and places like this have been fabulous, particularly for people like me who like wine and food! Maggie Beer is based in the Barossa and all of the things that she is doing very much complement the wine industry. Even though her business has grown so much, she remains very passionate about the Barossa and her home remains here.

Barossa Vintage Festival Parade

She could have that business anywhere, but she's very much passionate about the produce that you can get in the Barossa.

"The Barossa Farmers Market in Angaston is without doubt the best place for produce. If you want the best smoked ham, duck and veal sausages and meat, Schulz's butchery in Angaston is just fantastic and unique. It's carried on the tradition of the old Barossa and you can now buy it all across Australia. We always buy their bacon for our B&B because it's fantastic. And whenever we have a BBQ at home, we buy their duck and veal sausages because they're just sensational. People always say, 'Where the hell do you get those things?!' If you look at it as a country area, the towns are pretty small, and to be able to get these things is quite amazing.

"The interesting thing about food in the Barossa is that every township has its own favourites and we'll always champion our own as better than yours. That's part of the culture. I live in Tanunda and the Apex Bakery run by the Fechners is our favourite. We know the Fechners and they're good people. They still have a wood-fired oven and they wood fire everything. But everyone in Nuri would say that Linke's Bakery is the best!"

"I always buy bread and cake at the Lyndoch bakery," says Wolf. "That's a German bakery if ever there's been one! It is a real German style building in construction, and they make very fine bread. On the restaurant side, I think you have to be guided a little by who you're going to be with. If you want something a bit up market you probably have to go to Appellation."

Angas Park dried fruits are world class, according to Chris. "It's just fascinating to go in there and the things that you can buy are fantastic. There's also a great antique shop in Angaston called 'Antiques and More at 24'. It's two guys, Aaron Penley and Graham Butler,

Wolf Blass vineyard

who used to run Seppeltsfield, before they ran a gourmet delicatessen in Angaston. We call them the 'boys,' they're lovely guys."

Wolf Blass Visitor Centre

It's not something you might expect to hear from the Chief Winemaker of Australia's biggest wine company, but Chris Hatcher openly admits that "wine was very elitist when I first came into the industry and I hated going into cellar doors because I felt intimidated! You thought that if you didn't know anything about wine, the person behind the counter would look down on you. That's one thing that I've seen change, and Wolf has had a big impact on this. Today it's not like that at all. You can come to the Wolf Blass Visitor Centre and feel comfortable to talk at any level to the person behind the counter. They are very open to talking about the wines and they're well versed on what the Barossa is all about.

"I've had so many comments back from people on how the staff in the Visitor Centre are open to different levels of experience and they really help people to understand what wine's about. To me, that's part of the experience. In a couples situation, often one partner is more interested in wine than the other, so you really need to be able to cater for both, and I think that's something they do particularly well.

"There's no pressure to buy. That's why we call it a Visitor Centre, not a cellar door. The key is that it's about the visitor's experience, so when you go back home you can be familiar with the brand. It caters for all levels and we offer the opportunity to taste right across the range, so if you're someone who's interested in sweet wines then you can taste sweet wines. If you know more about wine you can do a specialist tasting and have a look at Platinum Label and Black Label and Grey Label. There is a separate tasting room and a small charge. There's no need to book in advance.

"The Centre is unique because there is nowhere else in the Barossa that has a museum of the founder and how he created the business."

Barossa Taxis

Wolf Blass knows the Barossa taxi service well. "We have an excellent taxi service here," he says. "If you're going to book into any one of the little hotels or units or whatever, you only have to press one button and, bang, a taxi is there! From a safety perspective, this is very important."

Birchwood on Bridge

Accommodation

"When I first came to the Barossa, accommodation was ordinary," recalls Chris. "There were two motels and there were pubs — they were the only places you could stay. There are now some professional large groups like the Novotel, the very premium mid-size Louise group and an enormous number of B&Bs, so there's a very diverse range of accommodation — something to suit everybody.

"My wife Annie and I run our own B&B in Tanunda, called Birchwood on Bridge. It's an 1870s marble-fronted cottage, full of antiques — although I hate lacy doilies and all that kind of stuff! It has a brand new kitchen, two new bathrooms and a nice garden. We run it to be completely independent. You get the key and the food's in the fridge. I hate B&Bs where you've got someone hovering over you!"

Cottage near Angaston
Dragan Radocaj Photography

Wroxton Grange Homestead, 1870

wroxton wines

Flaxman's Valley Rd via Angaston

Ph (08) 8565 3227

www.wroxton.com.au

wine@wroxton.com.au

Est 1920

Tastings at Taste Eden Valley in Angaston

Bed & breakfast

Price range $25

Key Wines: Eden Valley Riesling, Eden Valley Shiraz

Ian and Jo Zander are third-generation Eden Valley grape growers who produce two small-volume wines from estate grown, old vine vineyards. The wines are sold largely to guests who frequent their B&B, also operated under the Wroxton name, on the property that has been in the family since 1920.

My Place

"Our place is a special part of the world, and one we enjoy sharing with others," says Jo. "The great part about operating a B&B is that we get to meet so many interesting people from all over the world, people who come here, time and again, to absorb the unique lifestyle of the Eden Valley."

Food matches

"I can't think of a better match than our Eden Valley Riesling with freshly caught trout out of our dam. Guests are welcome to drop in a line at any time and can use the BBQ when they get lucky!"

Sam dying for a drink

TOP OF THE RANGE

yalumba

"When my great, great grandfather, Samuel Smith, established Yalumba in 1849, he could not have imagined that his fledgling enterprise of fourteen acres and a thatch-roofed winery would enjoy the reputation it holds today," says Robert Hill Smith, fifth generation proprietor of Yalumba. In 1989, Robert and his bother Sam purchased all shares in the company not held by their family at the time, making it Australia's oldest family owned winery.

With 160 years of continuous family winemaking, Yalumba is one of the country's most active wine exporters and is rightfully regarded as one of Australia's most progressive and successful wine companies. Its historic buildings and picturesque gardens make it a delightful place to visit in any season, and the wines that you will discover are among the best value anywhere in the world.

Visiting Yalumba

Visitors to Yalumba are invited to wander the grounds between the Wine Room and the historic Clocktower Building. It's a peaceful place with seasonal gardens and plenty of room for kids to run around. You can lay out a picnic rug or make use of the Pétanque piste to throw a few boules, which are on hand in the Wine Room.

A unique offering at Yalumba is its range of Viogniers. "There are not many wineries in the Barossa where you can taste Viognier in a range of different styles," says Winemaker Louisa Rose, who is regarded as Australia's leading authority on the variety. "Our Viogniers range from pure, fruit driven styles, through to those made with more winemaking complexity." The complete Viognier and

Eden Valley Road
Angaston

Map F14 Winery 73

Ph (08) 8561 3200

www.yalumba.com

info@yalumba.com

Est 1849

Wine Room tastings open Mon-Sun 10-5

Tutored tastings, cooperage, espresso, historical buildings, gardens

Price range $19-$150

Key Barossa Wines: The Signature Cabernet Sauvignon Shiraz, Single Site Tri-Centenary Grenache, The Virgilius Viognier, Bush Vine Grenache, Barossa Patchwork Shiraz, Barossa Shiraz Viognier, The Scribbler Cabernet Sauvignon Shiraz, Pewsey Vale The Contours Eden Valley Riesling, Pewsey Vale Eden Valley Riesling

Shiraz Viognier range is available to taste at the Wine Room, including Yalumba's pre-eminent white wine, 'The Virgilius' Viognier. "We also make an eau de vie from Viognier, called 'V de Vie', which is distilled in the Hill Smith family's historic Still House at the winery," says Louisa. "Visitors can see the Still House, located near the Wine Room."

Director of Winemaking, Brian Walsh, has been with Yalumba since moving to the

Robert Hill Smith and Louisa Rose

Brian Walsh

Yalumba Clocktower Building
Dragan Radočaj Photography

Barossa in 1988 and has been an avid supporter of Yalumba's journey with Viognier since day one. "I tell people we are now the world's most influential producer of Viognier as no other winemaker has the vineyard resources, the experience or the offerings up and down the price and diversity range that we do."

Along with the range of Viogniers there is always a selection available for tasting from the premium end of the range. "We do have four or five wines we normally don't pour at the Wine Room, but there's a fair chance one of them will be open" Brian explains. "There's hardly a day that goes by when we don't have a tasting with a buyer or journalist who has come to spend time with us. When the tasting is over, we always send the bottles down to the Wine Room to share with our customers."

For the driver or the weary taster at the end of a long day, we serve espresso and organic teas "which is also reassuring if you're not quite ready for a big glass of wine when you arrive," says Brian.

Barossa dirt

Yalumba has long held a reputation as a master blender of Barossa wines. "We take the best from the Barossa subregions to create a single variety wine, or the best from different varieties, like Cabernet and Shiraz and blend together," explains Robert. "We consider Cabernet Shiraz to be a great Barossa blend." As a champion of Viognier, Yalumba has also been an Australian pioneer of the Shiraz Viognier blend, which it now produces at three different price points.

In the early 1990s, Yalumba established a dedicated program to identify the vineyard blocks of greatest importance in the Barossa. "We've been looking into subregionality by

211

Top Yalumba Wine Room
Below Yalumba Harvest Market
Dragan Radocaj Photography

introducing a new range of single site wines from individual vineyards in the Barossa and Eden Valleys," explains Robert.

"We make three Shirazes from the same vintage in essentially the same way, which is a great way to explore the diversity of different sites in the Barossa," Louisa explains. Produced in very small volumes, Yalumba Single Site Wines are quite rare, but can be purchased from the Wine Room.

Old Vine Charter

As a champion of old Barossa vines, Yalumba established an old vine charter, which was recently extended, modified and adopted by the region to become the official Barossa Old Vine Charter.

"Presently in Australia there is no definition in our wine law to prescribe what constitutes an 'old vine', leaving it open to individual interpretation," points out Robert. "However, 'seriously' old vines appear to have an advantage in their consistent ability to make wines of great structure, concentration and power. At least that's our experience in the Barossa. Add to this the noble appearance of these gnarled survivors in an age of rapid redundancy, and there seems good cause to celebrate.

"The Old Vine Charter is dedicated to the recognition, preservation and promotion of these old vines, and we at Yalumba hope this Charter may play a small role in ensuring that in the unlikely event of another vine-pull scheme, it is not the oldest vines that are destroyed – as was the case in the 1980s!

"In the perception of drinkers of serious wines in the world, the Old World owns the integrity to old vineyards and tradition and the authenticity of great wine. To take an Old Vine Charter to the world is going to cause a lot of people who take Australia for granted to think again. This charter for us is about integrity and about hoping that the wines we put in front of people do express place and variety. It is a necessary evolution that signifies a 'growing up' of Australia."

In launching the Barossa Old Vine Charter, Brian explained that, "We figure, from one company to one region to one nation we might take on the world and define a position that actually establishes old vines in some sort of a logical hierarchy around the world. We want to celebrate these great old vines."

Yalumba Cooperage

Yalumba Cooperage

Yalumba established an on-site Cooperage at the turn of the 20th Century to craft its own oak barrels. Today it is the only winery in Australia to do so. While there are a small number of wineries with coopers who mend their own barrels, "no other Australian winemaker crafts their barrels from go to whoa, as we do," says Robert. "Oak plays an important part in the winemaking process so through our on site cooperage we have the advantage of being able to have full control of the quality of oak used to age our wines."

The Yalumba Cooperage is operational during the week and open for self-guided tours. Many of the historical barrel-making implements are on display, with story boards describing the traditional craft. While the Cooperage doesn't make complete barrels every day, there's a good chance that when people visit they will see the coopers busy at work. "When they're firing the barrels the toasty smell is quite inviting," says Robert. "Not to mention the warmth, which makes the Cooperage an ideal place to visit on a winter's day."

Eden Valley Riesling

Pewsey Vale Riesling is a legendary wine, made by the Hill Smith family since 1966, and sold to this day for a fraction of its true worth. "The great thing about Riesling is its purity," says Winemaker Louisa Rose. "Pewsey Vale vineyard has the ability to produce wines with

213

lovely fruit definition, so we make sure we apply minimal winemaker intervention in the process to ensure these characters remain intact. The thing that sets Eden Valley apart is not only its beautiful citrus flavour but its soft acid and minerality. It gives it a little more flesh and approachability as a young wine."

Riesling was among the first vines planted in the Eden Valley in 1847 by Joseph Gilbert. "When you drive through Eden Valley and see the rocks rising out of the ground you realise why the wines display that distinctive mineral character associated with the region," Louisa explains.

"Eden Valley is a peaceful place, with small pockets of vineyards spread out amongst the undulating hills and farming estates, which makes it a great place to explore. The Eden Valley Wine Grape Growers has a little exploring map to guide you through the region. Yalumba is a good place to start. From here you can take a drive past Heggies Vineyard and Pewsey Vale, which are both near the Kaiser Stuhl National Park. Whether you choose to drive, walk or ride, you'll get a feel for the rugged yet picturesque landscapes of these vineyards."

Museum cellar

Yalumba's Museum is one of the most remarkable collections of wine in the country, delving back into a century of wine history. It is from this collection that Robert Hill Smith selects the wines for the legendary Yalumba Museum Tastings, held on rare occasions around the world.

This cellar is living evidence of the way Barossa wines can blossom with age, as are the wines Yalumba showcases in the Wine Room. "The Reserve Cabernet Sauvignon Shiraz comes out in special years as a six-year-old release," explains Brian. "The Signature Cabernet Sauvignon Shiraz comes out at four years of age, but generally it's still pretty closed, brooding and restrained at this stage, with pretty profound tannins. I always reckon that it's ideal at ten years, when the secondary development is kicking in."

Louisa recently discovered half a dozen bottles of 1992 The Signature stuck away "in my not so great cellaring system! That's a long time to keep wine, but they were phenomenal and drinking beautifully."

Riesling is the Eden Valley's great ageing white wine. "Pewsey Vale Riesling really comes together at five years and it's great up to eight years, and even longer if you like the toasty characters that it develops," suggests Louisa. Pewsey Vale The Contours Riesling is released as a five-year-old wine.

The Hill Smith family recently opened up a warren of 1960s underground wine tanks to extend the Museum. Situated beneath the historic Clocktower, a selection of these tanks have been restored and fitted out for exclusive and intimate tasting and dining experiences.

Local knowledge

The Yalumba Harvest Market was introduced in 1995 as a Barossa Vintage Festival event, born of Robert and wife Annabel's passion for Barossa food and produce. The Yalumba winery grounds and cellars are transformed into a two-day celebration of uniquely Barossa food and produce.

Yalumba tasting room
Dragan Radocaj Photography

Yalumba Harvest Market

"Like all good things, it was born out of necessity", says Robert. "Back then there were so many cottage industries emerging in the Barossa. Harvest Market presented a way to bring them all together and to assist aspiring producers to reach wider markets." Six years later, the Harvest Market concept inspired the establishment of Food Barossa and, later, the Barossa Farmers Market.

"The Barossa Farmers Market held every Saturday morning is a must when you're in the region," says Louisa. "The quality and selection of produce are exemplary, and you'll always find great local characters who'll tell you a story or two about the region."

The strength of the Barossa food culture drives the quality of its restaurants. "The food is always great at Vintners Bar & Grill," says Louisa. "You can make it as casual or as formal as you like, and you can always be guaranteed you'll see a winemaker or two – or half a dozen. The wine list is impressive, and there's a good selection of interstate and international wines,

which is welcomed by the locals. We don't want to feel like a tourist in our own home!

"For something quite refined, Appellation is fantastic. It offers both à la carte and degustation menus with matching wines usually themed around Barossa styles. The main street of Angaston recently welcomed a new initiative called 'Taste Eden Valley,' an intimate wine shop offering Eden Valley wines for tasting from a range of small producers who are yet to establish their own cellar door."

Winemaking for the future

"Yalumba has a commitment to sustainable winemaking which we hope will sustain Yalumba for a further 160 years," says Robert. "We believe we have created an environmental program that leaves nothing to chance when it comes to protecting the essential elements that make up wine – air, water, soil and energy. We believe our efforts in protecting our natural resources are reflected in the quality of the wines we share with the world."

yelland and papps

Yelland and Papps might sound like a firm of high-powered lawyers, but Susan Yelland and Michael Papps are in reality a passionate husband and wife team who would much rather talk wine than affidavits. Having established their family business in 2005, their focus is on making hand-crafted Shiraz and Grenache blends from old vines in the Greenock subregion of the Barossa.

My Place

"Wine is our passion," says Susan. "We've embraced the challenge of crafting it from the ground up. When people come to taste our wines they sit with us in our house and share our home and the fruits of our labours. That's what we love most about being involved in the wine industry."

Local knowledge

"Our favourite spot in the Valley is the Greenock Creek Tavern," says Michael. "It's casual and relaxed, with a country feel, full of good people and well-priced beer!"

Food matches

"We're quite partial to pancetta, olive and sundried tomato pizza with a glass of our Yelland and Papps Grenache."

Ph (08) 8562 8434

www.yellandandpapps.com

sales@yellandandpapps.com

Est 2005

Tastings by appointment

Price range $17-$30

Key Wines: Greenock Shiraz, Old Vine Grenache, Cabernet Sauvignon

YELLAND&PAPPS
BAROSSA VALLEY

Wining kids

"Bring your kids along when you visit us. We've just started a family so we're with the program!"

Michael, Peyton and Susan Papps in a 120 year old Grenache vineyard

View of Rifle Range Road
Dragan Radocaj Photography

z wines

Janelle and Kristen Zerk are the dynamic duo behind Z Wines. Despite a grape-growing history in the Barossa that dates back to 1846, Janelle was the first Zerk family member to pursue a winemaking vocation. Sister Kristen studied wine marketing and together they started Z Wines in 1998, sourcing grapes from their father's Lyndoch-based estate to create a small portfolio of wines.

My Place

"With 150 acres of family vines in the Lyndoch area it was probably inevitable that we would end up making wine," suggests Janelle. "We set out to create wines under the Z label that were quintessentially Barossa, which for us meant that they had style, soul, and irresistibility. Our hand-crafted, tiny batch wines capture a sense of the past and at the same time express a modern, sophisticated style."

Barossa dirt

"Visit the Small winemakers centre at Chateau Tanunda to discover secret gems that are otherwise hard to find. You can taste Z Wines there, too."

Ph 0422 802 220

www.zwines.com.au

info@zwines.com.au

Est 1998

Tastings at Chateau Tanunda Small Winemakers Centre

Price range $15-$45

Key Wines: Shiraz, Riesling

Local knowledge

"The word on the street at this end of the Valley is that the Williamstown bakery makes a killer Shiraz pie!"

Food matches

"Try our Z Shiraz with a flame grilled fillet of beef and creamy blue cheese sauce."

217

This is the place to locate all the places worth visiting in the Barossa that aren't wineries or cellar doors. The following directory will point you to everything from parks to lookouts, B&Bs to hotels, restaurants to shops and bushwalks to helicopters. It's not a comprehensive list, it's much more than that – this is your 'best of' selection of Barossa highlights. These are all the places that have been recommended throughout this book by the local wine folk who know and love them.

directory
of recommended
places
to visit

Hutton Vale

barossa wine traveller 🍷

1918 Bistro & Grill

94 Murray Street, Tanunda
Open Lunch 12-2:30, dinner Mon-
Sat 6:30-9, Sun 6-8
Ph 08 8563 0405
www.1918.com.au
enquiries@1918.com.au

Angas Park Fruit Co

3 Murray Street, Angaston
Open Mon-Sat 9-5, Sun 10-5
Ph 08 8561 0830
Fax 08 8564 2686
www.angaspark.com.au
shop@angaspark.com.au

Angas Park Hotel

28 Murray Street, Nuriootpa
Ph 08 8562 1050

Angas Recreation Park, Angaston

Washington Street, Angaston
Ph 08 8563 8444
www.barossa.sa.gov.au/site/page.
cfm?u=685&c=16115
barossa@barossa.sa.gov.au
Contact the Barossa Council

Angaston Mobil Roadhouse

Nuriootpa Road (Corner of
Stockwell Rd), Angaston
Ph 08 8564 2480

Angaston Roaring 40's Café

30 Murray Street, Angaston
Ph 08 8564 2901
Fax 08 8564 2982
Mob 0407 471 772
www.40scafe.com.au
40s@40scafe.com.au
Open 9am-late daily

Angaston Tudor Bed & Breakfast

81 Murray Street, Angaston
Ph 08 8524 4825
Fax 08 8524 4046
Mob 0427 202 791

Antiques and More at 24

24 Murray Street, Angaston
Ph 08 8564 2310
Fax 08 8562 4246
am24@bigpond.net.au

Apex Bakery

Elizabeth Street, Tanunda
Ph 08 8563 2483
Fax 08 8563 0000
apexbakery@internode.on.net

Appellation

Seppeltsfield Road, Marananga
Open 7 days 7pm - late
Ph 08 8562 4144
www.appellation.com.au
dine@appellation.com.au

Atrium at Greenock Creek

Greenock Creek
Ph 08 8562 3714
www.atriumresidence.com.au
stay@atriumresidence.com.au

Ballycroft Artisan Cheese

Po Box 719, Greenock
Ph 08 8562 8184
Fax 08 8562 8162
http://ballycroft.com
ballycroft@chariot.net.au
Available at various outlets
throughout the Barossa

Barossa Bowland

Menge Road, Tanunda
Ph 08 8563 3177
Fax 08 8563 3148
http://barossabowland.com
barossabowland@bigpond.com.au

Barossa Brewing Company

Mill Street, Greenock
Ph 08 85634041
Mob 0419 811 525
www.barossabrewingcompany.com
sales@barossabrewingcompany.com

Barossa Farmers Market

Vintner's Shed behind Vintners Bar
& Grill, Corner of Stockwell and
Nuriootpa Roads, Angaston
Open every Sat 7.30am - 11.30am
Mob 0402 026 882
www.barossafarmersmarket.com
info@barossafarmersmarket.com
Country bacon & egg rolls available
for breakfast

Top Apex Bakery bread coming out of the wood oven
Middle Bread from The Lyndoch Bakery
Bottom Yalumba Harvest Market

directory of recommended places to visit

Barossa Helicopters

Hoffnungsthal Road, Lyndoch
Ph 08 8524 4209
www.barossahelicopters.com.au
fly@barossahelicopters.com.au

Barossa Valley Cheese Co.

67b Murray Street, Angaston
Open M-F 10-5, Sat 10-4, Sun 11-3
Ph 08 8564 3636
www.barossacheese.com.au
sales@barossacheese.com.au
Cheese Cellar open for tastings/sales

Barossa Valley Golf Club

Golf Course Road, Nuriootpa
Ph 08 8562 1589
Fax 08 8562 1589
www.barossavalleygolfclub.websyte.
com.au
admin@barossavalleygolf.com

Barossa Visitor Information Centre

66-68 Murray Street, Tanunda
Open Mon-Fri 9-5, Sat-Sun 10-4
Ph 08 8563 0600
Fax 08 8563 0616
www.barossa.com
info@barossa.com
Free call 1300 852 982

Barossa Wurst Haus and Bakery

86a Murray Street, Tanunda
Ph 08 8563 3598

Benno's Kiosk

See 'Seppeltsfield' winery

Bethany Lutheran Church

Bethany Road, Bethany
Ph 08 8563 2089
Fax 08 8663 3831
http://www.lca.org.au/search/
church/cong.php?EntityID=168
hergergechristi.bethany.sa@lca.org.au

Bethany Reserve

Bethany Road, Bethany
Open Mon-Fri 9am-5pm
Ph 08 8563 8444
www.barossa.sa.gov.au/site/page.
cfm?u=685&c=16145
barossa@barossa.sa.gov.au
Contact the Barossa Council

Birchwood on Bridge

34 Bridge Street, Tanunda
Ph 08 8563 1516
Fax 08 8563 1516
Mob 0409 097 947
www.birchwoodbarossa.com.au
escape@birchwoodbarossa.com.au
See 'Wolf Blass' winery

Blond Coffee, Angaston

Murray Street, Angaston
Open Mon-Fri 7:30-5:30, Sat 8:30-
5:30, Sun & public hols 9-5:30
Ph 08 8564 3444
www.blondcoffee.com.au
info@blondcoffee.com.au

Bowland

See 'Barossa Bowland'

The Branch

15 Murray Street, Nuriootpa
Open 7 days for breakfast and lunch
from 8am
Ph 08 8562 4561
www.thebranch.com.au
bookings@thebranch.com.au

Brauhaus Hotel

41 Murray Street, Angaston
Ph 08 8564 2014
Fax 08 8564 3573

Buck's Bistro, Springton

Main Street, Springton
Open M, W-Sat 10-8:30, Sun 10-5
Ph 08 8568 2999
bucksbistro@aapt.net.au
See 'Poverty Hill' winery

Carême Pastry

PO Box 184, Tanunda
Ph 08 8563 1490
Fax 08 8563 1470
Mob 0439 803 117
www.caremepastry.com
claire@caremepastry.com
At the Barossa Farmers Market every
Saturday. Pre-orders taken.

Chateau Yaldara Garden Bistro

Gomersal Road, Lyndoch
See 'McGuigan Barossa Valley' winery

Top Appellation Chef Mark McNamara at Barossa Slow
Middle Barossa Slow banquet **Bottom** Barossa preserves
Simon Casson Photography

221

barossa wine traveller 🍷

Company Kitchen

27 Valley Road, Angaston
Ph 08 8564 2725
Fax 08 8564 3258
www.sacompanystore.com.au
sacompanystore@bigpond.com

Corner Store Bakery, Williamstown

1-3 Queen Street, Williamstown
Ph 08 85246246

Eden Valley Hotel

11 Main Street, Eden Valley
Ph 08 8564 1072

Farm Follies

See 'Hutton Vale' winery

Farmers Market

See 'Barossa Farmers Market'

Gnadenberg Lutheran Church

Gnadenberg Road, Moculta
Ph 08 8563 2248
Fax 08 8563 3831
http://www.lca.org.au/search/
church/cong.php?EntityID=387
zion.moculta.sa@lca.org.au

Greenock Creek Tavern

Kapunda Road, Greenock
Open lunch Thu-Sun; dinner Thu-Sat
Ph 08 8562 8136

Gully Gardens Dried Fruits

Gawler Park Road, Angaston

Helicopters

See 'Barossa Helicopters'

Herbig Family Tree

Angaston Road, Springton
Open Always
Ph 08 8568 2287
http://www.southaustralia.
com/9000986.aspx

Heritage Wines B&B

106a Seppeltsfield Road, Marananga
Ph 08 8562 2880
Fax 08 8562 2692
www.heritagewinery.com.au
enquiries@heritagewinery.com.au
See 'Heritage' winery

Hutton Vale Lamb

See 'Hutton Vale' winery

Jellicoe House

Sawpit Gully Road, Mt McKenzie
Ph 08 8564 2741
Fax 08 8564 2437
Mob 0418 847 939
www.sorbyadamswines.com
Jellicoe@sorbyadamswines.com
See 'Sorby Adams' winery

Kaiser Stuhl Conservation Park

Tanunda Creek Road, off Mengler
Hill Road, Tanunda
www.barossa.sa.gov.au/site/page.
cfm?u=685&c=16170

Kathy's Old Fashioned Sweet Shop

86d Murray Street, Tanunda
Open 7 days 10-4:30
Ph 08 8563 1166
www.kathyssweetshop.com.au

Keg Factory

Lot 10 St Hallett Road, Tanunda
Ph 08 8563 3012
Fax 08 8563 0152
www.thekegfactory.com.au
enquiries@thekegfactory.com.au

Kegel Bowling

See 'Tanunda Recreation Park'

Keils Fine Food & Coffee

1/63 Murray Street, Tanunda
Ph 08 8563 1468

Kohlhagen Cottage

9 Maria Street, Tanunda
Ph 08 8563 3220

Krondorf Road Café

See 'Kabminye' winery

La Buona Vita

89 Murray St Tanunda
Open noon-10pm daily
Ph 08 8563 2527
Fax 08 8563 3477
labuonavita@ozemail.com.au

Top Keith and his free range eggs at the Barossa Farmers Market
Middle and bottom Step back in time in Bethany
Dragan Radocaj Photography

directory of recommended places to visit

Lavender Farm

See 'Lyndoch Lavender Farm'

Lindsay House

Lindsay Street, Angaston
Ph 08 8524 6380
Fax 08 8563 2325
Mob 0409 902 961

Linke's Bakery & Tea Rooms

40 Murray Street, Nuriootpa
Ph 08 8562 1129
Fax 08 8562 3410
linbake@dove.net.au

Linke's Central Meat Store

27 Murray Street, Tanunda
Ph 08 8562 1143

Lodge Country House

Sec 106 Seppeltsfield Road, Greenock
Ph 08 8562 8277
Fax 08 8562 8344
www.thelodgecountryhouse.com.au
stay@thelodgecountryhouse.com.au

Lord Lyndoch Hotel

23 Barossa Valley Way, Lyndoch
Open Mon-Fri 10-late; Sat, Sun &
Public Hols 9:30-late
Ph 08 8524 5440
Fax 08 8524 5441
bookings@lordlyndoch.com

Louise

See 'The Louise'

Lyndoch Bakery

Barossa Valley Highway, Lyndoch
Ph 08 8524 4422
Fax 08 8524 5222
www.lyndochbakery.com.au
lyndochbakery_rest@bigpond.com

Lyndoch Lavender Farm

Corner of Hoffnungsthal and
Tweedies Gully Roads, Lyndoch
Ph 08 8524 4538
www.lyndochlavenderfarm.com.au
llf@lyndochlavenderfarm.com.au

Lyndoch Recreation Park

Barossa Valley Way, Lyndoch
Ph 08 8563 8444

www.barossa.sa.gov.au/site/page.
cfm?u=685&c=16148
barossa@barossa.sa.gov.au
Contact the Barossa Council

Lyndoch Valley Meats

38 Barossa Highway Lyndoch
Ph 08 8524 4078

Maggie Beer's Farm Shop

Pheasant Farm Road, Nuriootpa
Open 7 days 10.30am-5pm,
Ph 08 85624477
Fax 885624757
www.maggiebeer.com.au
farmshop@maggiebeer.com.au
Cooking demonstration 2pm daily,
food & wine tastings, all day picnic
fare

Meadow Springs B&B

Sugarloaf Hill Road, Mt McKenzie
Ph 08 8565 3214
Mob 0418 139 383
petkiptyltd@bigpond.com

Mengler's Hill Lookout

See 'Sculpture Park'

Moculta Park

Truro Road, Moculta
Ph 08 8563 9074
www.barossa.sa.gov.au/site/page.
cfm?u=685&c=16150

Monkey Nut Café

See 'Kies' winery

Mount Crawford Forest

Warren Road, Williamstown
www.barossa.sa.gov.au/site/page.
cfm?u=685&c=16166

Mt Pleasant Butcher

98-100 Melrose Street, Mount
Pleasant
Ph 08 8568 2019

Mt Pleasant Hotel

43 Melrose Street, Mount Pleasant
Open 8:30am – 8:30pm
Ph 08 8568 2015
Fax 08 8568 2488
brett.tbg@bigpond.com

Top Hand picked carrots at the Barossa Farmers Market
Middle and bottom Ziegenmarkt
Dragan Radocaj Photography

223

barossa wine traveller 🍷

Murdock Indulge

31 Murray Street, Angaston
Ph 08 8564 3666
See 'Murdock' winery

Murdock Restaurant

See 'Murdock' winery

Naimanya Cottage

Pohlner Road via Tanunda
Ph 08 8565 3275
Fax 08 8565 3275
Mob 0418 893 130
www.naimanya.com.au
christadeans@bigpond.com

Novotel Barossa Valley Resort

Golf Links Road, Rowland Flat
Ph 08 8524 0000
www.novotelbarossa.com
H3026-re01@accor.com

Old Mill Gallery and Café

32 Murray Street, Tanunda
Open Mon-Fri 9-5, Sat-Sun 10-4
Ph 08 8563 0222

Roaring 40's Café

See 'Angaston Roaring 40's Café'

Salters Restaurant

See 'Saltram' winery

Sandy Creek YHA Hostel (Barossa Valley Farmhouse YHA)

Pimpala Rd, Sandy Creek
Conservation Park
Ph 08 8414 3000
Fax 08 8414 3014
www.yha.com.au
tanya@yhasa.org.au

Schulz's Butchers

42 Murray Street, Angaston
Ph 08 8564 2145
www.barossafinefoods.com
sales@barossafinefoods.com.au

Sculpture Park

Mengler Hill Road, Tanunda
Ph 08 8563 2381
www.barossa.sa.gov.au/site/page.
cfm?u=685&c=16123

Seppeltsfield Vineyard Cottage

Gerald Roberts Road, Seppeltsfield
Ph 08 85634059
Fax 08 8563 4003
Mob 0412 455 553
www.seppeltsfieldvineyardcottage.
com.au
stay@seppeltsfieldvineyardcottage.
com.au

Skate Park, Nuriootpa

See 'Tolley Reserve'

Sonntag House
Bethany Road, Bethany
Fax 08 8563 0200
Mob 0419 814 349
www.sonntaghouse.com.au
sonntaghouse@bigpond.com.au

Springton Hotel

16 Miller Street, Springton
Ph 08 8568 2290

Sunrise Bakery

28b Murray Street, Angaston
Ph 08 8564 2070

Tabor Lutheran Church

77 Murray Street, Tanunda
Ph 08 8563 2089
Fax 08 8563 3831
http://www.lca.org.au/search/
church/cong.php?EntityID=17
tabor.tanunda.sa@lca.org.au

Tanunda Bakery

181 Murray Street, Tanunda
Open Mon-Fri 8:30-5:30, Sat 8:30-
1:30, Closed Public holidays
Ph 08 8563 0096

Tanunda Cellars

14 Murray Street, Tanunda
Open 9am-7pm daily
Ph 08 8563 3544
www.tanundacellars.com.au
chris@tanundacellars.com.au

Tanunda Club

45 MacDonnell Street, Tanunda
Open 7 days, Lunch 12-2:30, Dinner
6-8:30
Ph 08 8563 2058

This page Barossa Vintage Festival Parade
Dragan Radocaj Photography

224

directory of recommended places to visit

Tanunda Hotel

51 Murray Street, Tanunda
Ph 08 8563 2030
Fax 08 8563 2165
www.tanundapub.com
info@tanundapub.com

Tanunda Pines Golf Club

Golf Links Road, Rowland Flat
Ph 08 8563 1200
Fax 08 8563 1211
www.tanundapines.com.au
info@tanundapines.com.au

Tanunda Recreation Park

Elizabeth Street, Tanunda
Ph 08 8563 8444
www.barossa.sa.gov.au/site/page.
cfm?u=685&c=16114
barossa@barossa.sa.gov.au
Contact the Barossa Council

Taste Eden Valley

36a Murray Street, Angaston
Open Wed-Mon 11am-5pm
Ph 08 8564 2435
Fax 08 8564 2435
www.tasteedenvalley.com.au
info@tasteedenvalley.com.au

The Louise

Seppeltsfield Road, Marananga
Ph 08 8562 2722
www.thelouise.com.au
stay@thelouise.com.au

Thorns Quality Meats

Elizabeth St, Tanunda
Ph 08 8563 2728

Tolley Reserve, Nuriootpa

Murray Street, Nuriootpa
Ph 08 8563 8444
www.barossa.sa.gov.au/site/page.
cfm?u=359&c=16159
barossa@barossa.sa.gov.au
Contact the Barossa Council

Tourist Information Centre

See 'Barossa Visitor Information
Centre'

Train Park, Nuriootpa

See 'Tolley Reserve'

Valley Hotel

73 Murray Street, Tanunda
Ph 08 8563 2039

Vintners Bar & Grill

Nuriootpa Road, Angaston
Open Lunch 7 days from 12; dinner
Mon-Sat from 6:30
Ph 08 8564 2488
Fax 08 8564 2433
www.vintners.com.au
chef@vintners.com.au

Whispering Wall

Whispering Wall Road, off Yettie
Road, Williamstown
www.barossa.sa.gov.au/site/page.
cfm?u=685&c=16162

Whistler Farm B&B

Samuel Road, Nuriootpa
Mob 0415 139 758
www.whistlerfarm.com.au
stay@whistlerfarm.com.au
See 'Whistler' winery

**Woodbridge Farm Cottage Bed &
Breakfast**

Gomersal Road, Gomersal
Ph 08 8563 2059
Fax 08 8563 2581
www.woodbridgefarm.com
woodbridgefarm@bigpond.com

Wroxton Grange B&B

Flaxmans Valley Road, Angaston
Ph 08 8565 3227
Fax 08 8565 3312
Mob 0439 653 312
www.wroxton.com.au
info@wroxton.com.au

Wurst Haus

See 'Barossa Wurst Haus and Bakery'

Zimmy's Barossa Valley Produce

Box 413, Tanunda
Ph 08 8563 2477
Fax 08 8563 2477
zimmys@bigpond.com.au
Available at various outlets
throughout the Barossa

This page Barossa Vintage Festival Parade
Dragan Radocaj Photography

225

index of wineries and recommended places to visit

index of wineries and recommended places to visit

Jenke Vineyard
Dragan Radocaj Photography

Simon Casson
Photography

FOOD

BAROSSA

thank yous

It has taken a cast of thousands to produce this book, and we are grateful to every one of you. It would fill another book just to name you all.

Barossa winemakers – In opening your homes, your lives and your stories to us, you have given us a glimpse of the Barossa as you see it. Like you, we have fallen in love with it.

Grape growers of the Barossa – You are the foundation of the Barossa community. We thank you for six generations of getting your hands dirty.

Wayne – This book was your vision. Two years later, we humbly present these pages to you in the hope that they might somehow reflect the dream.

The Wine Barossa Committee – Thank you for catching the vision and cheering us on.

Sam, Barbara and the Barossa Grape & Wine Association – From your little office, you run one of the most efficient and innovative wine bodies in the country. This book is a credit to your initiative.

Dragan – You have an eye for capturing the Barossa like no one has ever seen. Thank you for bringing these pages to life.

Greg and the Openbook team – This is our tenth book through your press. We still couldn't do it without you.

Rachael and Nikki – You are our inspiration and our joy. Thank you for two years of patience and a million sacrifices. We owe you a long holiday!

A small part of the cast to whom this book owes its existence.
John Kruger Photography

229

the authors

Tyson Stelzer is the author and publisher of ten wine books. He writes freelance articles for Wine Spectator, America's largest selling wine publication, Decanter Magazine (UK), WBM, Australia's Wine Business Magazine, Vintage Cellar's Cellar Press and Wine Selector. He pens a monthly wine page for Style Magazine, is a benchmark wine reviewer for WINE100 and a regular online writer for Wineaway. He is a contributor to The Oxford Companion to Wine Third Edition, which names him as the most prolific writer in the world on the topic of screw caps.

As an international speaker, Tyson has presented at wine conferences in Australia, New Zealand, South Africa, Japan and the United Kingdom. He is a regular judge at wine shows in Australia including the National Wine Show of Australia, The Royal Melbourne Wine Show, The Sydney Royal Wine Show and many regional shows. He is a co-creator with UK wine writer Matthew Jukes of The Great Australian Red Competition.

He co-authors the annual guide Taste Food & Wine with Matthew Jukes. The book was the winner of the Award for the Best Food and Wine Writing in the Australian Food Media Awards in 2008. Tyson was a finalist for the International Wine and Spirit Competition's Communicator of the Year 2006.

Tyson lives in Brisbane with his wife Rachael and son Linden and plays guitar and saxophone at his church, Our Saviour Lutheran. As a descendent of a Barossa Lutheran, he lays claim to Stelzer Road behind Tanunda, where his grandfather grew up in the Stelzer Homestead and was a member of the Gnadenfrei Lutheran Church, pictured on the cover of this book.

Grant Dodd has been a wine and feature writer for Australian Golf Digest since 2003 and has contributed to Gourmet Traveller Wine Magazine. He is a sports commentator for golf on Network TEN and a partner in Haskell Vineyards in Stellenbosch, South Africa.

In 2008 he initiated The Dombeya Scholarship to offer disadvantaged South African winemaking graduates the opportunity to work and study in Australia. Kaesler Wines (Barossa), Adelaide University, and Voyager Estate (Margaret River) are key partners in the the scholarship.

As a wine judge, Grant has judged in The Great Australian Red competition and at the Wine Magazine South Africa judging of Australia/France/South Africa Shiraz. He was a presenter at the ROI Seminar at Cape Wine International in 2008.

Grant lives on the Gold Coast with his wife Nikki, daughter Abby and son Alex. He plays the occasional game of golf, surfs irregularly (and badly) and likes to listen to old Ben Harper and Soundgarden CDs whenever he can wrest The Wiggles out of the player.